1st Workshop on NLP for Positive Impact (NLPPosImpact 2021)

Held online due to COVID-19

Bangkok, Thailand
5 August 2021

ISBN: 978-1-7138-3382-6

Printed from e-media with permission by:

Curran Associates, Inc.
57 Morehouse Lane
Red Hook, NY 12571

CURRAN ASSOCIATES INC. proceedings.com

Some format issues inherent in the e-media version may also appear in this print version.

Association for Computational Linguistics
209 N. Eighth Street
Stroudsburg, Pennsylvania 18360

Phone: 1-570-476-8006
Fax: 1-570-476-0860

acl@aclweb.org

Additional copies of this publication are available from:

Curran Associates, Inc.
57 Morehouse Lane
Red Hook, NY 12571 USA
Phone: 845-758-0400
Fax: 845-758-2633
Email: curran@proceedings.com
Web: www.proceedings.com

NLP4PosImpact 2021

The 1st Workshop on NLP for Positive Impact

Proceedings of the Workshop

August 5, 2021
Bangkok, Thailand (online)

Introduction

The widespread and indispensable use of language-oriented AI systems presents new opportunities to have a positive social impact. Much existing work on NLP for social good focuses on detecting or preventing harm, such as classifying hate speech, mitigating bias, or identifying signs of depression. However, NLP research also offers the potential for positive proactive applications that can improve user and public well-being or foster constructive conversations. Nevertheless, "positive impact" remains difficult to define, and well-intentioned NLP technology can raise concerns about ethics and privacy.

This volume contains the proceedings of the First Workshop on NLP for Positive Impact held in conjunction with the Joint Conference of the 59th Annual Meeting of the Association for Computational Linguistics and the 11th International Joint Conference on Natural Language Processing (ACL-IJCNLP 2021). The workshop received 40 submissions of technical papers of which 27 were accepted (16 archival and 11 non-archival), for an acceptance rate of 65%. Non-archival papers are included in the schedule and presented during the workshop, but are not included in the proceedings, whereas archival papers are included. We thank Program Committee members for providing high quality reviews in assembling these proceedings. These papers cover diverse aspects of NLP for positive impact, including developing NLP technology for applications like healthcare, criminal law, education, social media analyses, and consumer privacy as well discussing challenges and ethical implications of using NLP in these areas.

In addition to technical papers, this workshop also features invited keynote speakers and panelists to facilitate discussion and enhance knowledge of NLP for positive impact.

Keynote speakers:
Ndapa Nakashole, University of California, San Diego
Yulia Tsvetkov, University of Washington
Jason Weston, Facebook AI Research

Panelists:
Yejin Choi, University of Washington/Allen Institute for AI
Pascale Fung, Hong Kong University of Science and Technology
Inioluwa Deborah Raji, Mozilla Foundation
Baobao Zhang, Cornell University

We are grateful to all the people who have contributed to this workshop, including speakers, authors, reviewers, and attendees, and we would additionally like to thank Microsoft for providing funds for registration fee waivers.

We hope that our workshop can encourage future work on pro-social NLP and we look forward to welcoming you all to our virtual event!

- Anjalie, Shrimai, Maarten, Zhijing, Jieyu, and Chris

Organizing Committee
Anjalie Field, Carnegie Mellon University
Shrimai Prabhumoye, Carnegie Mellon University
Maarten Sap, University of Washington
Zhijing Jin, Max Planck Institute
Jieyu Zhao, University of California, Los Angeles
Chris Brockett, Microsoft Research

Program Committee
Tal August, University of Washington
Laura Biester, University of Michigan
Su Lin Blodgett, Microsoft Research
Luke Breitfeller, Carnegie Mellon University
Dallas Card, Stanford University
Serina Chang, Stanford University
Elizabeth Clark, University of Washington
Thomas Davidson, Cornell University
Lucas Dixon, Google Research
Pablo Duboue, Textualization Software Ltd.
Saadia Gabriel, University of Washington
Behzad Golshan, Megagon Labs
Alon Halevy, Facebook AI Research
Xiaochuang Han, Carnegie Mellon University
Oana Ignat, University of Michigan
Divyansh Kaushik, Carnegie Mellon University
Ashiqur KhudaBukhsh, Carnegie Mellon University
Sachin Kumar, Carnegie Mellon University
Nayeon Lee, Hong Kong University
Lucy Lin, University of Washington
Li Lucy, University of California, Berkeley
Aman Madaan, Carnegie Mellon University
Thomas Manzini, Microsoft Research
Julia Mendelsohn, University of Michigan
Sewon Min, University of Washington
Adam Miner, Stanford University
Negar Mokhberian, University of Southern California
Eda Okur, Intel
Tanmay Parekh, Carnegie Mellon University
Chan Young Park, Carnegie Mellon University
Hannah Rashkin, Google Research
Sofia Serrano, University Of Washington
Qinlan Shen, Carnegie Mellon University
Sameer Singh, Allen Institute for Artificial Intelligence
Jeffrey Sorensen, Google Research
Swabha Swayamdipta, Allen Institute for Artificial Intelligence
Lucy Vanderwende, University Of Washington
Rob Voigt, Northwestern University
Eric Wallace, University of California, Berkeley
Zijian Wang, Stanford University
Zeerak Waseem, University of Sheffield
Kellie Webster, Google Research

Michael Yoder, Carnegie Mellon University
Xuhui Zhou, University of Washington

Invited Speakers
Ndapa Nakashole, University of California, San Diego
Yulia Tsvetkov, University of Washington
Jason Weston, Facebook AI Research

Invited Panelists
Yejin Choi, University of Washington/Allen Institute for AI
Pascale Fung, Hong Kong University of Science and Technology
Inioluwa Deborah Raji, Mozilla Foundation
Baobao Zhang, Cornell University

Table of Contents

Conference Program

August 5, 2021 [UTC+0]

1:00PM–1:15PM Opening Remarks

1:15PM–2:15PM Invited talk: Jason Weston

2:15PM–2:30PM Break

2:30PM–4:00PM Poster Session 1

Conversations Gone Alright: Quantifying and Predicting Prosocial Outcomes in Online Conversations
Jiajun Bao, Junjie Wu, Yiming Zhang, Eshwar Chandrasekharan and David Jurgens

Effects of Online Self-Disclosure on Receiving Social Support During the COVID-19 Pandemic
Jooyoung Lee, Sarah Rajtmajer, Eesha Srivatsavaya and Shomir Wilson

Restatement and Question Generation for Counsellor Chatbot
John Lee, Baikun Liang and Haley Fong

The Climate Change Debate and Natural Language Processing
Manfred Stede and Ronny Patz

Methods for Detoxification of Texts for the Russian Language
Daryna Dementieva, Daniil Moskovskiy, Varvara Logacheva, David Dale, Olga Kozlova, Nikita Semenov and Alexander Panchenko

Towards Knowledge-Grounded Counter Narrative Generation for Hate Speech
Yi-Ling Chung, Serra Sinem Tekiroğlu and Marco Guerini

Cartography of Natural Language Processing for Social Good (NLP4SG): Searching for Definitions, Statistics and White Spots
Paula Fortuna, Laura Pérez-Mayos, Ahmed AbuRa'ed, Juan Soler-Company and Leo Wanner

Conversational Receptiveness: Improving Engagement with Opposing Views
Michael Yeomans, Julia Minson, Hanne Collins and Francesca Gino

August 5, 2021 [UTC+0] (continued)

Guiding Principles for Participatory Design-inspired Natural Language Processing
Tommaso Caselli, Roberto Cibin, Costanza Conforti, Enrique Encinas and Maurizio Teli

Using Word Embeddings to Analyze Teacher Evaluations: An Application to a Filipino Education Non-Profit Organization
Francesca Vera

Analyzing Stereotypes in Generative Text Inference Tasks
Anna Sotnikova, Yang Trista Cao, Hal Daumé III and Rachel Rudinger

Theano: A Greek-speaking conversational agent for COVID-19
Nikoletta Ventoura, Kosmas Palios, Yannis Vasilakis, Georgios Paraskevopoulos, Nassos Katsamanis and Vassilis Katsouros

Are we human, or are we users? The role of natural language processing in human-centric news recommenders that nudge users to diverse content
Myrthe Reuver, Nicolas Mattis, Marijn Sax, Suzan Verberne, Nava Tintarev, Natali Helberger, Judith Moeller, Sanne Vrijenhoek, Antske Fokkens and Wouter van Atteveldt

Use of Formal Ethical Reviews in NLP Literature: Historical Trends and Current Practices
Sebastin Santy, Anku Rani and Monojit Choudhury

Automatic Sentence Simplification in Low Resource Settings for Urdu
Yusra Anees and Sadaf Abdul Rauf

4:00PM–5:00PM Invited Talk: Yulia Tsvetkov

August 5, 2021 [UTC+0] (continued)

5:00PM–5:30PM Break

5:30PM–6:30PM Invited talk: Ndapa Nakashole

6:30PM–9:30PM Break

9:30PM–11:00PM Poster Session 2

Challenges for Information Extraction from Dialogue in Criminal Law
Jenny Hong, Catalin Voss and Christopher Manning

Detecting Hashtag Hijacking for Hashtag Activism
Pooneh Mousavi and Jessica Ouyang

Breaking Down Walls of Text: How Can NLP Benefit Consumer Privacy?
Abhilasha Ravichander, Alan W Black, Thomas Norton, Shomir Wilson and Norman Sadeh

Conversation-Level Resilience to Bad Actors in Reddit Communities
Charlotte Lambert and Eshwar Chandrasekharan

NLP for Consumer Protection: Battling Illegal Clauses in German Terms and Conditions in Online Shopping
Daniel Braun and Florian Matthes

A Research Framework for Understanding Education-Occupation Alignment with NLP Techniques
Renzhe Yu, Subhro Das, Sairam Gurajada, Kush Varshney, Hari Raghavan and Carlos Lastra-Anadon

Dialogue Act Classification for Augmentative and Alternative Communication
E. Margaret Perkoff

Improving Policing with Natural Language Processing
Anthony Dixon and Daniel Birks

Empathy and Hope: Resource Transfer to Model Inter-country Social Media Dynamics
Clay H. Yoo, Shriphani Palakodety, Rupak Sarkar and Ashiqur KhudaBukhsh

How Good Is NLP? A Sober Look at NLP Tasks through the Lens of Social Impact
Zhijing Jin, Geeticka Chauhan, Brian Tse, Mrinmaya Sachan and Rada Mihalcea

A Speech-enabled Fixed-phrase Translator for Healthcare Accessibility
Pierrette Bouillon, Johanna Gerlach, Jonathan Mutal, Nikos Tsourakis and Hervé Spechbach

A Grounded Well-being Conversational Agent with Multiple Interaction Modes: Preliminary Results
Xinxin Yan and Ndapa Nakashole

11:00PM–12:30AM [+1] Panel Discussion: Yejin Choi, Pascale Fung, Inioluwa Deborah Raji, Baobao Zhang

12:30AM [+1]–12:45AM [+1] Closing Remarks

Restatement and Question Generation for Counsellor Chatbot

John S. Y. Lee, Baikun Liang, Haley H. M. Fong
Department of Linguistics and Translation
City University of Hong Kong
Hong Kong SAR, China
{jsylee, baikliang2, heimfong3}@cityu.edu.hk

Abstract

Amidst rising mental health needs in society, virtual agents are increasingly deployed in counselling. In order to give pertinent advice, counsellors must first gain an understanding of the issues at hand by eliciting sharing from the counsellee. It is thus important for the counsellor chatbot to encourage the user to open up and talk. One way to sustain the conversation flow is to acknowledge the counsellee's key points by restating them, or probing them further with questions. This paper applies models from two closely related NLP tasks — summarization and question generation — to restatement and question generation in the counselling context. We conducted experiments on a manually annotated dataset of Cantonese post-reply pairs on topics related to loneliness, academic anxiety and test anxiety. We obtained the best performance in both restatement and question generation by fine-tuning BertSum, a state-of-the-art summarization model, with the in-domain manual dataset augmented with a large-scale, automatically mined open-domain dataset.

1 Introduction

Advances in dialog modeling have facilitated chatbot use in many domains (Li et al., 2016; Zhou et al., 2020; Wang et al., 2020a). They are now also increasingly deployed for mental health assistance, including counselling (Fitzpatrick et al., 2017).

Dialogs in counselling share some common characteristics with those in other domains. Advice generation, for example, can be implemented with a Q&A model that retrieves counselling materials from a knowledge base (Liu et al., 2013; Huang et al., 2015). Empathetic language — words that reflect the feelings of one's interlocutors — is conducive to establishing rapport with the counsellee. Research in empathetic response generation has led to systems that can recognize the emotional state of the user, and generate responses tailored to that state (Lubis et al., 2018; Lin et al., 2019). The counsellor must also encourage the counsellee to open up and talk in order to gain an adequate understanding of the issues at hand. A common strategy to sustain the conversation flow is to use "encouragers" (Ivey and Ivey, 2003), such as back-channel phrases, restatements and questions. A good restatement acknowledges main points from the counsellee by paraphrasing or summarizing them. A helpful question elicits elaboration on a key point and invites collaborative problem solving. Table 1 shows some examples.

This paper focuses on automatic generation of restatements and questions for counselling dialogs. Specifically, it addresses two research questions:

- Text summarization and question generation are NLP tasks that are potentially relevant to the counselling domain. Can we adapt models designed for these tasks to produce high-quality restatements and questions for a counsellor chatbot?

- Dialog data for domain-specific tasks such as counselling is often limited. Can we leverage open-domain dialog data to improve restatement and question generation?

Our experiments compare a number of summarization, question generation and dialog models for the single-turn reply generation task. We obtained the strongest model by fine-tuning BertSum (Liu and Lapata, 2019), a state-of-the-art summarization model, with an in-domain, manually annotated dataset augmented with a large-scale, automatically mined open-domain dataset.

After summarizing previous work (Section 2) and presenting our dataset (Section 3), we describe our approach for restatement and question generation (Section 4). We then report experimen-

Proceedings of the 1st Workshop on NLP for Positive Impact, pages 1–7
Bangkok, Thailand (online), August 5, 2021.

Post	Restatement	Question
(a) 每逢測驗都一定會夜晚唔食飯 專心溫習 同自己講 我一定唔可以輸 Before a test, I skip dinner to study and I say to myself, "I must not lose"	你一定唔可以輸 You must not lose	你同邊個比賽呀？ Who are you competing with?
(b) Professor教書教得咁廢考試又出勁難 The professor teaches poorly and gives a really hard exam	考試勁難 Exam is extremely hard	你考試係咪唔識做？ Are there questions you can't answer in the exam?
(c) 我估我到考試果陣會頭痛，我以前都試過系咁 I just knew I'll get a headache during the exam, like I did before.	你擔心考試時會頭痛 You worry you'll get a headache during the exam	你有冇試過去搵醫生睇睇呢? Have you tried to consult a doctor?
(d) 朋友真係咁易識咩...唔想要損友... Making friends is not so easy ... [I] don't want bad friends ...	你覺得唔容易識朋友 You think it's not easy to make friends	係咪覺得損友好冇益？ You think bad friends are bad for you?

Table 1: Example post-statement and post-question pairs from our manually annotated dataset (Section 3.1) addressing issued related to (a,b) academic anxiety; (c) test anxiety; and (d) loneliness

tal results (Section 5) and conclude (Section 6). Our datasets are available for download from https://github.com/CantoneseCounsellorChatbot

2 Previous work

While chatbot response generation has exploited models from machine translation (Ritter et al., 2011) and question answering (Liu et al., 2013), there has been less effort in leveraging those from other NLP tasks such as text summarization and question generation. This section reviews research in these two fields.

2.1 Text summarization

Text summarization models, which condense an input text into a shorter version, can generate short summaries or headlines (Rush et al., 2015). Pretrained language models such as BERT (Devlin et al., 2019) have been shown to boost the quality of summarization, among many other NLP tasks. Among the best-performing models is BertSum, which uses a document-level BERT-based encoder to express the semantics of the input text document and obtain sentence representations (Liu and Lapata, 2019). Its fine-tuning schedule adopts different optimizers for the encoder and the decoder, and has been shown to improve performance by alleviating the mismatch between them.

Compared to open-domain dialogs, a human counsellor more often gives shorter replies and reflects the points made by the counsellee. Summarization models can therefore potentially be helpful in generating restatements in the counselling domain. Generic summarization models, however, likely need to be fine-tuned since restatements are not identical to summaries. In Table 1(c), for instance, the perspective changes from first person to second person ('I'll get a headache' $\rightarrow$ 'You'll get a headache'); empathetic words are also inserted to diagnose the counsellee's emotion ('You worry ...'). To our knowledge, this is the first reported evaluation on applying a summarization model to counselling dialog generation.

2.2 Question generation

A question generation model composes a question from an input text. Neural question generation algorithms have recently attained state-of-the-art performance. For example, a sequence-to-sequence model with an attention mechanism has been proposed by Du et al. (2017). Answer separation techniques have further improved question quality (Kim et al., 2019).

Question generation is slightly different in the dialog context in that the answer should generally not be found in the input text, i.e., the previous utterances, so that the question would not seem redundant. Question generation models have been deployed to engage users in a conversation (Mostafazadeh et al., 2016), but the research was focused on images. Template-based approaches, as exemplified by ELIZA (Weizenbaum, 1983), can also transform the user's statements into questions. These templates are labor-intensive to

Post-reply type	Pairs	Length	
		post	reply
Post-restatement	12,634	40.1	7.9
Post-question	9,036	36.8	11.1

Table 2: Statistics on manual dataset (average length in number of characters)

Post-reply type	Method	Pairs	Length	
			post	reply
Post-restatement	Extraction	72.6K	13.6	6.3
	Matching	36.9K	47.6	6.2
Post-question	Extraction	80.7K	12.0	6.3
	Matching	33.1K	22.8	10.9

Table 3: Statistics on automatically mined dataset (average length in number of characters)

construct, however, and may not provide sufficient coverage.

3 Data

Our data consists of *post-reply pairs*, a term that will be used henceforth to refer to both post-restatement and post-question pairs. This section describes the construction process of two datasets, which contain in-domain, manually crafted (Section 3.1) and open-domain, automatically mined (Section 3.2) post-reply pairs, respectively.

3.1 Manual dataset

We recruited 10 undergraduate students to collect Cantonese social media posts with content concerning loneliness, academic and test anxiety. For each of the 6,294 posts collected, human annotators marked a text span as their "target phrase", and composed a restatement and/or question for that phrase. As shown in Table 2, the dataset contains 12,634 post-restatement pairs and 9,036 post-question pairs. There are on average 2.2 gold restatements per post, and 1.6 gold questions per post.

3.2 Automatically mined dataset

This dataset was automatically mined from the LCCC dataset (Wang et al., 2020b), which consists of 6.8 million Mandarin dialogs; and from 89K post-reply pairs crawled from Cantonese discussion forums in Hong Kong. We used two methods to generate post-reply pairs:

Extraction. To produce post-restatement pairs, we identified the longest common string of the post and the reply in each post-reply pair in the open-domain corpora above. We extracted all pairs whose longest common string contains at least four characters, and used the repeated string in the post as the restatement. To extract post-question pairs, we identified post-reply pairs whose reply starts with a short question, defined as a question mark preceded by no more than 10 characters.

Matching. We identified all posts that contain a text span that matches a target phrase in the manual dataset (Section 3.1). We then reused the restatement and/or question for that target phrase to form a new post-restatement and/or post-question pair.

4 Approach

We first construct and evaluate models for restatement generation and for question generation separately (Section 4.1). We then combine these models to interleave restatements and questions in a counselling dialog (Section 4.2).

4.1 Restatement and Question Generation

We focus on generation-based rather than retrieval-based models, in order to tailor restatements and questions specifically to the content in the post. For each of the following approaches, we trained a restatement generation model by fine-tuning the pre-trained model with post-restatement pairs in the manual dataset (Section 3.1); we then separately trained a question generation model in a similar fashion.

DialoGPT We used *GPT2 for Chinese chitchat*[1], a dialog model that is based on DialoGPT (Zhang et al., 2020) and trained on GPT2-Chinese (Du, 2019). We fine-tuned the pre-trained model with our post-reply pairs (Section 3.1).[2]

mT5 Competitive question generation models can be built by fine-tuning the Google T5 model (Pan et al., 2021). Adopting a similar approach with mT5 (Xue et al., 2021), a multilingual variant of T5, we fine-tuned the mT5-base model with our post-reply pairs.[3]

[1]https://github.com/yangjianxin1/GPT2-chitchat

[2]We used AdamW with a learning rate of 1.5e-4 and 2000 warmup steps as the optimizer. We fine-tuned the model for 50 epochs with batch size 32.

[3]We used a learning rate of 1e-4 and fine-tuned the model for 10 epochs with batch size 32, with the software provided at http://github.com/patil-suraj/question_generation

BertSum BertSum is a state-of-the-art summarization model (Liu and Lapata, 2019). We used the abstractive summarization model, which uses a standard encoder-decoder framework. The encoder is the pre-trained Bert and the decoder is a 6-layered Transformer with random initialization. We fine-tuned its pre-trained bert-base-chinese model with our post-reply pairs.[4]

Global Encoding The Global Encoding framework, which has shown competitive result in text summarization, seeks to improve the representations of the source-side information by using global information of the source context (Lin et al., 2018). Similar to above, we fine-tuned the pre-trained model with our post-reply pairs.[5]

Oracle Retrieval To gauge the maximum performance of a retrieval-based paradigm, this algorithm selects the highest-scoring reply in the training set in terms of ROUGE-L.

We further fine-tuned the DialoGPT, mT5, BertSum and Global Encoding models with the automatically mined dataset (Section 3.2). The resulting models are denoted as DialoGPT$^+$, mT5$^+$, BertSum$^+$, and Global Encoding$^+$.

4.2 Interleaving restatements and questions

A conversation becomes monotonous and even irritating if the counsellor repeatedly gives restatements or asks questions. Using DialoGPT and BertSum$^+$, the two strongest models for question generation (Table 5), we investigated the following methods to choose between a restatement candidate and question candidate as the reply.

BertSum$^+_{R+Q}$ This model is trained with the same settings as BertSum$^+$ (Section 4.1), except that it is fine-tuned with *both* post-restatement and post-question pairs.

BertSum$^+$ (threshold) This algorithm responds with a question when the BertSum$^+$ model for questions surpasses a confidence threshold; otherwise, it responds with a restatement. The tuning of the threshold will be described in Section 5.3.

BertSum$^+$ (random) This algorithm randomly chooses either the BertSum$^+$ model for restatements or the BertSum$^+$ model for questions.

BertSum$^+$ (ceiling) Designed to measure the maximum performance of BertSum$^+$, this algorithm identifies the subset of posts for which BertSum$^+$ generates the highest-scoring questions in terms of ROUGE-L. It replies to these posts with the generated questions, and to the remainder with restatements.

DialoGPT (ceiling) Same as above, the algorithm uses DialoGPT rather than BertSum$^+$.

5 Experimental results

All results are based on 5-fold cross-validation on the manual dataset (Section 3.1). Following previous research, our evaluation metrics include BLEU (Papineni et al., 2002) and ROUGE (Lin, 2004). In addition, we report results with METEOR (Banerjee and Lavie, 2005) and BertScore (Zhang et al., 2019).

5.1 Restatement generation

Table 4 shows the results for restatement generation. When fine-tuned on the manual dataset only, DialoGPT yielded a ROUGE-L score of 0.5525, outperforming Global Encoding (0.4031), mT5 (0.4960) and BertSum (0.4938).

When augmented with the automatically mined post-restatement pairs, BertSum$^+$ achieved the best ROUGE-L score (0.7142). It also outperformed other models in terms of BLEU, METEOR and BertScore. In terms of ROUGE-L, it even surpassed Oracle Retrieval (0.6932), which means that the restatements generated by the model were superior to the best available in the training set.

5.2 Question generation

Generally, automatically generated questions have lower ROUGE scores than restatements (Table 5). DialoGPT achieved only 0.4160 ROUGE, compared to 0.5525 for restatements. It outperformed both Global Encoding (0.3766) and BertSum (0.3602).

[4] We used two Adam optimizers with $\beta_1 = 0.9$ and $\beta_2 = 0.999$ for the encoder and the decoder, respectively, and learning rate $lr_E = 0.002$ and $lr_D = 0.1$. All models were trained for 200,000 steps. Model checkpoints were saved and evaluated on the validation set every 2,500 steps. We selected the best checkpoint based on their evaluation loss on the validation set.

[5] We used Adam with learning rate 0.0003 and learning rate decay parameter 0.5. We fine-tuned the model for 30 epochs with batch size 64.

Model	ROUGE-1	ROUGE-2	ROUGE-L	BLEU	METEOR	BertScore
DialoGPT	0.5587	0.4369	0.5525	0.5010	0.5135	0.4954
DialoGPT$^+$	0.5740	0.4656	0.5681	0.5038	0.5303	0.5127
Global Encoding	0.4114	0.2588	0.4031	0.3200	0.3347	0.3511
Global Encoding$^+$	0.6136	0.5079	0.6073	0.5449	0.5738	0.5508
mT5	0.5004	0.4133	0.4960	0.4102	0.4332	0.4276
mT5$^+$	0.5550	0.4787	0.5520	0.4751	0.5051	0.4712
BertSum	0.5013	0.3171	0.4938	0.4315	0.3986	0.3618
BertSum$^+$	**0.7184**	**0.6362**	**0.7142**	**0.6518**	**0.6881**	**0.6647**
Oracle Retrieval	0.6902	0.6011	0.6932	0.6709	0.6878	0.6604

Table 4: Model performance on restatement generation (the + superscript means the training set includes the automatically generated data)

Model	ROUGE-1	ROUGE-2	ROUGE-L	BLEU	METEOR	BertScore
DialoGPT	0.4252	0.2601	0.4160	0.4157	0.3605	0.4273
DialoGPT$^+$	0.3952	0.2360	0.3848	0.3803	0.3251	0.3905
Global Encoding	0.3845	0.2085	0.3766	0.3658	0.3082	0.3820
Global Encoding$^+$	0.4073	0.2516	0.3990	0.3887	0.3372	0.4004
mT5	0.3807	0.2415	0.3699	0.3669	0.3184	0.4152
mT5$^+$	0.3564	0.2293	0.3472	0.3338	0.2975	0.3932
BertSum	0.3676	0.1718	0.3602	0.3568	0.2591	0.2992
BertSum$^+$	**0.4752**	**0.3171**	**0.4665**	**0.4390**	**0.4002**	**0.4658**
Oracle Retrieval	0.6597	0.5612	0.6538	0.6401	0.6111	0.6626

Table 5: Model performance on question generation (the + superscript means the training set includes the automatically generated data)

When augmented with the automatically mined dataset, BertSum$^+$ again showed significant gains in performance. It achieved the highest ROUGE-L score (0.4665), followed by Global Encoding$^+$ (0.3990) and DialoGPT$^+$ (0.3848). Although mT5 is designed for question generation, its output scored lower than the other models in ROUGE-L, both when it is trained without (0.3699) and with the automatically mined data (0.3472).

5.3 Interleaving restatements and questions

Since it is more challenging to generate questions than restatements, a fair comparison between the algorithms requires a constant *question frequency* — i.e., the proportion of posts in the evaluation data to which the chatbot offers a question as response. The BertSum$^+_{R+Q}$ model generated questions 27.1% of the time and restatements 72.9% of the time.[6] We therefore set the confidence threshold for the BertSum$^+$ (threshold) model such that its question frequency would also be 27.1%. We likewise configured the BertSum$^+$ (random) model to randomly choose 27.1% of the posts to reply with questions.

As shown in Table 6, BertSum$^+$ (threshold) achieved the best performance at 0.7013 ROUGE-L, higher than its random counterpart (0.6730), BertSum$^+_{R+Q}$ (0.6702), as well as DialoGPT (ceiling) (0.5604). It suffered only a degradation of 0.04 in comparison to BertSum$^+$ (ceiling), which picks the optimal posts for question generation. This result suggests the effectiveness of selecting reply type with a confidence threshold.

One advantage of BertSum$^+$ (threshold) over BertSum$^+_{R+Q}$ is the ease with which question frequency can be adjusted to suit different conversation styles. Figure 1 plots its ROUGE-L score at various question frequencies. Since question generation is more difficult, the score decreases as questions are selected as the reply to a larger proportion of posts. BertSum$^+$ (threshold) outperformed both its random counterpart and DialoGPT (ceiling) at all question frequencies.

[6]The output is considered a question if it achieves a higher ROUGE-L score with the gold output in the post-question pair than the post-restatement pair (Section 3.1).

Model	ROUGE-1	ROUGE-2	ROUGE-L	BLEU	METEOR	BertScore
BertSum$^+_{R+Q}$	0.6752	0.5703	0.6702	0.6670	0.6308	0.6379
BertSum$^+$ (random)	0.6793	0.5664	0.6730	0.6884	0.6376	0.6412
BertSum$^+$ (threshold)	**0.7071**	**0.6061**	**0.7013**	**0.7232**	**0.6673**	**0.6621**
BertSum$^+$ (ceiling)	0.7504	0.6610	0.7456	0.7548	0.7137	0.7122
DialoGPT (ceiling)	0.5679	0.4371	0.5604	0.5156	0.5111	0.5147

Table 6: Model performance on response generation of either restatement or question (the + superscript means the training set includes the automatically generated data)

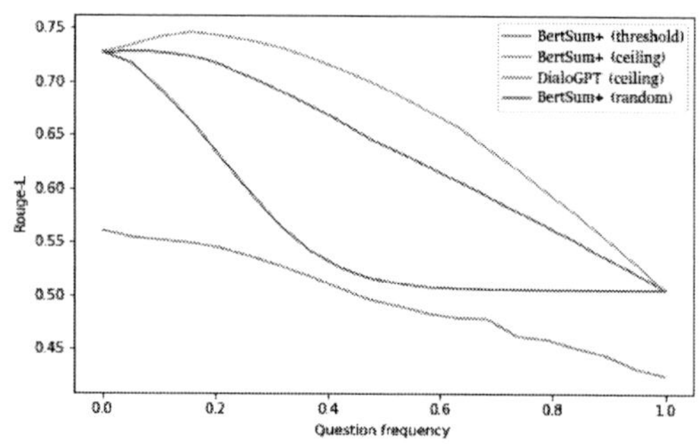

Figure 1: ROUGE-L score of BertSum$^+$ (threshold), BertSum$^+$ (ceiling), BertSum$^+$ (random) and DialoGPT (ceiling) at various question frequencies.

6 Conclusion

Restatements and questions are common conversation strategies in counselling. This paper has investigated automatic generation of these two reply types by exploiting models of two closely related NLP tasks — summarization and question generation. We obtained the best generation performance for both reply types by fine-tuning BertSum, a state-of-the-art summarization model, with an in-domain, manually annotated dataset augmented with a large-scale, automatically mined open-domain dataset. We then showed that restatements and questions can be interleaved with a confidence score threshold.

To the best of our knowledge, this is the first reported application of summarization models on chatbot response generation in the counselling domain. It is hoped that our proposed techniques can improve the quality of a counsellor chatbot for the public. Further research is needed to take into account the progress of the counselling session when selecting a reply (Althoff et al., 2016; Zhang and Danescu-Niculescu-Mizil, 2020), and to measure correlation with counselling outcomes.

Acknowledgments

This work was supported by a grant from the Health and Medical Research Fund (project #17180961), the Food and Health Bureau, The Government of the Hong Kong Special Administrative Region.

References

Tim Althoff, Kevin Clark, and Jure Leskovec. 2016. Large-scale Analysis of Counseling Conversations: An Application of Natural Language Processing to Mental Health. *Transactions of the Association for Computational Linguistics*, 4:463–476.

Satanjeev Banerjee and Alon Lavie. 2005. Meteor: An automatic metric for mt evaluation with improved correlation with human judgments. In *Proceedings of the acl workshop on intrinsic and extrinsic evaluation measures for machine translation and/or summarization*, pages 65–72.

Jacob Devlin, Ming-Wei Chang, Kenton Lee, and Kristina Toutanova. 2019. BERT: Pretraining of Deep Bidirectional Transformers for Language Understanding. In *Proc. NAACL-HLT*.

Xinya Du, Junru Shao, and Claire Cardie. 2017. Learning to Ask: Neural Question Generation for Reading Comprehension. In *Proceedings of the 55th Annual Meeting of the Association for Computational Linguistics (ACL)*.

Zeyao Du. 2019. Gpt2-chinese: Tools for training gpt2 model in chinese language. `https://github.com/Morizeyao/GPT2-Chinese`.

K. K. Fitzpatrick, A. Darcy, and M. Vierhile. 2017. Delivering Cognitive Behavior Therapy to Young Adults with Symptoms of Depression and Anxiety using a Fully Automated Conversational Agent (Woebot): A Randomized Controlled Trial. *JMIR Mental Health*, 4(2):e19.

Jing Huang, Qi Li, Yuanyuan Xue, Taoran Cheng, Shuangqing Xu, Jia Jia, and Ling Feng. 2015. TeenChat: A Chatterbot System for Sensing and Releasing Adolescents' Stress. *LNCS*, 9085:133–145.

Allen E. Ivey and Mary Bradford Ivey. 2003. *Intentional Interviewing and Counseling: Facilitating Client Development in a Multicultural Society*. Brooks Cole.

Yanghoon Kim, Hwanhee Lee, Joongbo Shin, and Kyomin Jung. 2019. Improving Neural Question Generation Using Answer Separation. In *Proc. 33rd AAAI Conference on Artificial Intelligence (AAAI-19)*.

Jiwei Li, Michel Galley, Chris Brockett, Jianfeng Gao, and Bill Dolan. 2016. A persona-based neural conversation model. In *Proc. ACL*.

Chin-Yew Lin. 2004. ROUGE: A package for automatic evaluation of summaries. In *Text Summarization Branches Out*, page 74–81, Barcelona, Spain.

Junyang Lin, Xu Sun, Shuming Ma, and Qi Su. 2018. Global Encoding for Abstractive Summarization. In *Proc. ACL*.

Zhaojiang Lin, Andrea Madotto, Jamin Shin, Peng Xu, and Pascale Fung. 2019. MoEL: Mixture of Empathetic Listeners. In *Proceedings of the 2019 Conference on Empirical Methods in Natural Language Processing and the 9th International Joint Conference on Natural Language Processing (EMNLP-IJCNLP)*, page 121–132.

Yang Liu and Mirella Lapata. 2019. Text Summarization with Pretrained Encoders. In *Proc. 2019 Conference on Empirical Methods in Natural Language Processing and the 9th International Joint Conference on Natural Language Processing*, page 3730–3740.

Yuanchao Liu, Ming Liu, Xiaolong Wang, Limin Wang, and Jingjing Li. 2013. PAL: A Chatterbot System for Answering Domain-specific Questions. In *Proc. 51st Annual Meeting of the Association for Computational Linguistics (ACL)*, pages 67–72.

Nurul Lubis, Sakriani Sakti, Koichiro Yoshino, and Satoshi Nakamura. 2018. Eliciting Positive Emotion through Affect-Sensitive Dialogue Response Generation: A Neural Network Approach. In *Proc. 32nd AAAI Conference on Artificial Intelligence (AAAI-18)*.

Nasrin Mostafazadeh, Ishan Misra, Jacob Devlin, Margaret Mitchell, Xiaodong He, and Lucy Vanderwende. 2016. Generating Natural Questions About an Image. In *Proc. 54th Annual Meeting of the Association for Computational Linguistics (ACL)*.

Liangming Pan, Wenhu Chen, Wenhan Xiong, Min-Yen Kan, and William Yang Wang. 2021. Unsupervised Multi-hop Question Answering by Question Generation. In *Proc. NAACL*.

Kishore Papineni, Salim Roukos, Todd Ward, and Wei-Jing Zhu. 2002. BLEU: a Method for Automatic Evaluation of Machine Translation. In *Proc. ACL*.

Alan Ritter, Colin Cherry, and William B. Dolan. 2011. Data-Driven Response Generation in Social Media. In *Proc. EMNLP*.

Alexander M. Rush, Sumit Chopra, and Jason Weston. 2015. A neural attention model for abstractive sentence summarization. In *Proc. EMNLP*.

Xiaofeng Wang, Shuai Chen, Tao Li, Wanting Li, Yejie Zhou, Jie Zheng, Qingcai Chen, Jun Yan, and Buzhou Tang. 2020a. Depression Risk Prediction for Chinese Microblogs via Deep-Learning methods: Content Analysis. *JMIR Medical Informatics*, 8(7).

Yida Wang, Pei Ke, Yinhe Zheng, Kaili Huang, Yong Jiang, Xiaoyan Zhu, and Minlie Huang. 2020b. A large-scale chinese short-text conversation dataset. In *Proc. CCF International Conference on Natural Language Processing and Chinese Computing*, pages 91–103.

Joseph Weizenbaum. 1983. ELIZA–A Computer Program For the Study of Natural Language Communication Between Man and Machine. *Communications of the ACM*, 26(1):23–28.

Linting Xue, Noah Constant, Adam Roberts, Mihir Kale, Rami Al-Rfou, Aditya Siddhant, Aditya Barua, and Colin Raffel. 2021. mT5: A Massively Multilingual Pre-trained Text-to-Text Transformer. In *Proc. NAACL*.

Justine Zhang and Cristian Danescu-Niculescu-Mizil. 2020. Balancing Objectives in Counseling Conversations: Advancing Forwards or Looking Backwards. In *Proc. ACL*.

Tianyi Zhang, Varsha Kishore, Felix Wu, Kilian Q Weinberger, and Yoav Artzi. 2019. Bertscore: Evaluating text generation with bert. *arXiv preprint arXiv:1904.09675*.

Yizhe Zhang, Siqi Sun, Michel Galley, Yen-Chun Chen, Chris Brockett, Xiang Gao, Jianfeng Gao, Jingjing Liu, and Bill Dolan. 2020. DIALOGPT : Large-Scale Generative Pre-training for Conversational Response Generation. In *Proc. ACL*.

Li Zhou, Jianfeng Gao, Di Li, and Heung-Yeung Shum. 2020. The Design and Implementation of XiaoIce, an Empathetic Social Chatbot. *Computational Linguistics*, 46(1):53–93.

The Climate Change Debate and Natural Language Processing

Manfred Stede
Applied Computational Linguistics
University of Potsdam
Potsdam/Germany
stede@uni-potsdam.de

Ronny Patz
Hertie School
Berlin/Germany
patz@hertie-school.de

Abstract

The debate around climate change (CC)—its extent, its causes, and the necessary responses—is intense and of global importance. Yet, in the natural language processing (NLP) community, this domain has so far received little attention. In contrast, it is of enormous prominence in various social science disciplines, and some of that work follows the "text-as-data" paradigm, seeking to employ quantitative methods for analyzing large amounts of CC-related text. Other research is qualitative in nature and studies details, nuances, actors, and motivations within CC discourses. Coming from both NLP and Political Science, and reviewing key works in both disciplines, we discuss how social science approaches to CC debates can inform advances in text-mining/NLP, and how, in return, NLP can support policy-makers and activists in making sense of large-scale and complex CC discourses across multiple genres, channels, topics, and communities. This is paramount for their ability to make rapid and meaningful impact on the discourse, and for shaping the necessary policy change.

1 Introduction

Anthropogenic climate change (CC) has become a central topic of global, national, and local debates across multiple arenas and channels that involve virtually all branches of society. From private talk to public social media exchanges, from scientific papers to journalistic articles in traditional mass media, from statements by stakeholders (industry, civil society groups, etc.) to political deliberations in national parliaments or in international organizations—no sphere is without references to climate change. While climate scientists have reached a consensus that climate change is real, that it is caused by human activity on the planet, and that is has and will have adverse effects for humanity and the biosphere around the planet (Cook et al., 2016), public debates on CC and on the policy implications remain highly controversial (see, e.g., (Hulme, 2009)).

Natural Language Processing (NLP) is well-positioned to help study the dynamics of the large-scale and complex discourse on CC. Activists and policy-makers need NLP tools through which they can filter, order, and make sense of the vast amount of textual data produced on CC. However, within the NLP community, the amount of work done so far on CC remains limited. In the words of Luo et al. (2020, p. 3296), the topic of climate change "has received little attention in NLP despite its real world urgency". This is in contrast to the attention that CC discourses receive in climate and environmental science and in various social sciences.

We argue in this paper that the research questions, insights and methods applied in these disciplines can provide useful orientation for NLP practitioners. And conversely, the general advances in NLP can provide more reliable and valid tools to actors aiming at shaping policy and influencing individual behavior. Such tools for monitoring the discourses across the multitude of channels, genres, speakers, and topics can enable policy-makers and activists to more rapidly respond to discourse shifts, which is of huge importance given the speed of the ongoing climate change.

To set the stage, in Section 2, we explain what we mean by CC "discourses" and we delineate the different readings of the term. Next, Section 3 takes the viewpoint of the NLP community and summarizes work that has been done in the field so far. Section 4 describes key studies taken from the social science literature, which study CC discourse in different ways and to different ends. Our emphasis here is on the methodological choices that are being made. Section 5 provides a comparative analysis and proposes points of synergy that we regard as

Proceedings of the 1st Workshop on NLP for Positive Impact, pages 8–18
Bangkok, Thailand (online), August 5, 2021. ©2021 Association for Computational Linguistics

recommendations for NLP work. Our conclusions on the potential positive impact of NLP for making sense of the CC debate are presented in Section 6.

2 Climate Change "Discourses"

The term *discourse* is both polysemous and vague. In NLP and its branch of 'discourse processing', its default reading refers to a single text or a single dialogical interaction that becomes an object of study, involving phenomena that cross sentence boundaries (anaphoric reference, coherence relations, and so on). That reading is largely irrelevant for our purposes here.

In the social sciences, theories and definitions of *discourse(s)* and methods of *discourse analysis* are highly diverse. In the context of environmental policy, Hajer and Versteeg (2005, p. 175) define a discourse as the "ensemble of ideas, concepts and categories through which meaning is given to social and physical phenomena, and which is produced and reproduced through an identifiable set of practices". Thus, when we refer to the *climate change discourse*, we refer to the ensemble of practices of writing about or debating CC-related matters by one or multiple actors in various physical or digital arenas.

In much of the empirical literature on CC debates that we review below, this results in a focus on one of two dimensions of discourse:

- Discourse$_1$: Focus on exchanges on different technical media ("channels") and in different genres:
  - Traditional news media
  - Social media
  - Scientific exchange
  - Parliamentary debate
  - ...
- Discourse$_2$: Focus on social communities engaged in the topic-specific interaction, possibly using multiple channels (but studies often focus on single channels):
  - Grouped by role in the social constellation:
    * Politicians
    * Scientists
    * Industrial stakeholders
    * Interest groups (environmental, etc.)
    * Individuals
    * ...
  - Grouped by stance toward the topic:
    * Climate change believers/accepters
    * Climate change sceptics/deniers
    * ...

Once one zooms in on the stances on CC more closely, further dimensions of Discourse$_2$ become visible. For example, Anshelm and Hultman (2015) develop a more fine-grained stance classification distinguishing between "industrial fatalism", "Green Keynesian", "eco-socialist" and "climate-sceptic" discourses.[1]

Whether studies on CC detect a divided debate or a relatively unified conversation (Wetts, 2020) will depend on the types of discourse dimensions studied as well as on the level of analysis. This should be important also for NLP practitioners when they select a set of data for their work, as certain differences in nuances on stances may remain inconsequential in a social media debate between individuals, but can have significant policy implications when uttered by political leaders in a parliamentary debate.

3 CC discourse: Research in the NLP community

The difference between this and the following section is one of scientific community: In the present section, we briefly summarize work that has been done on CC-related data and was presented at NLP/Computational Linguistics or AI meetings. The number of such publications is small, so we mention them here in chronological order. Henceforth, we use lowercased "cc" and "gw" as shorthand for "climate change" and "global warming", respectively, as a search bigram employed by researchers for retrieving their data.

Diakopoulos et al. (2014) crawled 1.5 mio posts from 3,000 blogs, found by the query term cc or one from a short list of other terms, and manually coded a selection of blogs as belonging to sceptic or accepter discourse. 133 topical terms of CC discourse are taken from previous work, and for each term, correlations with "virtue" and "vice" words

[1]"Industrial fatalism": apocalyptic scenarios are to be answered by technologcial solutions; "green Keynesian": CC is but one symptom of an institutional ecological crisis that requires redistribution of global resources; "eco-socialist": CC is a result of the pathological growth ideology of industrial capitalist society; "climate-sceptic": emissions with anthropogenic causes are not responsible for climate change, and no huge interventions are necessary.

(from the General Inquirer lexicon) are computed for both groups of blogs. Then visual analytics are applied to manually compare the discourses. Differences between blogs are found to be mainly in the framing of "climate science" and "quality of life". In continuation of this work, Salway et al. (2016) built a corpus of CC blog posts in three languages. They applied network analysis to the graph of blog linkages and detected four prominent communities of bloggers.

The CC topic became more visible in the NLP community when (Mohammad et al., 2016) introduced the new SemEval task "stance detection of tweets", where "Climate change is a real concern" was one of five statements for which a dataset was built. Beyond this, however, CC was not addressed in any more specific way.

Pathak et al. (2017) collected tweets around the 2015 UN CC conference in Paris, using about 20 search keywords and a similar number of hashtags, as well as three Twitter accounts dedicated to the conference. Term lists for CC subtopics are constructed by extending seed words with similar words gathered by a word2vec model. Then, opinion and emotion analysis tools are applied. Results are plotted in particular for correlations of emotions and topics and the role of "influencers" versus less prominent accounts.

Jiang et al. (2017) gathered 11,000 newspaper articles from four British broadsheets over the years 2007-2016. The search criterion was that cc has to occur at least three times. They use LDA to find sentiment targets in the texts, and by employing SentiWordNet to label keywords in the associated topics, they found some differences between newspapers in their topic-sentiment association.

Recently, Luo et al. (2020) were the first to apply a broad range of current NLP techniques to the CC domain. They introduce a corpus of 2,000 CC sentences from 63 US news sources (2000-2020), which were labeled by crowdworkers for stance toward "climate change is a real concern" (cf. (Mohammad et al., 2016) above). The base corpus of 56,000 articles was built with four bigram and two unigram query terms. Dependency parsing and coreference resolution are applied to enable extraction of opinion statements using a set of hand-coded patterns. These statements allow to distinguish self-affirming versus opponent-doubting frames in quoting sources of information. A BERT model is employed for stance classification, allowing to identify accepter and sceptic media.

Recently, Koenecke and Feliu-Fabà (2020) study whether CC sentiment in tweets changed in response to five natural disasters occurring in the US in 2018. Tweets had to contain one of the terms cc or gw, plus at least one instance of a set of natural-disaster terms. This yielded 800 pre-event and 6,000 post-event tweets. An array of standard ML tools were tested for classifying accepter versus sceptic tweets. RNNs with GloVe embeddings performed best, yielding an accuracy of 75%. A cohort-level analysis then shows that the 2018 hurricanes yielded a statistically significant increase in average tweet sentiment affirming CC, while other disasters did not.

Summary In the absence of any "standard CC dataset", the NLP research so far has been scattered. Types of target texts (Discourse$_1$) were limited to news (Jiang et al., 2017; Luo et al., 2020), blogs (Diakopoulos et al., 2014; Salway et al., 2016) and Twitter (Pathak et al., 2017; Koenecke and Feliu-Fabà, 2020); no comparisons across genres or channels were made, and there was no attention on political arenas or on statements by individuals and interest groups that are meant to directly influence policy-making. In terms of methods and goals we found network analysis for detecting communities (Salway et al., 2016; Pathak et al., 2017), sentiment/stance classification for Discourse$_2$ grouping (Diakopoulos et al., 2014; Pathak et al., 2017; Jiang et al., 2017; Luo et al., 2020; Koenecke and Feliu-Fabà, 2020), topic modeling for computing topic/sentiment correlations (Jiang et al., 2017), and fine-grained framing distinction (Luo et al., 2020).

4 CC discourse: Research in the social sciences

In the following we provide a synthesis of a subjective selection of papers from journals in communication science, political science, and climate/environmental science that address CC discourse. All selected contributions take a "text-as-data" approach (Grimmer and Stewart, 2013) and use either semi-automatic methods such as corpus-linguistic collocation analysis or fully-automatic text mining methods. The papers we chose are either frequently cited or representative for widespread methodological approaches; a few are selected because they are innovative, either in terms of method or in terms of the text genre(s) being addressed.

We group the discussion along the targeted text genres or media (i.e., our Discourse_1 dimension), to illustrate the range of underlying social science research questions and the data used to answer them. Then, in the second subsection, we summarize and assess the methods used, and we close the section with remarks on the relation between qualitative and quantitative research.

4.1 Genres and research questions

News media News text has for a long time been a highly prominent object of study in quantitative text analysis in the social sciences. In an early paper on CC, Trumbo (1996) determined how much coverage the topic received in 5 US newspapers, and he manually coded texts for using frames in the sense of Entman (1993) (see Sct. 5). Frames were also studied intensively by Hoffman (2011), who hand-coded 800 newspaper op-eds for (i) overall stance (convinced, sceptical, neutral, unclear); (ii) topical frame categories (science, risk, technology, economics, religion, political ideology, national security); and (iii) whether arguments used diagnostic, prognostic or motivational frames (Entman, 1993). Findings included that in the press, accepter articles usually come from journalists, while sceptical texts tend to be letters to the editor. Yet another conception of frames was recently used by Stecula and Merkley (2019) who employed supervised classification to obtain 14,000 articles on the CC topic. The authors found that frames of "economic decline as a result of mitigating CC" are on the decline, and that frames highlighting scientific uncertainty (rather than CC consensus) are in sharp decline.

A different question was investigated by Boykoff and Boykoff (2007), who studied CC coverage on TV and in newspapers to determine whether adherence to the "journalistic norms" of personalization, drama, novelty, authority-order and balance contributed to impediments in covering anthropogenic CC. They found that the goals of balance and drama lead to fringe scientists getting more attention than would be proportionally warranted.

A different, in some sense more "modest", line of work is interested in the amount of coverage of CC in the press, and possible correlations with important events. Lyytimäki and Tapio (2009) studied 4,000 texts from the Finnish press, with manual coding of topical relevance following an automatic retrieval. Other work in this vein added the aspect of cross-country comparison: Grundmann and Krishnamurthy (2010), for example, worked with newspapers from four countries. Besides comparing attention to CC across the countries, they offered observations on the basis of word frequencies and collocation lists. Schmidt et al. (2013) extended the comparison of attention to an impressive list of 27 countries with a corpus spanning 15 years. In contrast, O'Neill et al. (2015) focused specifically on the coverage of newly-released IPCC reports in newspapers, and also on TV and in Twitter. Studying the frames used in reporting about specific IPCC working groups, the authors proposed some recommendations on how to communicate particular kinds of information in future climate science reports.

Topic modeling is generally a popular tool in "text-as-data" research. Applying it to a corpus of 78,000 CC articles from 52 US newspapers, Bohr (2020) identified 28 themes related to climate change, whose prevalence (according to his interpretation) partly depends on the political orientation of the respective editorial boards.

Social media Key questions in research on CC discourse in social media concern how discursive networks and "discursive landscapes" (Schoenfeld et al., 2018) form, and what drives the polarization in CC debates. For example, Elgesem et al. (2014) aimed to "chart the entire structure of the climate change blogosphere". They crawled 1.3 mio posts from 3,000 blogs and ran community detection algorithms. Blogs were manually classified as sceptic, accepter, or neutral; after running LDA, certain associations between blogger subcommunities and topics were found. Similarly, Pérez-González (2020) used concordance and visualization tools on 450,000 tokens from five blogs and show that terms such as "bias", "dogma" or "peer review" are framed with different motifs depending on the bloggers ideological orientation.

Many studies are performed on Twitter data. As an example of a largely descriptive analysis, Dahal et al. (2019) collected 360,000 tweets with five CC-related bigrams, and plotted distributions over topics (via LDA), countries and time. Veltri and Atanasova (2015) collected 60,000 tweets representing a random week (using the bigams cc and gw), built cooccurrence networks over weighted terms and used centrality measures to determine the salient topics. Further, using an emotion lexicon revealed that emotionally arousing text was more likely to be shared. Samantray and Pin (2019) worked with 14 mio Tweets from 3.5 mio users, written over 10 years (also found with the bigrams cc, gw). They classified Tweets and users for stance believer/denier/neutral, and with sentiment and emotion lexicons they computed correlations between polarizing language and the degree of interaction between people with similar versus antagonistic viewpoints.

Parliamentary debate and political speech Though the amount of available data from CC-dedicated political debate is small, the research perspectives taken here show that attention to different genres is crucial for moving beyond the foci on measuring coverage and polarization. For instance, by working with a speech corpus of 100,000 words from the UK parliament's debate on the 2008 Climate Change Bill, Willis (2017) found that climate change is presented through "strongly scientific, technical and economic language", and he thus derived a tendency to de-politicize CC in parliament, and to frame it as a technical issue that is amenable to straightforward policy action.

More advanced research questions at the intersection of social science and linguistics also come with somewhat more elaborate computational methods. Majdik (2019) worked with US congressional records from 1994 to 2016 and retrieved 30,000 instances of speech mentioning cc or gw. After POS tagging and extracting bigrams, regular expressions are employed to analyze the context of selected combinations of cc/gw and verbs, which lead to a comparison of "active-agentive" to "passive-agentive" mentions in the speeches. On a related genre, (Calderwood, 2020) took a random sample of presidential speeches, ranging from Georg H. Bush to Obama, querying with "climat*" and "warm*". One resulting observation showed certain patterns of invoking CC when the speech is given in specific geographical locations.

Institutional text and reports Documents from specific institutions play an important role for many social science research questions. When Barkemeyer et al. (2016) compared the "summary for policymakers" of IPCC reports to other scientific communication, they found that the summaries have a low readability and differ notably in terms of "optimism scores" as derived with a sentiment dictionary. Other types of documents reveal a shift in the CC discourse from prevention to mitigation: Jaworska (2018) studied corporate social responsibility and environmental reports that were produced by major oil companies from 2000 to 2013. Using corpus-linguistic tools she found a trend toward highlighting the risks of CC. This suggests that future research may find a new divide, not between deniers and accepters but between the attitudes "we can do something" and "CC is an unpredictable risk". A different trend was found by Wetts (2020) in a corpus of 1,700 institutional press releases (1985 to 2013). With topic modeling and cluster analysis she found the discourse among interest groups to become "post-political", i.e., less polarized, over time.

Looking specifically at CC denial, Boussalis and Coan (2016) used LDA on 16,000 documents from 19 organizations to find typical topics that contrarian actors link to CC. Going a significant step further, Farrell (2019) turned to intentional misinformation. Using the Stanford NER system he detected 28,000 different names of individuals and organizations connected to the American "Philantropy Roundtable" organization (in magazines, almanacs and other online sources). Similarly he built a list of people known to be associated with deliberate misinformation, and then he computed the intersection with an approximate string matching algorithm.

Other genres Finally, we mention two examples of work on corpora from other sources. Hulme et al. (2018) built a CC subcorpus of the editorials of the *Nature* and *Science* journals, ranging from the mid 1960s to 2017. Eight frame categories, similar to those mentioned above for (Hoffman, 2011), were manually assigned to the texts. Observing the shifting frames over time and the differences between Europe and North America underscores that scientific communication around the CC discourse is not homogeneous and deserves continued attention.

Citizens' voices on CC can be found not only on social media. Devaney et al. (2020) compiled a small corpus of 1,885 citizen submissions to the Irish Citizens' Assembly on climate change. Combining LDA with a qualitative analysis of a 10 per cent sample, they drew lessons "for enhancing environmental literacy by improving climate crisis communication and engagement strategies". Beyond the polarization question, the submissions show what issues citizens care about when they talk about climate change—which in turn can advise policy-makers in shaping policy solutions.

4.2 Methods applied

We briefly summarize the text mining/NLP methods that have been used in the work mentioned above (and in some other social science research), vaguely in the order of increasing complexity or sophistication.

- perform bigram matching for finding texts about climate change (often just the two bigrams cc and gw; sometimes more extensive Boolean queries, as in (Schmidt et al., 2013)), occasionally followed by manual filtering (e.g., (Lyytimäki and Tapio, 2009; Hulme et al., 2018)
- run straightforward term frequency and collocation analysis as a preparation for manual corpus inspection (e.g., (Willis, 2017)); sometimes with sophisticated visualisation (Pérez-González, 2020)
- compute bigram frequencies, or combine POS tagging with regex search to find verb usage patterns (Majdik, 2019)
- apply lexicons (sentiment, emotions, LIWC, etc.) "out of the box" (e.g., (Barkemeyer et al., 2016))
- apply supervised classification to find CC texts and detect the presence of frames (economy, ideology, uncertainty) (Stecula and Merkley, 2019)
- apply topic modeling, usually LDA, without much further intepretation (e.g., (Dahal et al., 2019)) or with extensive subsequent interpretation (e.g., (Boussalis and Coan, 2016))
- apply topic modeling and combine this with other methods, such as network analysis (Elgesem et al., 2014) or cluster analysis (Wetts, 2020), in order to study a dedicated research question
- combine multiple techniques (sentiment, emotion, network analysis) to arrive at a fairly complex concept like "credibility of a tweet" (Samantray and Pin, 2019)

4.3 Qualitative and quantitative research

We wish to point out that in the social sciences, the body of qualitative research on CC-related discourse is hardly smaller or less diverse than that of the quantitative work. Qualitatively-oriented studies show, for example, that effective communication on CC policy can result in citizen assemblies supporting specific policy proposals (Muradova et al., 2020). Carpenter (2002) traced how shifts in interest group discourses impacted negotiations of states at the COP-6. And studies on public opinion demonstrated that the quantity of media coverage on CC did not impact public opinion as much as "elite cues" represented through partisan press releases or voting. A common theme, in any case, is that one needs to study CC discourse *across* channels and communities in order to understand the (lack of) impact on opinion or policy.

5 Analyzing the CC debate: Goals and methods

In the social sciences, three criteria are often used to assess the quality of research (see, e.g., (Kantner and Overbeck, 2020)):

- **Reliability:** Are analyses stable over time and can they be reproduced by other researchers?
- **Representativeness:** Does the selected data represent the variability in the underlying textual population?
- **Validity:** Do the analyses on the data actually measure the theoretically-derived (or underlying) concepts, i.e., are they helpful for the research question?

The first point corresponds quite clearly to the goal of reproducibility in NLP and does not require further comment here. In this section, we will thus reflect on the other two points. An the end, we summarize the takeaway messages that we propose for NLP.

5.1 Representativeness

Unless a certain dataset trvially represents the totality of a target discourse (e.g., all CC submissions to the Irish Citizens' Assembly; (Devaney et al., 2020)), the work starts with assembling the subcorpus of texts that are relevant for the research question. As we pointed out in Section 4, the majority of studies employ just two bigrams (cc, gw), while a few use longer flat lists of terms (Pathak et al.,

2017) or combine terms into elaborate Boolean queries (Schmidt et al., 2013). In comparison, climate change is a relatively "friendly" domain in this respect, as the cc bigram intuitively promises relatively good quality in terms of both precision and recall. Nonetheless, one has to be aware of pitfalls, for instance when working with older text, where "global warming" and "greenhouse effect" in many discourses were the central representative terms. These questions have consequences for comparing the results and insights of different studies, for example on polarization; as noted by Calderwood (2020): "climate change" and "global warming" can be used as politically-sensitive terms, while others like "carbon emission" are more neutral.

A follow-up question concerns the "degree of topicality" of texts. The vast majority of work discussed above ran algorithms on the retrieved set of documents under the assumption that they are of equal relevance. However, in our own (ongoing) work on building a CC subcorpus of newspaper articles, we noted that querying the cc bigram also yields plenty of wine discussions and restaurant reviews. Depending on the size of the dataset, either noise is to be tolerated, or a step of manual filtering can be undertaken to improve precision, as also noted for news text by Lyytimäki and Tapio (2009) and for *Science/Nature* editorials by Hulme et al. (2018). On the latter corpus, ongoing work in our group found that supervised topic-frame classification works better for those texts that have a higher degree of "climate topicality", in comparison to texts that only mention CC in passing.

In general, supervised classification has not yet received a great deal of attention in the social science work, the exception in our survery being the study by Stecula and Merkley (2019), who used it both for finding topical texts in a large corpus and for identifying framing categories within the texts. They did not provide any evaluation of these steps, though; this is a point where established NLP research routines could inform the social science methodology.

5.2 Validity

Grimmer and Stewart (2013) stressed the danger of applying automatic tools to a text corpus without thorough reflection on what they actually measure. In the studies discussed in the previous sections, we find different attitudes toward this caution. Sometimes, the output of topic modeling or sentiment analysis is rather straightforwardly used to plot correlations with media types, time, or geographical regions. Stipulating such correlations based on NLP measures becomes much more critical when people or communities are directly affected, for example when Farrell (2019) relies on out-of-the-box NER to find out which people or organizations are associated both with philanthropy and with misinformation campaigns. Awareness of the risks of noisy or imprecise tool behavior is important for social scientists. The NLP community thus needs to consider its responsibility for making quality measures and domain or genre dependencies for their tools transparent, so that they are not used where their validity is low. One example of this discussion is the realm of sentiment lexicons, where the political science community found "one of their own" domain-specific tools (Young and Soroka, 2012) to be more trustworthy than so-called general-purpose lexicons.

Notwithstanding this note of caution, we believe that social science research should be open to embracing NLP tools that move beyond the well-established bag of words models and lexicon matching, especially where it increases validity. We agree with Grimmer and Stewart (2013) that NLP starts when the analysis goes beyond bags and "digs deeper" into the linear order of words and sentences for the purpose of extracting information. We think that, for example, word embeddings could receive more attention in social science in contexts where the meaning of CC terms is complex or shifting. Similarly, dependency parsing as a preparatory step to deeper content analysis can be highly relevant (also in conjunction with manual rules), as demonstrated for CC texts by Luo et al. (2020).

The "deeper analysis" concerns in particular the notion of *framing*, which is well-known to be highly ambiguous and vague (Scheufele and Iyengar, 2014, p. 6). This problem directly concerns the axiom of validity in quantitative research: what is, actually, being analyzed or measured? The majority of work discussed in Section 4 refers to Entman (1993), who stated that "to frame is to select some aspects of a perceived reality and make them more salient in a communicating text, in such a way as to promote a particular problem definition, causal interpretation, moral evaluation, and/or treatment recommendation". However, while much research refers to Entman, we noted only one paper that actually uses his categories for annotation and analysis (Trumbo, 1996). Most other frame sets are, essentially, *topic perspectives*, as the list by Hoffman (2011) (quoted above) illustrates. Similar lists have been defined by, inter alia, Hulme et al. (2018) and O'Neill et al. (2015).

Whether frames are conceived as topics or as epistemic categories (e.g., (Entman, 1993; Luo et al., 2020)) makes a huge difference for validity of measurement in different research questions: The mere presence of a topic-frame in a text is to be distinguished from the stipulation that an intentional communicative act of selecting or emphasizing has been performed. The computational identification of subtle and purposeful framing requires approaches that most certainly have to go beyond bags of words. Linguistically-inspired NLP researchers can help in sorting out these phenomena, e.g., by systematically relating forms of framing to types of subjectivity analysis that are established in the NLP community, such as stance, aspect-based sentiment or argument mining.

Our final remark is that many interesting phenomena in discourse analysis are simply too subtle for automatic mining and instead require human analysis to increase validity. Here, NLP has an important role in preparing and annotating the corpora, and also in making them available to analysts in effective and comfortable ways.

5.3 Key takeaways for NLP

Considering the discussion in the previous sections, we summarize our main recommendations for how the NLP community can contribute to sense-making of the CC debate and of similar debates that are being studied in the social sciences.

- Given the importance of subcorpus building to the interdisciplinary study of the CC discourse, NLP can provide advanced and effective methods of finding topic-relevant cc texts without relying on a few predefined bigrams.
- By studying "smaller" genres such as political speech or citizen voices on CC, NLP can increase its relevance for policy debates even where it does not deal with "big data", viz. by increasing efficiciency and reliability/reproducibility of analyses.
- NLP can contribute to tools that provide for valid cross-channel and cross-genre analyses to understand how CC discourses travel across communities, genres, and time.
- NLP tools regularly need to be adapted to domains and genres that are relevant for social science questions on CC discourses, as opposed to just using them "out of the box". This includes clarifying in what way a tool depends on its training data or other sources and how well it can be expected to perform elsewhere.
- While social scientists studying CC may have the domain expertise, the linguistic expertise from the NLP community can help understanding how notions of "framing" correspond to established NLP tasks in subjectivity analysis and topic classification, so that social science can adopt tools that are relevant for such tasks.
- More attention can be given to the connections between network analysis (actors and their social relations) and NLP analyses, for example to extend multiplex community detection or to trace CC-related frame diffusion in online and offline social networks.
- For phenomena that eschew fully-automatic analysis, NLP and social sciences can collaborate on developing tools that support the human analyst and/or annotator in tracing CC discourses, for example by easy corpus filtering or visual analytics of frames, speaker-topic networks and the like.

6 Conclusions: Climate change, NLP, and the impact for social good

In this contribution, we have argued that NLP and social science can enrich each other to more comprehensively study the complex discourse(s) on climate change across channels, genres, communities, and topics. This is important because the CC debate is unfolding among three large and diverse actor communities:

- the general public,
- the policy-making communities (governments, public administrations, interest groups) at national or international levels, and
- the scientific communities.

Each community uses different genres, registers, and terminologies to communicate with each other and with other communities about CC. These communities shape individual and collective ideas, frames, and, ultimately, the behavior that is consequential for the future evolution of anthropogenic climate change. While social scientists explore this complex discourse in qualitative and quantitative research, they lack the full toolbox to do so at scale. And while NLP researchers are continuously expanding the general NLP toolbox, they have so far been selective in the channels and questions they focus on when it comes to CC, more or less choosing "the usual suspects".

The positive impact of combining both perspectives is not guaranteed, but possible. As societies increase their ability of "making sense" of the CC discourse, they get better at understanding and evaluating the politics and discourse landscape: Who is trying to frame CC discussions, on what channel, in what way, and for what interests? Is the CC debate polarized, controversial, fragmented into echo chambers or simply nuanced in an attempt to find socially and politically accepted solutions? Which frames are intentionally placed, and which are taken over, consciously and subconsciously, in traditional and new media? Why are some frames more successful and thus more likely to shape ideas that define public policy or collective behavior in relation to CC?

Where NLP can help answer these questions in reliable/reproducible, representative, and valid ways, it can have a positive impact for the social good beyond enriching the social sciences: Ultimately, it may provide each of the three communities mentioned above with the ability to judge in what direction one of the most important debates of our time—the climate change discourse—is evolving, and to respond accordingly.

Acknowledgments

We thank the anonymous reviewers for detailed constructive suggestions for improving the previous version of the paper.

References

Jonas Anshelm and Martin Hultman. 2015. *Discourses of Global Climate Change – Apocalyptic framing and political antagonisms.* Cambridge UP, Cambridge.

Ralf Barkemeyer, Suraje Dessai, Beatriz Monge-Sanz, Barbara Gabriella Renzi, and Giulio Napolitano. 2016. Linguistic analysis of IPCC summaries for policymakers and associated coverage. *nature climate change*, 6:311–317.

Jeremiah Bohr. 2020. Reporting on climate change: A computational analysis of U.S. newspapers and sources of bias, 1997–2017. *Global Environmental Change*, 61(102038).

Constantine Boussalis and Travis G. Coan. 2016. Text-mining the signals of climate change doubt. *Global Environmental Change*, 36:89–100.

Maxwell Boykoff and Jules Boykoff. 2007. Climate Change and Journalistic Norms: A Case-Study of US Mass-Media Coverage. *Geoforum*, 38(6):1190–2004.

Kevin J. Calderwood. 2020. Going Global: Climate Change Discourse in Presidential Communications. *Environmental Communication*, 14(1):52–67.

Chad Carpenter. 2002. Businesses, Green Groups and The Media: The Role of Non-Governmental Organizations in the Climate Change Debate. *International Affairs*, 77(2):313–328.

John Cook, Naomi Oreskes, Peter T Doran, William R L Anderegg, Bart Verheggen, Ed W Maibach, J Stuart Carlton, Stephan Lewandowsky, Andrew G Skuce, Sarah A Green, Dana Nuccitelli, Peter Jacobs, Mark Richardson, Bärbel Winkler, Rob Painting, and Ken Rice. 2016. Consensus on consensus: a synthesis of consensus estimates on human-caused global warming. *Environmental Research Letters*, 11(4).

Biraj Dahal, Sathish A. P. Kumar, and Zhenlong Li. 2019. Topic modeling and sentiment analysis of global climate change tweets. *Social Network Analysis and Mining*, 9(24).

Laura Devaney, Pat Brereton, Diarmuid Torney, Martha Coleman, Constantine Boussalis, and Travis G. Coan. 2020. Environmental literacy and deliberative democracy: a content analysis of written submissions to the Irish Citizens' Assembly on climate change. *Climatic Change*, 162:1965–1984.

Nicholas Diakopoulos, Amy X. Zhang, Dag Elgesem, and Andrew Salway. 2014. Identifying and analyzing moral evaluation frames in climate change blog discourse. In *Proceedings of the Eighth International AAAI Conference on Weblogs and Social Media*, pages 583–586.

Dag Elgesem, Lubos Steskal, and Nicholas Diakopoulos. 2014. Structure and Content of the Discourse on Climate Change in the Blogosphere: The Big Picture. *Environmental Communication*, 9(2).

R.M. Entman. 1993. Framing: Toward clarification of a fractured paradigm. *Journal of Communication*, 43(4):51–58.

Justin Farrell. 2019. The growth of climate change misinformation in US philanthropy: evidence from natural language processing. *Environmental Research Letters*, 14:034013.

Justin Grimmer and Brandon M. Stewart. 2013. Text as Data: The Promise and Pitfalls of Automatic Content Analysis Methods for Political Texts. *Political Analysis*, 21:267–297.

Reiner Grundmann and Ramesh Krishnamurthy. 2010. The Discourse of Climate Change: A Corpus-based Approach. *Critical Approaches to Discourse Analysis across Disciplines*, 4(2):113–133.

Maarten Hajer and Wytske Versteeg. 2005. A decade of discourse analysis of environmental politics: Achievements, challenges, perspectives. *Journal of Environmental Policy & Planning*, 7(3):175–184.

Andrew J. Hoffman. 2011. Talking Past Each Other? Cultural Framing of Skeptical and Convinced Logics in the Climate Change Debate. *Organization & Environment*, 24(1):3–33.

Mike Hulme. 2009. *Why we disagree about climate change: Understanding controversy, inaction and opportunity*. Cambridge UP, Cambridge.

Mike Hulme, Noam Obermeister, Samuel Randalls, and Maud Borie. 2018. Framing the challenge of climate change in Nature and Science editorials. *nature climate change*, 8:515–521.

Sylvia Jaworska. 2018. Change But no Climate Change: Discourses of Climate Change in Corporate Social Responsibility Reporting in the Oil Industry. *Int'l Journal of Business Communication*, 55:194–219.

Ye Jiang, Xingyi Song, Jackie Harrison, Shaun Quegan, and Diana Maynard. 2017. Comparing attitudes to climate change in the media using sentiment analysis based on Latent Dirichlet Allocation. In *Proceedings of the 2017 EMNLP Workshop: Natural Language Processing meets Journalism*, pages 25–30, Copenhagen, Denmark.

Cathleen Kantner and Maximilian Overbeck. 2020. Exploring soft concepts with hard corpus-analytic methods. In Nils Reiter, Axel Pichler, and Jonas Kuhn, editors, *Reflektierte algorithmische Textanalyse*. De Gruyter, Berlin.

Allison Koenecke and Jordi Feliu-Fabà. 2020. Learning twitter user sentiments on climate change with limited labeled data. In *Proceedings of the 14th International AAAI Conference on Web and Social Media*.

Yiwei Luo, Dallas Card, and Dan Jurafsky. 2020. Detecting stance in media on global warming. In *Findings of the Association for Computational Linguistics: EMNLP 2020*, pages 3296–3315, Online.

J. Lyytimäki and P. Tapio. 2009. Climate change as reported in the press of Finland: From screaming headlines to penetrating background noise. *International Journal of Environmental Studies*, 66(6):723–735.

Zoltan P. Majdik. 2019. A Computational Approach to Assessing Rhetorical Effectiveness: Agentic Framing of Climate Change in the Congressional Record, 1994–2016. *Technical Communication Quarterly*, 28(3):207–222.

Saif Mohammad, Svetlana Kiritchenko, Parinaz Sobhani, Xiaodan Zhu, and Colin Cherry. 2016. SemEval-2016 task 6: Detecting stance in tweets. In *Proceedings of the 10th International Workshop on Semantic Evaluation (SemEval-2016)*, pages 31–41, San Diego, California.

Lala Muradova, Hayley Walker, and Francesca Colli. 2020. Climate change communication and public engagement in interpersonal deliberative settings: evidence from the irish citizens' assembly. *Climate Policy*, 20(10):1322–1335.

Saffron O'Neill, Hywel T. P. Williams, Tim Kurz, Bouke Wiersma, and Maxwell Boykoff. 2015. Dominant frames in legacy and social media coverage of the IPCC Fifth Assessment Report. *nature climate change*, 5:380–385.

N. Pathak, M.J. Henry, and S. Volkova. 2017. Understanding social media's take on climate change through large-scale analysis of targeted opinions and emotions. In *AAAI Spring Symposia: AI for the Social Good*.

Luis Pérez-González. 2020. 'Is climate science taking over the science?': A corpus-based study of competing stances on bias, dogma and expertise in the blogosphere. *Humanities and Social Sciences Communications*, 7(92).

Andrew Salway, Dag Elgesem, Knut Hofland, Øystein Reigem, and Lubos Steskal. 2016. Topically-focused blog corpora for multiple languages. In *Proceedings of the 10th Web as Corpus Workshop*, pages 17–26, Berlin.

Abhishek Samantray and Paolo Pin. 2019. Credibility of climate change denial in social media. *palgrave communications*, 5(127).

D.A. Scheufele and S. Iyengar. 2014. The state of framing research. In Kate Kenski and Kathleen Hall Jamieson, editors, *The Oxford Handbook of Political Communication Vol 1*. Oxford University Press, Oxford.

Andreas Schmidt, Ana Ivanova, and Mike S. Schäfer. 2013. Media Attention for Climate Change around the World: A Comparative Analysis of Newspaper Coverage in 27 Countries. *Global Environmental Change*, 23(5):1233–1248.

Mirco Schoenfeld, Steffen Eckhard, Ronny Patz, and Hilde van Meegdenburg. 2018. Discursive Landscapes and Unsupervised Topic Modeling in IR: A Validation of Text-As-Data Approaches through a New Corpus of UN Security Council Speeches on Afghanistan. *Computing Research Repository*, arxiv:1810.05572.

Dominik A. Stecula and Eric Merkley. 2019. Framing Climate Change: Economics, Ideology, and Uncertainty in American News Media Content From 1988 to 2014. *Frontiers in Communication*, 4(6).

Craig Trumbo. 1996. Constructing climate change: claims and frames in US news coverage of an environmental issue. *Publ. Underst. Science*, 5:269–283.

Giuseppe A. Veltri and Dimitrinka Atanasova. 2015. Climate change on Twitter: Content, media ecology and information sharing behaviour. *Public Understanding of Science*.

Rachel Wetts. 2020. Models and Morals: Elite-Oriented and Value-Neutral Discourse Dominates American Organizations' Framings of Climate Change. *Social Forces*, 98(3):1339–1369.

Rebecca Willis. 2017. Taming the Climate? Corpus analysis of politicians' speech on climate change. *Environmental Politics*, 26(2):212–231.

L. Young and S. Soroka. 2012. Affective News: The Automated Coding of Sentiment in Political Texts. *Political Communication*, 29(2):205–231.

Cartography of Natural Language Processing for Social Good: Definitions, Statistics and White Spots

Paula Fortuna[1], **Laura Pérez-Mayos**[1], **Ahmed AbuRa'ed**[1], **Juan Soler-Company**[1], **Leo Wanner**[2,1]
[1]NLP Group, Pompeu Fabra University,
[2]Catalan Institute for Research and Advanced Studies (ICREA)
paula.fortuna|laura.perezm|ahmed.aburaed|juan.soler|leo.wanner@upf.edu

Abstract

The range of works that can be considered as developing NLP for social good (NLP4SG) is enormous. While many of them target the identification of hate speech or fake news, there are others that address, e.g., text simplification to alleviate consequences of dyslexia, or coaching strategies to fight depression. However, so far, there is no clear picture of what areas are targeted by NLP4SG, who are the actors, which are the main scenarios and what are the topics that have been left aside. In order to obtain a clearer view in this respect, we first propose a working definition of NLP4SG and identify some primary aspects that are crucial for NLP4SG, including, e.g., tackled areas, ethics, privacy and bias. Then, we draw upon a corpus of around 50,000 articles downloaded from the ACL Anthology. Based on a list of keywords retrieved from the literature and revised in view of the task, we retrieve from this corpus articles that can be considered to be on NLP4SG according to our definition and analyze them. The result of the analysis is a map of the current NLP4SG research and insights concerning the white spots on this map.

1 Introduction

Measuring the social impact of NLP is not a trivial task. A priori, the range of works that can be considered as developing NLP for social good (NLP4SG) is enormous. It goes from more theoretical works (Cowls et al., 2021), language resources (Midrigan Ciochina et al., 2020; El-Haj et al., 2015) and models (Devlin et al., 2019) to concrete technologies of which many target the identification of hate speech (Fortuna et al., 2021) or fake news (Shu et al., 2017). But there are also others that address, e.g., text simplification or paraphrasing, which can be used to alleviate consequences of dyslexia (Rello et al., 2015), conversational agents for mental health treatment (Gaffney et al., 2019), or eLearning applications, which support students with specific learning disabilities (Bjekić et al., 2014).

In general, many NLP technologies can be used for good but also for bad; at a larger scale, they may affect the lives of many people, and it is difficult to predict in the first place all the potential positive or negative sides resulting from the application of these technologies. In order to discard at this stage uncontrolled "collateral" positive or negative technology influence, we can assume that social good does not come as a side effect when researching certain fields and developing technologies. Even more: if we do not address directly, measure and intentionally promote and control social good, we can cause more harm than good. Therefore, it is of paramount importance to define what we mean when we say "NLP for Social Good", what aspects of peoples' lives are improved by NLP4SG and how, and what suitable strategies are to promote and measure the impact of technological solutions related to NLP. However, so far, there is no clear picture of what areas are targeted by NLP4SG, who are the actors, which are the main scenarios and what are the topics that have been left aside. In this paper, we discuss what NLP for social good (NLP4SG) is, and how we can promote the development of more socially positive technologies. The contribution of this paper is twofold:

(i) we offer a working definition of NLP4SG and related concepts that can serve as a first orientation in the field;

(ii) we provide an analysis of the current state and the tendencies of the research on NLP4SG.

The remainder of this paper is structured as follows. Section 2 defines NLP4SG and introduces some other central aspects of it – the applications, collaboration, and ethics. Section 3 details the

Proceedings of the 1st Workshop on NLP for Positive Impact, pages 19–26
Bangkok, Thailand (online), August 5, 2021.

data, methodology, and results of our evaluation of the social impact in the NLP field. Section 4 elaborates on how to improve the current state of affairs. Section 5 addresses the limitations and ethical concerns, and Section 6, finally, summarizes the implications of our work and draws some conclusions.

2 Defining NLP4SG

Before we set out to provide an overview of the NLP4SG research and explore its characteristics, we need to define what we mean by NLP4SG. Let us start by analysing what is "social good". In the context of social science, Barak (2020) proposes a conceptual "social good" model according to which there are three elements needed to promote social good: innovative technologies, social good domains, and engaging unconventional systems of change, which in this work we also refer to as "collaborations". In the following subsections, we focus on each of these dimensions and dig into other NLP4SG related aspects.

2.1 Social good and NLP technologies

In order to address how NLP technologies can contribute to social good, we draw upon existing research in the broader area of Artificial Intelligence (AI), which intersects NLP problems and methodologies. AI for social good (AI4SG) has recently gained attraction. Floridi et al. (2020) define "social good" in the context of AI. We apply this definition to NLP by replacing 'AI' by 'NLP' and consider NLP4SG as:

> "Design, development, and deployment of **NLP** systems in ways that (i) prevent, mitigate or resolve problems adversely affecting human life and/or the well being of the natural world, and/or (ii) enable socially preferable and/or environmentally sustainable developments."

In what follows, we review the domains and the contexts in which NLP4SG is carried out.

2.2 Applications for Social Good

In research and ethics, the definition of social good focused so far on its use in application areas that generally have a direct positive impact on the society. Several lists of such areas have been worked with. For instance, Shi et al. (2020) highlights agriculture, education, environment sustainability, healthcare, combating information manipulation, social care and urban planning, public safety and transportation; Floridi et al. (2020) focuses on healthcare, education, equality, climate change, and environmental protection; and Hager et al. (2019) deals with justice, economic development, workforce development, public safety, policing, education, public health, transportation, and public welfare. In the analysis presented in this paper, we draw upon Shi et al. (2020) to compose an adapted list of NLP4SG areas, keeping agriculture, education, environmental sustainability, healthcare, public safety and transportation. We exclude "social care and urban planning", as they may refer to different aspects, and we rephrase "combating information manipulation" as "media corrupted communication" because we want to include not only fake news, but also abusive language. Finally, to tackle specific NLP health-related issues, we extend the list by "language disorders". Consider the first column of Table 1 for the list of areas that we take into account.

2.3 Collaborations for social good

Tomašev et al. (2020) details how AI4SG projects should be approached as a collaborative effort in bringing communities together in order to carefully assess the complexities of designing AI systems. Community involvement assures integration and inclusiveness, and it brings more information to the decision on the design of a technology, including knowledge about the contexts in which design decisions are going to have an impact. Furthermore, community involvement adds other perspectives to the design since researchers alone cannot anticipate all the needs of the users and all the possible usages of a technology. Along the same lines, we propose that NLP4SG needs the collaboration of users, activists, minorities, grassroots movements, businesses, non-governmental organizations (NGOs), and social entrepreneurs to achieve a social positive technological development.

2.4 NLP and Ethics

To achieve a positive impact, technological solutions need to adhere to ethical principles, e.g., guidelines provided by the European Commission, the Organisation for Economic Co-operation and Development, or the Montreal Declaration for Responsible AI (Tomašev et al., 2020). Naturally, this also applies to NLP. Technology based on human data can be potentially harmful, and the presence of ethics in NLP is therefore much needed. There are three primary topics that frequently underlie ethical issues in NLP research: privacy, bias and dual use (Bender et al., 2020).

Privacy tackles how to protect the privacy of data authors used in the training or evaluation of NLP systems. It has been more widely discussed, e.g., in (Hovy and Spruit, 2016).

Dual use anticipates how a developed technology could be repurposed for negative applications and thus helps design systems such that they do not cause harm; cf., e.g., (Bender et al., 2020).

Bias is about understanding how over- and under-sampling of different populations will affect datasets and models that are built using these datasets. Potential solutions include building less biased datasets, debiasing trained models and matching appropriate training data to a given use case (Bender et al., 2020).

3 Evaluation of social good in NLP

Evaluating the current state of NLP for social good is a crucial step towards the identification of the gaps and promotion of a more impactful technology development. For this purpose, we build upon the *NLP Scholar Dataset* (Mohammad, 2020) and analyse existent features together with new classifications on social good aspects. In what follows, we describe in detail the data and the procedure of our analysis. We make the code available to the community[1].

3.1 Data

The *NLP Scholar Dataset* provides access to more than 50k instances from both ACL Anthology (AA) and Google Scholar (GS), and includes authors' names, year of publication, venue of publication, etc. We use the version of this dataset from June 2020 (Mohammad, 2020). The dataset includes some entries that are not really papers (e.g., forewords, prefaces, programs, schedules, indexes, invited talks, appendices, etc.). After discarding them, we are left with 52,288 papers. Regarding the available paper descriptors, we use: Title, Year, Authors, NS paper type, NS paper venue and GS citations. This data is enriched with some other fields introduced in the next subsection.

[1] https://github.com/paulafortuna/NLP4SG_NLP4PI_paper

3.2 Methodology

We enrich the available dataset with the abstracts of the papers and automatically annotate the NLP4SG-related variables. To validate our automatic annotation procedure, we extract 200 papers as validation set, gathering one opinion per paper with respect to the quality of the annotation.

Retrieving paper abstracts. For each instance (paper) of the dataset, we collect the pdf file of the paper, and extract its abstract using Grobid[2]. Then, we use Microsoft Academic Graph API[3] to complete the missing abstracts. In total, we have been able to retrieve the abstracts for 95.8% of the papers in our dataset.

Annotation as *explicit NLP4SG* For each considered NLP-application area, we compile a list of keywords. This allows us to match NLP publications with the obtained "keyword lexicon" and assess the positive impact in the field.

To come up with the keyword lexicon, we use a set of keywords from (Shi et al., 2020),[4] enriching it further with keywords extracted from the Wikipedia page for language disorders,[5] and with words extracted from the UN Sustainable Development Goals[6]. To filter the final keyword lists, two annotators, instructed with the definitions of NLP4SG from Section 2, reviewed the titles and abstracts of the papers retrieved by each keyword, discarding those with a high percentage of false positives. For instance, the "genetic" keyword is present in the *health* set of the original list from Shi et al. (2020). As this keyword retrieves a high percentage of papers referring only to genetic algorithms we opted to remove it.

The final keyword list is divided into two sets: *areas for social good* and *other dimensions of social good*; cf. Tables 1 and 2. *Areas for social good* keywords correspond to social good applications. As previously outlined in Section 2.2, the main areas are *Agriculture*, *Education*, *Environmental sustainability*, *Healthcare*, *Public safety*, *Social care*, *Transportation* and *Urban planning*.

[2] https://github.com/kermitt2/grobid

[3] https://www.microsoft.com/en-us/research/project/microsoft-academic-graph/

[4] https://github.com/csinguva/NLP4SocialGood/blob/master/keywords.py

[5] https://en.wikipedia.org/wiki/List_of_language_disorders

[6] https://sdgs.un.org/goals

Area	Example keywords
Agriculture	sustainable agriculture, farmer, vegetation, livestock
Education	tutor, pedagogy, tuition, textbook
Environmental sustainability	sustainability, wildlife, pollution, biodiversity, climate action
Healthcare	cancer, covid, autism, impairment
Media corrupted communication	fake news, polarization, politic, toxicity
Public safety	crime, police, safety, fraud, terrorism
Social care	gender gap, racism, migrants, social justice
Transportation	carpool, passenger, railroad, traffic
Urban planning	emergency, cost of living, low-income, sustainable cities
Language disorders	dyslexia, coprolalia, echolalia, glossolalia

Table 1: Social good areas' example keywords.

Other Dimensions	Example keywords
Ethics	ethical, bias, privacy, data statement
Social good	interpretability, accountability, social good, social impact
Systems of change and collaboration	NGO, activist, inclusive, financial cost

Table 2: Social good general example keywords.

To these main areas we add two areas of particular relevance to the NLP field, namely *Language disorders* and *Media corrupted communication*. To account for areas that are not explicitly related to applied research, we provide an alternative taxonomy that covers *Other dimensions of social good*: *Ethics*, *General social good* and *Systems of change and collaboration*. For the *other dimensions of social good* we add keywords in accordance with the definitions provided in Section 2

We automatically annotate the set of papers as *explicit NLP4SG* vs. *non-explicit NLP4SG* by using keyword matching. The term 'explicit' intends to highlight here that keyword matching is robust enough to capture only those papers that explicitly mention any of the NLP4SG keywords that we are looking for, and, therefore, it is possible that we misses papers that tackle NLP4SG in a more subtle manner. Papers of the dataset that are not tagged as 'explicit NLP4SG', i.e., that do not match any of the keywords, are tagged as 'non-explicit NLP4SG'.

The outcome of the automatic annotation task has been manually validated by a meta-annotator, who approved the assignment of the *explicit NLP4SG* tags in 95% of the times.

3.3 Results and Discussion

It has been stated that the number of publications in NLP has been increasing over the last years (Mohammad, 2020). Our results confirm that this is also the case for *explicit NLP4SG* works (cf. Figure 1). Our results indicate that until 2010, the percentage of *explicit NLP4SG* papers per year was more constant (around 5%). The majority of the papers until 2010 is related to social good mostly because the research focused on some specific areas. More recently, this trend has been changing. During the last 10 years, not only is the percentage of *explicit NLP4SG* increasing, but the percentage of papers mentioning *other dimensions of social good* has been increasing as well; cf. Figure 1. The year with most *explicit NLP4SG* publications has been so far 2020, where more than 20% of the publications already mention social good-related terms or areas. This figure also shows that the percentage of NLP4SG publications referring to our NLP4SG *areas* is higher than the percentage of publications referring to *other dimensions* of NLP4SG, and only a minority of publications refers to both sets of terms at same time.

Figures 2 and 3 show the different *areas* and *other dimensions* of NLP4SG in terms of verified frequencies. *Healthcare* is the preferred area of investigation, followed by *social care*, *media corrupted communication* and *education*. *Public safety*, *transportation*, *urban planning*, *environmental sustainability* and *language disorders* are areas with less publications. Regarding other social good dimensions, we can state that the research has been focusing mostly on *ethical* issues, directly mentioning *general social good* and related concepts, but rarely referring to *systems for change and collaboration*.

The observed tendency over time and the corresponding detailed analysis show that NLP research is increasingly conscious about its implications for the society and begins to directly address these implications. Still, some particular aspects such as, e.g., collaboration with actors outside NLP, remain to be addressed. In addition, despite having increased considerably over the last years, the percentage of NLP4SG-related research can further be improved.

In order to buttress this claim, we compiled some telling numbers that contrast *explicit NLP4SG* with *non-explicit NLP4SG*; cf. Table 3. These numbers point to the lack of prominence of social good in

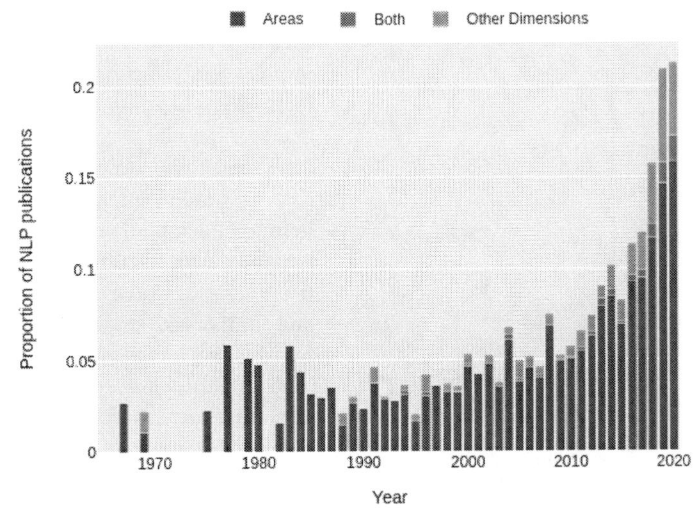

Figure 1: Social good publications per year in proportion to the total of NLP papers. Each bar represents the accumulation of papers that matched general keywords (green), areas (blue) or both (red).

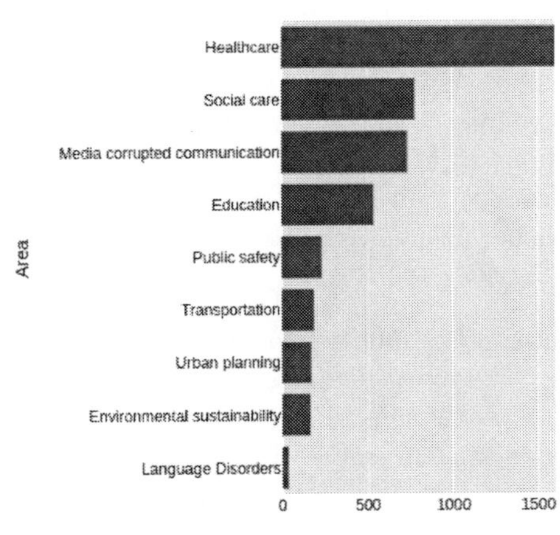

Figure 2: *Explicit NLP4SG* paper areas frequencies.

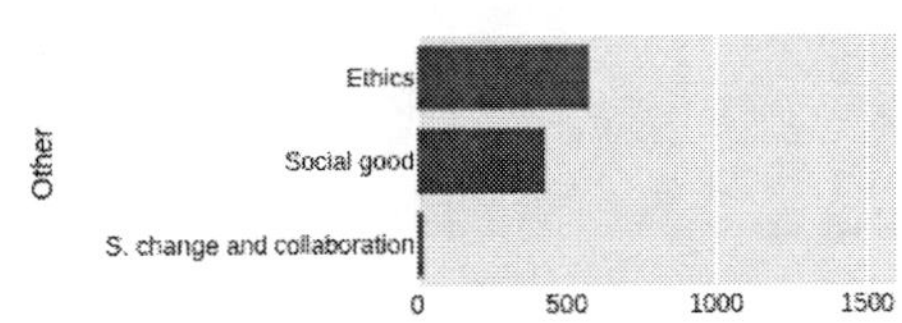

Figure 3: *Explicit NLP4SG* paper Other dimensions frequencies.

the field. Our results show that *explicit NLP4SG* papers, accounting for 9.63% of the total, tend to have, in average, more authors per paper and less citations. Moreover, 24.02% of the authors have published at least one paper belonging to *explicit NLP4SG*. Shared tasks, workshops and system demonstration are the venues publishing *explicit NLP4SG*; cf. Figure 4. The percentages keep decreasing for conferences, miscellaneous, top-tier conferences, tutorials and journals. Regarding the particular venues, the non-SemEval shared task, RANLP, Workshops, student Research, and Demo lead the top five of venues with the highest percentage of *explicit NLP4SG* papers; cf. Figure 5.

4 Improving the current state of affairs

As shown in the previous section, the NLP field is recently more attentive to social good related issues. Nevertheless, we do believe that there are certain aspects that need further attention by the community. In what follows, we enumerate these aspects, along with some hints on how to address them.

Metrics	Explicit NLP4SG	Non-explicit NLP4SG
Total number of papers in percentage	9.63%	90.37%
Average number of Google Scholar citations per paper	25.87	42.03
From the total authors publishing in NLP	24.02%	75.98%
Mean number of authors per paper	3.65	2.97

Table 3: *Explicit* vs. *Non-explicit NLP4SG* papers statistics.

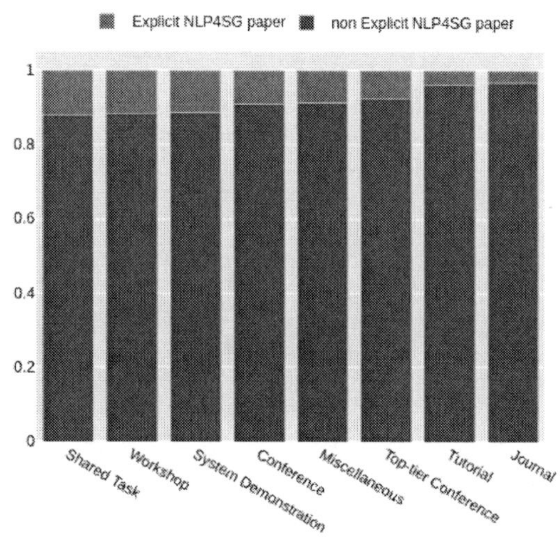

Figure 4: Percentage of *explicit NLP4SG* publications per type of venue.

Social good areas with less research. Areas that we identified as producing less NLP for social good publications are, e.g., *language disorders*, *environmental sustainability*, *urban planning*, *transportation*, and *public safety*. While it is natural that areas that are less related to language receive less attention in NLP, e.g., transportation, they still offer room for many NLP-applications, which can be tackled with a positive impact.

The discussion on which percentage of the research in NLP is appropriate for the different areas still remains open – if it can be resolved at all.

More than social good areas. Although we follow previous research in an attempt to measure NLP4SG by matching keywords of certain areas (Shi et al., 2020), we must be cautious when looking at the obtained results: while research in a certain area may imply social good, it may also imply social harm, depending on how a certain technology is going to be used (e.g., a fake news detector may be used to detect, but also to generate fake news). Another analysis over the same data may aid to interpret the achieved results and help to understand whether the approaches of the previous work to address social good areas lead to positive or negative outcomes. With this in mind, and for the sake of a broader analysis of research impact, we include into our consideration other NLP4SG dimensions such as ethics, social good terms and systems of change and collaboration. As a guideline for future research, we may conclude that providing data statements and terms of use for the developed technologies would help preventing potential misuses.

Other social good dimensions. When we look at the *explicit NLP4SG*, papers from the considered *areas* are more frequent than papers related to *other dimensions*, and it is only in recent years that *other dimensions*-related papers are increasing in number and have more weight. We believe that research in NLP would benefit from a wider discussion on social good dimensions such as ethics, positive impact and collaborations. In particular, questions such as how the development of NLP applications may involve end-users and include knowledge about their context of use require more attention.

Social good should not be the researcher's enemy. We show that *explicit NLP4SG* publications tend to have less citations in average and are published in smaller venues. The reduced number of authors of explicit NLP4SG papers suggests that there is a smaller NLP4SG community within the larger NLP community. We believe that it is urgent to actively encourage research to tackle social good areas, and, in particular, also to promote the formation of an interconnected social good community across different academic disciplines. Pushing towards this objective will benefit both the field and the society that is impacted by the technology that we produce.

5 Limitations and Ethical Concerns

As mentioned in Section 3.2, our keyword matching approach to the identification of NLP publications as being relevant to NLP4SG is robust and

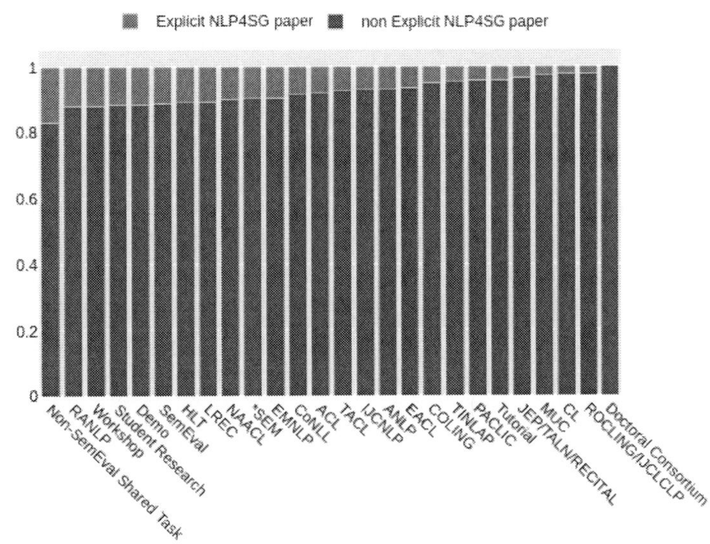

Figure 5: Percentage of *explicit NLP4SG* publications per venue.

performative enough only for a subset of the publications, namely those that contain one of the keywords that we are looking for. The term *explicit NLP4SG* intends to highlight this limitation. It is possible (or even likely) that it misses some papers tackling NLP4SG in a more subtle manner. This means that the results presented in this paper serve as a lower bound baseline.

As far as the collection of the used keyword is concerned, we started by using an initial sample of terms specifically conceived for Artificial Intelligence. We tried then to add some NLP related expressions and remove terms that were bringing misleading results. However, in the course of the presented analysis it became clear that a more systematic method could have revealed more social good NLP related terms. Furthermore, when discussing definitions of social good, we should bear in mind that what is considered to be a "positive impact" depends on the context and set of values. For instance, ethical concerns and guidelines are different according to different countries (Hovy and Spruit, 2016; Berberich et al., 2020) and are not absent of social and political interests (Washington and Kuo, 2020). As a consequence, we must acknowledge the limitation of our analysis in this regard since we follow an Eurocentric perspective and focus only on ACL publications.

6 Conclusions

The goals of this paper have been to help to draw a clearer picture of what NLP4SG is and where we stand in the current state of NLP. We established working definitions of NLP4SG and identified some aspects that are crucial for the analysis of NLP publications with respect to their relevance to NLP4SG, namely *technologies*, *areas*, *collaborations*. NLP-specific *ethical* aspects formed another perspective of our analysis. We drew upon the ACL Anthology corpus and annotated papers in terms of *explicit* vs. *non-explicit NLP4SG* to show a clearer view of the evolution of the field. We identified social good-relevant NLP areas with less research, as well as other social good dimensions that are important to address, and proposed a non-exhaustive list of aspects that need further attention by the community.

The results of the research in NLP have a huge impact on the whole society, and we strongly believe that it is urgent for the community to potentiate and encourage research that not only includes ethical consideration, but also actively addresses social good.

Acknowledgments

The first author is supported by the research grant SFRH/BD/143623/2019, provided by the Portuguese national funding agency for science, research and technology, Fundação para a Ciência e a

Tecnologia (FCT), within the scope of Operational Program *Human Capital* (POCH), supported by the European Social Fund and by national funds from MCTES. The work of the Juan Soler-Company and Leo Wanner has been supported by the European Commission in the context of the H2020 Research Program under the contract numbers 700024 and 786731.

References

Michàlle E. Mor Barak. 2020. The practice and science of social good: Emerging paths to positive social impact. *Research on Social Work Practice*, 30(2):139–150.

Emily M. Bender, Dirk Hovy, and Alexandra Schofield. 2020. Integrating ethics into the NLP curriculum. In *Proceedings of the 58th Annual Meeting of the Association for Computational Linguistics: Tutorial Abstracts, ACL 2020, Online, July 5, 2020*, pages 6–9. Association for Computational Linguistics.

Nicolas Berberich, Toyoaki Nishida, and Shoko Suzuki. 2020. Harmonizing artificial intelligence for social good. *Philosophy & Technology*, 33(4):613–638.

Dragana Bjekić, Svetlana Obradović, Milica Vučetić, and Milevica Bojović. 2014. E-teacher in inclusive e-education for students with specific learning disabilities. *Procedia – Social and Behavioral Sciences*, 128:128–133.

Josh Cowls, Andreas Tsamados, Mariarosaria Taddeo, and Luciano Floridi. 2021. A definition, benchmark and database of ai for social good initiatives. *Nature Machine Intelligence*, 3(2):111–115.

Jacob Devlin, Ming-Wei Chang, Kenton Lee, and Kristina Toutanova. 2019. BERT: pre-training of deep bidirectional transformers for language understanding. In *Proceedings of the 2019 Conference of the North American Chapter of the Association for Computational Linguistics: Human Language Technologies, NAACL-HLT 2019, Minneapolis, MN, USA, June 2-7, 2019, Volume 1 (Long and Short Papers)*, pages 4171–4186. Association for Computational Linguistics.

Mahmoud El-Haj, Udo Kruschwitz, and Chris Fox. 2015. Creating language resources for under-resourced languages: methodologies, and experiments with arabic. *Lang. Resour. Evaluation*, 49(3):549–580.

Luciano Floridi, Josh Cowls, Thomas C. King, and Mariarosaria Taddeo. 2020. How to design AI for social good: Seven essential factors. *Sci. Eng. Ethics*, 26(3):1771–1796.

Paula Fortuna, Juan Soler Company, and Leo Wanner. 2021. How well do hate speech, toxicity, abusive and offensive language classification models generalize across datasets? *Inf. Process. Manag.*, 58(3):102524.

Hannah Gaffney, Warren Mansell, and Sara Tai. 2019. Conversational agents in the treatment of mental health problems: Mixed-method systematic review. *JMIR Mental Health*, 6(10):e14166.

Gregory D. Hager, Ann W. Drobnis, Fei Fang, Rayid Ghani, Amy Greenwald, Terah Lyons, David C. Parkes, Jason Schultz, Suchi Saria, Stephen F. Smith, and Milind Tambe. 2019. Artificial intelligence for social good. *CoRR*, abs/1901.05406.

Dirk Hovy and Shannon L. Spruit. 2016. The social impact of natural language processing. In *Proceedings of the 54th Annual Meeting of the Association for Computational Linguistics, ACL 2016, August 7-12, 2016, Berlin, Germany, Volume 2: Short Papers*. The Association for Computer Linguistics.

Ludmila Midrigan Ciochina, Victoria Boyd, Lucila Sanchez-Ortega, Diana Malancea_Malac, Doina Midrigan, and David P. Corina. 2020. Resources in underrepresented languages: Building a representative Romanian corpus. In *Proceedings of the 12th Language Resources and Evaluation Conference*, pages 3291–3296, Marseille, France. European Language Resources Association.

Saif M. Mohammad. 2020. NLP scholar: A dataset for examining the state of NLP research. In *Proceedings of The 12th Language Resources and Evaluation Conference, LREC 2020, Marseille, France, May 11-16, 2020*, pages 868–877. European Language Resources Association.

Luz Rello, Miguel Ballesteros, and Jeffrey P. Bigham. 2015. A spellchecker for dyslexia. In *Proceedings of the 17th International ACM SIGACCESS Conference on Computers & Accessibility, ASSETS 2015, Lisbon, Portugal, October 26-28, 2015*, pages 39–47. ACM.

Zheyuan Ryan Shi, Claire Wang, and Fei Fang. 2020. Artificial intelligence for social good: A survey. *CoRR*, abs/2001.01818.

Kai Shu, Amy Sliva, Suhang Wang, Jiliang Tang, and Huan Liu. 2017. Fake news detection on social media: A data mining perspective. *SIGKDD Explor.*, 19(1):22–36.

Nenad Tomašev, Julien Cornebise, Frank Hutter, Shakir Mohamed, Angela Picciariello, Bec Connelly, Danielle CM Belgrave, Daphne Ezer, Fanny Cachat van der Haert, Frank Mugisha, et al. 2020. Ai for social good: unlocking the opportunity for positive impact. *Nature Communications*, 11(1):1–6.

Anne L. Washington and Rachel S. Kuo. 2020. Whose side are ethics codes on?: power, responsibility and the social good. In *FAT* '20: Conference on Fairness, Accountability, and Transparency, Barcelona, Spain, January 27-30, 2020*, pages 230–240. ACM.

Guiding Principles for Participatory Design-inspired Natural Language Processing

Tommaso Caselli, **Roberto Cibin**, **Costanza Conforti**
Enrique Encinas, **Maurizio Teli**
University of Groningen
Institute of Sociology of the Czech Academy of Sciences & Masaryk University
Rural Senses Ltd., University of Aalborg
t.caselli@rug.nl, roberto.cibin@soc.cas.cz,
stanze@ruralsenses.com, {eencinas@cs|maurizio@plan}.aau.dk

Abstract

We introduce 9 guiding principles[1] to integrate Participatory Design (PD) methods in the development of Natural Language Processing (NLP) systems. The adoption of PD methods by NLP will help to alleviate issues concerning the development of more democratic, fairer, less-biased technologies to process natural language data. This short paper is the outcome of an ongoing dialogue between designers and NLP experts and adopts a non-standard format following previous work by Traum (2000); Bender (2013); Abzianidze and Bos (2019). Every section *is* a guiding principle. While principles 1–3 illustrate assumptions and methods that inform community-based PD practices, we used two *fictional design scenarios* (Encinas and Blythe, 2018), which build on top of situations familiar to the authors, to elicit the identification of the other 6. Principles 4–6 describes the impact of PD methods on the design of NLP systems, targeting two critical aspects: data collection & annotation, and the deployment & evaluation. Finally, principles 7–9 guide a new reflexivity of the NLP research with respect to its *context*, *actors and participants*, and *aims*. We hope this guide will offer inspiration and a road-map to develop a new generation of PD-inspired NLP.

1 PD is about consensus and conflict

PD has its origin in Scandinavia forty years ago, when it was articulated as an *offensive strategy* for the trade union movement to promote industrial democracy (Group, 1981; Ehn, 1992). PD was seen as a way to allow workers to shape the technologies they would use at the workplace (Ehn, 2016).

As a form of system design performed *with and by* people (Briefs et al., 1983), PD entails a process of mutual learning among participants, among design researchers, and between design researchers and participants (Simonsen and Robertson, 2012). Traditionally, that means adopting a variety of research and design methods, from workshops (Ehn et al., 1996) to participant observations (Blomberg and Karasti, 2012a), passing through cards (Teli et al., 2017) or games (Vaajakallio and Mattelmäki, 2014), to include scenarios (Bødker, 2000), prototypes (Kannabiran and Bødker, 2020), and many others. The appropriate combination of methods and activities is determined, in a situated way, beginning with the involvement of different social groups (Bratteteig et al., 2012).

Historically, PD questions who is involved in the design process from various communities (DiSalvo et al., 2012) to specific socio-economic actors (Teli, 2015) and how. As a consequence, the design process can and should reflect on the visions for social transformation that the participants can develop (Huybrechts et al., 2020; Helgason et al., 2020), by translating those visions into alternatives to existing technologies (Korsgaard et al., 2016).

2 Design is an inherently disordered and unfinished process

Being based on nurturing relations between professional technology designers and members of the various social groups they interact with, PD methods and practices acknowledge that designing digital technologies with non-professionals does not follow a linear model (Callon, 2004; Cibin et al., 2020). Even when formalized (Bratteteig et al., 2012), the design process is disordered and unfinished. This character is well represented by the expressions *use-before-use* and *design-after-design* (Ehn, 2008; Fry, 2017).

[1]The principles are guided by the authors experience, primarily focused in Europe (with the exception of one of them). However, we would defend the applicability of most of them to a wider range of contexts, with the situated effort of appropriation and transformation that is an integral part of PD.

Proceedings of the 1st Workshop on NLP for Positive Impact, pages 27–35
Bangkok, Thailand (online), August 5, 2021.

		Principle	Description
PD principles	1.	*PD is about consensus and conflict*	• PD entails a process of mutual learning between researchers and community • PD adopts a variety of research and design methods (workshops, participants observation, cards, ...)
	2.	*Design is an inherently disordered and unfinished process*	• *Use-before-use*: tool's use is envisioned *before* the tool is actually implemented • *Design-after-design*: tool's design isn't exhausted with delivery, but will be modified by the users' appropriation, use, and feedback
	3.	*Communities are often not completely determined* a priori	• Communities are not a unitary whole, but can get formed within and through the design process
NLP tools	4.	*Data and communities are not separate things*	• The shift from *language as data* to *language as people*: language data are produced by human speakers • Communities should be involved in the different stages of the NLP pipeline
	5.	*Community involvement is not scraping*	• Collaboration with a community should imply ethical engagement practices based on respect, equity and reciprocity • Researchers should communicate to the community the usage of the collected data in a transparent and appropriate way
	6.	*Never stop designing*	• Community adaptation should be treated as a feature of an NLP system at the design stage
Researchers' reflexivity	7.	*Text is a means rather than an end*	• The linguistic output of NLP systems should serve people's needs rather than imitate people's production of language.
	8.	*The thin red line between consent and intrusion*	• Do not assume that community members are technology experts nor technologically illiterate • A community's refusal to collaboration is a risk that must be accepted
	9.	*The need to combine research goals, funding, and concrete social political dynamics*	• Designers and researchers as intermediaries between the interests of the different actors involved (project beneficiaries, investors, funding agencies, and other stakeholders' goals)

Table 1: Summary of guiding principles for developing PD-inspired NLP tools

Use-before-use addresses the common practice to build an image of the use of a product by people *before* use actually take place. The methods employed to favor people determination of use-before-use (e.g., workshops, design games, fictional scenarios, and prototyping) can become part of forms of *participation washing* (Sloan et al., 2020), that is the use of methods belonging to PD in processes in which participants do not have a significant influence on the outcome. When done properly, the keys in PD process are the articulation of transformative visions (Huybrechts et al., 2020), the ethnographic approach to design (Blomberg and Karasti, 2012b), and the reflexive discussion on the position of designers, communities, and institutions (Lyle et al., 2018; Teli et al., 2020).

Design-after-design addresses the possibility of people's manipulation of "finished" products. Design-after-design needs to be investigated and favored through concepts like *infrastructuring* (Karasti, 2014) or by looking at the connections between specific digital artifacts and wider artifacts ecologies (Bødker and Klokmose, 2012).

3 Communities are often not determined *a priori*

The last 20 years have seen a change in the subjects involved in PD, with the notion of *community* becoming one of the most relevant to describe the participants to PD projects (Dittrich et al., 2002; DiSalvo et al., 2012; Light and Miskelly, 2019).

The notion of community is complex and multifaceted. Long lasting criteria such as the sharing a place, an interest, or a condition have proven to be limited (Mosconi et al., 2017; Thinyane et al., 2018; Cibin et al., 2019; Teli et al., 2020). This paper defines a community as the presence of dense social relations and of, at least, an element - being it geography, interests, specific conditions, or structural position in society in terms of power - tying together its members. Each of these dimensions represents a challenge to current practices of design and realization of NLP systems.

Although the definition of community recalls an idea of a *unitary whole*, the ensemble of the participants to a project is not always completely determined *a priori* but it could get formed *within and through* the design process (Le Dantec and DiSalvo, 2013), which current sampling methods in NLP mostly fail to capture.

A consolidated tendency is to look at PD practices in terms of empowerment of marginalized groups (Ertner et al., 2010; Racadio et al., 2014). Their adoption and integration in the NLP pipeline can help to address underexposure of both language varieties and linguistic phenomena.

Mario is a scholar in Human-Computer Interaction and technology design. He works on a project to support the development of community radio stations by rural and isolated communities. One of the communities involved belongs to a village of about 600 inhabitants located between a river delta and the Black Sea in Romania. The inhabitants are mainly descendants of a group of Ukrainian Cossacks who immigrated there in the 18th century. In addition to speaking Romanian the residents speak a Ukrainian dialect. Together with a Romanian NGO specialising in human rights and media democracy, Mario works to involve the inhabitants as volunteers to run the radio station and create content for the programs. However, the Romanian broadcasting license obliges stations to transmit 24 hours a day, and the volunteers struggle to create enough content. Mario proposes to use a new and advanced natural language generation system, GPT-3, to generate content. Besides the fact that the machine does not "speak" the community's dialect and requires English translations, GPT-3 produces output with prejudices and negative stereotypes against the community.

4 Data and communities are not separate things

As we saw in the first three points, communities represent the core element of PD. One might expect that communities have a prominent role in the development of NLP systems. Indeed, communities are the producers of the oil that runs NLP research: language data.

We observe, however, that this is not the case. Searching for the term "community" in the ACL Anthology[2] returns 100 papers. However, by manually inspecting each of them, we discovered that only 9 present some sort of engagement with a community of speakers (Garcia et al., 2008; Levin, 2009; Bird et al., 2014; Everson et al., 2019; Kempton, 2017; Susarla and Challa, 2019; Conforti et al., 2020; Griscom, 2020; Le Ferrand et al., 2020). These works target endangered languages and propose technological solutions to an array of problems (e.g., archiving, documenting, or tooling). None of them presents an active and direct involvement of the communities *in the design process* of the suggested NLP solution. As pointed out by Bird (2020), people agency is absent and language is seen as data to be dug.

Compliance with PD methods requires for NLP to become more aware of the relationship between language data and the speakers who first produced. In this context, we advocate for a shift of paradigm, from *language as data* to *language as people*.

Mario's story exemplifies the danger of forgetting the link between NLP training data and its underlying producers: by not asking himself whether the language varieties behind GPT-3 are representative of the community he is trying to help, he ends up hurting it. The application of PD methods is a viable solution to overcome part of this predicament. The next principles will address two key steps of the development of NLP systems: data collection & annotation, and evaluation & deployment.

5 Community involvement is not scraping

The training of current SOTA language models (LMs) is based on large amounts of written text crawled from the Web, with no or little documentation (Bender et al., 2021). However, the attempt to calibrate a tool to the needs of a specific community demands *concrete* social interactions. This requires the development of ethical engagement practices based on respect, equity, and reciprocity to gain the trust of the gatekeepers of the community (Le Dantec and Fox, 2015; Hirmer et al., 2021; Bird, 2020). Gaining trust of communities is fundamental, especially when dealing with small groups of people. In that case, all information is sensitive and often considered a currency that can be devalued once made public (Giglitto, 2017).

Innovative, flexible and transparent approaches to data collection and annotation should be put in practice. In line with PD methods, the way this cannot be reduced to a check-list valid for each and every community: context-specificity, which affects participation practices, cannot be avoided (Sloan et al., 2020). Documenting, describing, explaining, and showing how the data a community makes available is processed by and used to create an NLP

[2] Accessed on April 30th, 2021

system is an essential step. It is up to the NLP researchers to gain trust by describing as best as they can the purpose of the work and the risks and benefits for the community. Additional advantages of designing NLP systems around the needs of a community are the possibilities of challenging existing power dynamics and also reduce risks of dual use. In this context, initiatives such as the *Feminist.AI*[3] collective and *Indigenous data sovereignty practices* (Kukutai and Taylor, 2016; Walter and Suina, 2019) are positive and innovative examples.

6 Never stop designing

Mario's scenario is a good example of a bottleneck in the deployment of NLP systems: in most cases, they will not fit the needs of a community and adapting them is a challenging task.

The adoption of Machine Learning techniques for developing NLP systems adopts a vision where statistical generalizations can be learned and applied to broader contexts (Sloan et al., 2020). Datasets are assumed to be good samples of language phenomena, but are actually deeply context-bound at different levels (e.g., time period, medium, population sample, among others). It is known that NLP tools struggle with tail phenomena (Ettinger et al., 2017) and are subject to bias (Bender and Friedman, 2018). Solutions are varied and focused on areas such as Domain Adaptation and Transfer Learning (Blitzer et al., 2006; Daumé III, 2007; Ma et al., 2014; Ganin and Lempitsky, 2015; Wu and Huang, 2016; Ruder et al., 2017; Ruder and Plank, 2017; Ramponi and Plank, 2020) or de-biasing (Gonen and Goldberg, 2019; Paul Panenghat et al., 2020; Liang et al., 2020; Zhou et al., 2021).

A PD-aware NLP tool should foresee this *community adaptation* feature at its design stage. This requires to overcome technical (i.e., access or manipulation of the code) and resource (financial and human) predicaments as well as the use of predatory practices of users' involvement (i.e., recognize participation as labor). Having access to continuous and updated feedback from a community is paramount for ensuring that tool adaptation effectively addresses their evolving needs. In this context, researchers should put in place appropriate socio-technical solutions considering the peculiarities of the community (e.g., developing an API to report bugs might not be appropriate in areas with limited internet connection). This open-ended evaluation process challenges existing industrial paradigm based on the idea of scaling.

Katie is a PhD candidate in Interaction Design working on a project on compliance to labor norms. She engages relatively small trade unions in understanding how the unions can communicate widely and effectively to the public, and to the large population of prospective new members. She has collected a variety of information, through interviews and workshops. During these activities, she has encountered two main challenges for her research: (i) she collected a large amount of textual data about labor conditions and used out-of-the-shelf NLP tools to run sentiment analysis on it; however, the tools provide predictions only in an aggregated, uninterpretable form, which prevents Katie from providing the unions with specific insights. She has also applied for funding to improve the tools' interpretability but her request has been conditionally accepted subject to changes in her research topic; (ii) although she is mindful of her role as a researcher, Katie has faced frictions when engaging with the unions as some of their members feel overtly exposed when sharing their experiences.

7 Text is a means rather than an end

Introducing PD methods in the design of NLP tools promotes and embraces a philosophical perspective on the interactions between humans and machines, and of Artificial Intelligence in general, as a problem-solving tool rather than as an adaptive mechanism mimicking human abilities (Winograd, 1997; Auernhammer, 2020). On the contrary, current trends in NLP are more oriented towards a rationalist perspective, attempting to develop *intelligent* systems that *understand* language (Bender and Koller, 2020).

This follows a logic of automation that attempts to ultimately remove human intervention (Crawford, 2021), reinforcing a vision of *language as data*. Language, however, is not a uniform entity but it adapts to the context where it is used. NLP systems have the potential to support the flow of meanings between contexts but in order to do so, and act as means rather than ends (Auger et al., 2017; Hanna et al., 2017), they must contend with the structural solidity of the categories on which its

[3] https://share.hek.ch/en/participatory-ai-how-to-make-better-ai/

algorithms are built (Bender et al., 2021). The tools Katie uses are unable to offer insightful information to her respondents because the output is uninterpretable (i.e., why a messages has been labeled in such a way?). To see NLP technologies aligned with participatory methods and tasks demands a shift in the conceptualization of the outputs, or products, of NLP systems. The linguistic output of NLP systems should be material that triggers iterations or refinements to serve people's needs rather than imitate people's production of language.

8 The thin red line between consent and intrusion

Katie's scenario highlights how common it is to take for granted that the community always wants to be helped authorizing researchers to use any tool. Refusing collaboration is a risk that must be accepted thus preventing or interrupting the development of a proposed technical solution.

Importantly, the community's consent can be considered authentic only if it was proceeded by appropriate communication. When introducing a technology or a tool to a community, researchers must avoid two unethical approaches. On one hand, using terminology with which a community is not familiar with might confuse more than explain, thus potentially resulting in uninformed consent (Tekola et al., 2009). Note, however, that researchers might also find themselves in the opposite situation. When approaching (small) communities, researchers can be misled by what is called a *deficit model* (Irwin and Wynne, 1996), i.e., taking for granted that the reference community whom one is going to collaborate with lacks of knowledge regarding science and technology. However, people are constantly immersed in an ecology of technologies (Bødker and Klokmose, 2012) and practical knowledge to which they refer when called upon to understand something new.

To avoid misunderstandings, one must offer transparent information about the actions that will be carried out, making use of metaphors and comparisons with existing artifacts, even if the complexity of the technological architecture represent a communication challenge (Bratteteig and Verne, 2018). And always keep in mind that this dialogue can steer people's eyes in the wrong place.

9 The need to combine research goals, funding, and concrete social political dynamics

All the cases observed highlight how a community-based collaboration between NLP and PD is an issue where multiple dimensions continuously interact. In addition to this, Katie's fiction introduces an additional challenge: the need to obtain external funding to conduct her research and the interests (and requests) of the funding providers/agencies.

These dynamics must take into account the goals of the researchers/designers, and of the communities involved, which cannot be completely overturned by the founders. It is evident that in this context the role of the designer/researcher becomes more and more that of an intermediary capable of translating and holding together the interests of the different stakeholders involved, without risking being co-opted and involved only in a token way (Cibin et al., 2020; Teli et al., 2020).

Acknowledgments

We thank the anonymous reviewers for their effort in reviewing this paper, their constructive feedback and suggestions. CC is grateful to the RuralSenses team for sharing experiences on participatory practices in sustainable project design.

References

Lasha Abzianidze and Johan Bos. 2019. Thirty musts for meaning banking. In *Proceedings of the First International Workshop on Designing Meaning Representations*, pages 15–27, Florence, Italy. Association for Computational Linguistics.

Jan Auernhammer. 2020. Human-centered ai: The role of human-centered design research in the development of ai. In *Synergy - DRS International Conference 2020*, Online. Design Research Society.

James Auger, Julian Hanna, and Enrique Encinas. 2017. Reconstrained design: Confronting oblique design constraints. *Nordes*, 7(1).

Emily M Bender. 2013. Linguistic fundamentals for natural language processing: 100 essentials from morphology and syntax. *Synthesis lectures on human language technologies*, 6(3):1–184.

Emily M. Bender and Batya Friedman. 2018. Data statements for natural language processing: Toward mitigating system bias and enabling better science. *Transactions of the Association for Computational Linguistics*, 6:587–604.

Emily M. Bender, Timnit Gebru, Angelina McMillan-Major, and Shmargaret Shmitchell. 2021. On the dangers of stochastic parrots: Can language models be too big? In *FAccT '21: 2021 ACM Conference on Fairness, Accountability, and Transparency, Virtual Event / Toronto, Canada, March 3-10, 2021*, pages 610–623. ACM.

Emily M. Bender and Alexander Koller. 2020. Climbing towards NLU: On meaning, form, and understanding in the age of data. In *Proceedings of the 58th Annual Meeting of the Association for Computational Linguistics*, pages 5185–5198, Online. Association for Computational Linguistics.

Steven Bird. 2020. Decolonising speech and language technology. In *Proceedings of the 28th International Conference on Computational Linguistics*, pages 3504–3519, Barcelona, Spain (Online). International Committee on Computational Linguistics.

Steven Bird, Lauren Gawne, Katie Gelbart, and Isaac McAlister. 2014. Collecting bilingual audio in remote indigenous communities. In *Proceedings of COLING 2014, the 25th International Conference on Computational Linguistics: Technical Papers*, pages 1015–1024.

John Blitzer, Ryan McDonald, and Fernando Pereira. 2006. Domain adaptation with structural correspondence learning. In *Proceedings of the 2006 conference on empirical methods in natural language processing*, pages 120–128. Association for Computational Linguistics.

Jeanette Blomberg and Helena Karasti. 2012a. Ethnography: Positioning ethnography within participatory design. In Jesper Simonsen and Toni Robertson, editors, *Routledge International Handbook of Participatory Design*, pages 106–136. Routledge, New York, NY.

Jeanette Blomberg and Helena Karasti. 2012b. Positioning ethnography within participatory design. In Jesper Simonsen and Toni Robertson, editors, *Routledge international handbook of participatory design*, pages 86–116. Routledge. Publisher: Routledge London.

Tone Bratteteig, Keld Bødker, Yvonne Dittrich, Preben Holst Mogensen, and Jesper Simonsen. 2012. Organising principles and general guidelines for Participatory Design Projects. In Jesper Simonsen and Toni Robertson, editors, *Routledge handbook of participatory design*, page 117. Routledge.

Tone Bratteteig and Guri Verne. 2018. Does ai make pd obsolete? exploring challenges from artificial intelligence to participatory design. In *Proceedings of the 15th Participatory Design Conference: Short Papers, Situated Actions, Workshops and Tutorial-Volume 2*, pages 1–5.

Ulrich Briefs, Claudio Ciborra, and Leslie Schneider. 1983. *Systems Design For, With, and by the Users: Proceedings of the Ifip Wg 9.1 Working Conference on Systems Design For, With, and by the Users, Riva Del Sole, Italy, 20-24 September 1982*. North Holland.

S. Bødker. 2000. Scenarios in user-centred design—setting the stage for reflection and action. *Interacting with Computers*, 13(1):61–75. Publisher: Oxford Academic.

Susanne Bødker and Clemens Nylandsted Klokmose. 2012. Dynamics in artifact ecologies. In *Proceedings of the 7th Nordic Conference on Human-Computer Interaction: Making Sense Through Design*, NordiCHI '12, pages 448–457, Copenhagen, Denmark. Association for Computing Machinery.

Michel Callon. 2004. The role of hybrid communities and socio-technical arrangements in the participatory design. *Journal of the center for information studies*, 5(3):3–10.

Roberto Cibin, Sarah Robinson, Maurizio Teli, Conor Linehan, Laura Maye, and Christopher Csíkszentmihályi. 2020. Shaping social innovation in local communities: The contribution of intermediaries. In *Proceedings of the 11th Nordic Conference on Human-Computer Interaction: Shaping Experiences, Shaping Society*, NordiCHI '20, New York, NY, USA. Association for Computing Machinery.

Roberto Cibin, Maurizio Teli, and Sarah Robinson. 2019. Institutioning and community radio. a comparative perspective. In *Proceedings of the 9th International Conference on Communities amp; Technologies - Transforming Communities*, Camp;T '19, page 143–154, New York, NY, USA. Association for Computing Machinery.

Costanza Conforti, Stephanie Hirmer, Dai Morgan, Marco Basaldella, and Yau Ben Or. 2020. Natural language processing for achieving sustainable development: the case of neural labelling to enhance community profiling. In *Proceedings of the 2020 Conference on Empirical Methods in Natural Language Processing (EMNLP)*, pages 8427–8444, Online. Association for Computational Linguistics.

Kate Crawford. 2021. *The Atlas of AI*. Yale University Press.

Hal Daumé III. 2007. Frustratingly easy domain adaptation. *ACL 2007*, page 256.

Carl DiSalvo, Andrew Clement, and Volkmar Pipek. 2012. Participatory design for, with, and by communities. In Jesper Simonsen and Toni Robertson, editors, *International Handbook of Participatory Design*, pages 182–209. Routledge, Oxford.

Yvonne Dittrich, Sara Eriksén, and Christina Hansson. 2002. PD in the Wild; Evolving Practices of Design in Use. In *Participatory Design Conference*.

Pelle Ehn. 1992. Scandinavian design: On participation and skill. In Paul S. Adler and Terry A. Winograd, editors, *Usability*, pages 96–132. Oxford University Press, Inc.

Pelle Ehn. 2008. Participation in design things. In *Proceedings of the Tenth Anniversary Conference on Participatory Design 2008*, PDC '08, pages 92–101, USA. Indiana University.

Pelle Ehn. 2016. Design, Democracy and Work: Exploring the Scandinavian Participatory Design Tradition. *Critical Design / Critical Futures.*

Pelle Ehn, Bengt Brattg\aard, E. Dalholm, R. C. Davies, Ann Hägerfors, Birgitta Mitchell, and Jörn Nilsson. 1996. The envisionment workshop-from visions to practice. In *Proceedings of the Participatory Design conference*, pages 141–152. MIT Boston.

Enrique Encinas and Mark Blythe. 2018. Research fiction and thought experiments in design. *Foundations and Trends in Human–Computer Interaction*, 12(1):1–105.

Marie Ertner, Anne Mie Kragelund, and Lone Malmborg. 2010. Five Enunciations of Empowerment in Participatory Design. In *Proceedings of the 11th Biennial Participatory Design Conference*, PDC '10, pages 191–194, New York, NY, USA. ACM.

Allyson Ettinger, Sudha Rao, Hal Daumé III, and Emily M Bender. 2017. Towards linguistically generalizable nlp systems: A workshop and shared task. In *Proceedings of the First Workshop on Building Linguistically Generalizable NLP Systems*, pages 1–10.

Rebecca Everson, Wolf Honoré, and Scott Grimm. 2019. An online platform for community-based language description and documentation. In *Proceedings of the Workshop on Computational Methods for Endangered Languages*, volume 1.

Tony Fry. 2017. Design after design. *Design Philosophy Papers*, 15(2):99–102. Publisher: Routledge _eprint: https://doi.org/10.1080/14487136.2017.1392093.

Yaroslav Ganin and Victor Lempitsky. 2015. Unsupervised domain adaptation by backpropagation. In *International conference on machine learning*, pages 1180–1189. PMLR.

Krissanne Kaye Garcia, Ma Angelica Lumain, Jose Antonio Wong, Jhovee Gerard Yap, and Charibeth Cheng. 2008. Natural language database interface for the community based monitoring system. In *Proceedings of the 22nd Pacific Asia Conference on Language, Information and Computation*, pages 384–390.

Danilo Giglitto. 2017. Community empowerment through the management of intangible cultural heritage in the isle of jura, scotland. *Imperial Journal of Interdisciplinary Research*, 3(5):567–578.

Hila Gonen and Yoav Goldberg. 2019. Lipstick on a pig: Debiasing methods cover up systematic gender biases in word embeddings but do not remove them. In *Proceedings of the 2019 Workshop on Widening NLP*, pages 60–63, Florence, Italy. Association for Computational Linguistics.

Richard Griscom. 2020. Mobilizing metadata: Open data kit (odk) for language resource development in east africa. In *Proceedings of the first workshop on Resources for African Indigenous Languages*, pages 31–35.

UTOPIA Project Group. 1981. The UTOPIA Project. On Training, Technology and Products Viewed from the Quality of Work Perspective.

Julian Hanna, James Auger, and Enrique Encinas. 2017. Reconstrained design: a manifesto.

Ingi Helgason, Michael Smyth, Enrique Encinas, and Ivica Mitrović. 2020. Speculative and critical design in education: Practice and perspectives. In *Companion Publication of the 2020 ACM Designing Interactive Systems Conference*, pages 385–388.

Stephanie Hirmer, Alycia Leonard, Josephine Tumwesige, and Costanza Conforti. 2021. Building representative corpora from illiterate communities: A reviewof challenges and mitigation strategies for developing countries. In *Proceedings of the 16th Conference of the European Chapter of the Association for Computational Linguistics: Main Volume*, pages 2176–2189, Online. Association for Computational Linguistics.

Dirk Hovy and Shannon L. Spruit. 2016. The social impact of natural language processing. In *Proceedings of the 54th Annual Meeting of the Association for Computational Linguistics (Volume 2: Short Papers)*, pages 591–598, Berlin, Germany. Association for Computational Linguistics.

Liesbeth Huybrechts, Maurizio Teli, Mela Zuljevic, and Mela Bettega. 2020. Visions that change. Articulating the politics of participatory design. *CoDesign*, 16(1):3–16.

Alan Irwin and Brian Wynne, editors. 1996. *Misunderstanding Science?: The Public Reconstruction of Science and Technology*. Cambridge University Press, Cambridge.

Gopinaath Kannabiran and Susanne Bødker. 2020. Prototypes as Objects of Desire. In *Proceedings of the 2020 ACM Designing Interactive Systems Conference*, pages 1619–1631. Association for Computing Machinery, New York, NY, USA.

Helena Karasti. 2014. Infrastructuring in participatory design. In *Proceedings of the 13th Participatory Design Conference: Research Papers - Volume 1*, PDC '14, pages 141–150, Windhoek, Namibia. Association for Computing Machinery.

Timothy Kempton. 2017. Cross-language forced alignment to assist community-based linguistics for low resource languages. In *Proceedings of the 2nd Workshop on the Use of Computational Methods in the Study of Endangered Languages*, pages 165–169.

Henrik Korsgaard, Clemens Nylandsted Klokmose, and Susanne Bødker. 2016. Computational alternatives in participatory design: putting the t back in socio-technical research. In *Proceedings of the 14th Participatory Design Conference: Full papers - Volume 1*, PDC '16, pages 71–79, New York, NY, USA. Association for Computing Machinery.

Tahu Kukutai and John Taylor. 2016. *Indigenous data sovereignty: Toward an agenda*. Anu Press.

Christopher A. Le Dantec and Carl DiSalvo. 2013. Infrastructuring and the formation of publics in participatory design. *Social Studies of Science*, 43(2):241–264.

Christopher A. Le Dantec and Sarah Fox. 2015. Strangers at the Gate: Gaining Access, Building Rapport, and Co-Constructing Community-Based Research. In *Proceedings of the 18th ACM Conference on Computer Supported Cooperative Work & Social Computing*, CSCW '15, pages 1348–1358, Vancouver, BC, Canada. Association for Computing Machinery.

Eric Le Ferrand, Steven Bird, and Laurent Besacier. 2020. Enabling interactive transcription in an indigenous community. In *Proceedings of the 28th International Conference on Computational Linguistics*, pages 3422–3428, Barcelona, Spain (Online). International Committee on Computational Linguistics.

Lori Levin. 2009. Adaptable, community-controlled, language technologies for language maintenance. In *13th Annual Conference of the European Association for Machine Translation*, page 8. Citeseer.

Paul Pu Liang, Irene Mengze Li, Emily Zheng, Yao Chong Lim, Ruslan Salakhutdinov, and Louis-Philippe Morency. 2020. Towards debiasing sentence representations. In *Proceedings of the 58th Annual Meeting of the Association for Computational Linguistics*, pages 5502–5515, Online. Association for Computational Linguistics.

Ann Light and Clodagh Miskelly. 2019. Platforms, Scales and Networks: Meshing a Local Sustainable Sharing Economy. *Computer Supported Cooperative Work (CSCW)*, 28(3):591–626.

Peter Lyle, Mariacristina Sciannamblo, and Maurizio Teli. 2018. Fostering Commonfare. Infrastructuring Autonomous Social Collaboration. In *Proceedings of the 2018 CHI Conference on Human Factors in Computing Systems*, CHI '18, pages 452:1–452:12, New York, NY, USA. ACM.

Ji Ma, Yue Zhang, and Jingbo Zhu. 2014. Tagging the web: Building a robust web tagger with neural network. In *Proceedings of the 52nd Annual Meeting of the Association for Computational Linguistics (Volume 1: Long Papers)*, volume 1, pages 144–154.

Gaia Mosconi, Matthias Korn, Christian Reuter, Peter Tolmie, Maurizio Teli, and Volkmar Pipek. 2017. From Facebook to the Neighbourhood: Infrastructuring of Hybrid Community Engagement. *Computer Supported Cooperative Work (CSCW)*, 26(4-6):959–1003.

Mithun Paul Panenghat, Sandeep Suntwal, Faiz Rafique, Rebecca Sharp, and Mihai Surdeanu. 2020. Towards the necessity for debiasing natural language inference datasets. In *Proceedings of the 12th Language Resources and Evaluation Conference*, pages 6883–6888, Marseille, France. European Language Resources Association.

Robert Racadio, Emma J. Rose, and Beth E. Kolko. 2014. Research at the margin: participatory design and community based participatory research. In *Proceedings of the 13th Participatory Design Conference on Short Papers, Industry Cases, Workshop Descriptions, Doctoral Consortium papers, and Keynote abstracts - PDC '14 - volume 2*, pages 49–52, Windhoek, Namibia. ACM Press.

Alan Ramponi and Barbara Plank. 2020. Neural unsupervised domain adaptation in NLP—A survey. In *Proceedings of the 28th International Conference on Computational Linguistics*, pages 6838–6855, Barcelona, Spain (Online). International Committee on Computational Linguistics.

Sebastian Ruder, Parsa Ghaffari, and John G Breslin. 2017. Data selection strategies for multi-domain sentiment analysis. *arXiv preprint arXiv:1702.02426*.

Sebastian Ruder and Barbara Plank. 2017. Learning to select data for transfer learning with bayesian optimization. In *Proceedings of the 2017 Conference on Empirical Methods in Natural Language Processing*, pages 372–382, Copenhagen, Denmark. Association for Computational Linguistics.

Jesper Simonsen and Toni Robertson. 2012. *Routledge International Handbook of Participatory Design*. Routledge, New York, NY.

Mona Sloan, Emanuel Moss, Olaitan Awomolo, and Laura Forlano. 2020. Participation is not a design fix for machine learning (pp. 1–7). In *Proceedings of the International Conference on Machine Learning, Vienna, Austria*.

Sai Susarla and Damodar Reddy Challa. 2019. A platform for community-sourced indic knowledge processing at scale. In *Proceedings of the 6th International Sanskrit Computational Linguistics Symposium*, pages 68–82, IIT Kharagpur, India. Association for Computational Linguistics.

Fasil Tekola, Susan J Bull, Bobbie Farsides, Melanie J Newport, Adebowale Adeyemo, Charles N Rotimi, and Gail Davey. 2009. Tailoring consent to context: designing an appropriate consent process for a biomedical study in a low income setting. *PLoS Negl Trop Dis*, 3(7):e482.

Maurizio Teli. 2015. Computing and the Common. Hints of a new utopia in Participatory Design. *Aarhus Series on Human Centered Computing*, 1(1):4.

Maurizio Teli, Antonella De Angeli, and Maria Menéndez-Blanco. 2017. The positioning cards: on affect, public design, and the common. *AI & SOCIETY*, pages 1–8.

Maurizio Teli, Marcus Foth, Mariacristina Sciannamblo, Irina Anastasiu, and Peter Lyle. 2020. Tales of Institutioning and Commoning: Participatory Design Processes with a Strategic and Tactical Perspective. In *Proceedings of the 16th Participatory Design Conference 2020 - Participation(s) Otherwise - Volume 1*, PDC '20, pages 159–171, Manizales, Colombia. Association for Computing Machinery.

Mamello Thinyane, Karthik Bhat, Lauri Goldkind, and Vikram Kamath Cannanure. 2018. Critical Participatory Design: Reflections on Engagement and Empowerment in a Case of a Community Based Organization. In *Proceedings of the 15th Participatory Design Conference: Full Papers - Volume 1*, PDC '18, pages 2:1–2:10, New York, NY, USA. ACM.

David R Traum. 2000. 20 questions on dialogue act taxonomies. *Journal of semantics*, 17(1):7–30.

Kirsikka Vaajakallio and Tuuli Mattelmäki. 2014. Design games in codesign: as a tool, a mindset and a structure. *CoDesign*, 10(1):63–77. Publisher: Taylor & Francis Ltd.

Maggie Walter and Michele Suina. 2019. Indigenous data, indigenous methodologies and indigenous data sovereignty. *International Journal of Social Research Methodology*, 22(3):233–243.

Terry Winograd. 1997. From Computing Machinery to Interaction Design. In Peter Denning and Robert Metcalfe, editors, *Beyond Calculation: The Next Fifty Years of Computing*, pages 149–162. Springer-Verlag.

Fangzhao Wu and Yongfeng Huang. 2016. Sentiment domain adaptation with multiple sources. In *Proceedings of the 54th Annual Meeting of the Association for Computational Linguistics (Volume 1: Long Papers)*, volume 1, pages 301–310.

Xuhui Zhou, Maarten Sap, Swabha Swayamdipta, Yejin Choi, and Noah Smith. 2021. Challenges in automated debiasing for toxic language detection. In *Proceedings of the 16th Conference of the European Chapter of the Association for Computational Linguistics: Main Volume*, pages 3143–3155, Online. Association for Computational Linguistics.

Theano: A Greek-speaking conversational agent for COVID-19

Nikoletta Ventoura[1], Kosmas Palios[1], Ioannis Vasilakis[1], Georgios Paraskevopoulos[1,2], Athanasios Katsamanis[1,3], Vassilis Katsouros[1]

[1] Institute for Language and Speech Processing, Athena Research Center, Athens, Greece
[2] School of ECE, National Technical University of Athens, Athens, Greece
[3] Behavioral Signals Technologies, Los Angeles, CA, USA

nikoletta.ventoura@athenarc.gr, kosmas.palios@athenarc.gr
yannis.vasilakis@athenarc.gr, g.paraskevopoulos@athenarc.gr
nkatsam@athenarc.gr, vsk@athenarc.gr

Abstract

Conversational Agents (CAs) can be a proxy for disseminating information and providing support to the public, especially in times of crisis. CAs can scale to reach larger numbers of end-users than human operators, while they can offer information interactively and engagingly. In this work, we present Theano, a Greek-speaking virtual assistant for COVID-19. Theano presents users with COVID-19 statistics and facts and informs users about the best health practices as well as the latest COVID-19 related guidelines. Additionally, Theano provides support to end-users by helping them self-assess their symptoms and redirecting them to first-line health workers. The relevant, localized information that Theano provides, makes it a valuable tool for combating COVID-19 in Greece. Theano has already conversed with different users in more than 170 different conversations through a web interface as a chatbot and over the phone as a voice bot.

1 Introduction

The current COVID-19 pandemic has presented a global challenge for citizens, health and government structures, and the global economy. One key characteristic of the current crisis is, that it cannot be combated with centralized handling alone, but requires a significant degree of cooperation from the public. Specifically, citizens adapt their lifestyle by adhering to measures limiting their daily contacts through physical distancing guidelines, stay-at-home orders, and curfews. Additionally, citizens are urged to avoid unnecessary visits to the hospitals. This transformation in everyday life has been a cause of stress for all areas of society. The best way to help people handle this crisis responsibly is to disseminate accurate information about the current state of affairs so that citizens are well-informed of expert recommendations and the status of the pandemic.

Intelligent conversational agents (CAs) can be a powerful tool for information dissemination and user support. Specifically, CAs have been extensively used for health applications, e.g., to help users quit smoking[1], for mental health support (Cameron et al., 2017, 2018; Grové, 2020), and HIV counselling (van Heerden et al., 2017). CAs have also been used for other social applications, e.g., fact checking (Gupta et al., 2021) and encouraging altruistic behavior (Wang et al., 2019). In the context of the COVID-19 crisis, CAs have been proposed for symptom self-checking, i.e., Clara[2], information dissemination, i.e., HealthyBuddy+[3], and combating misinformation, i.e., Jennifer[4] (Li et al., 2020).

One issue that arises is that most CAs are created for English-speaking demographics, but in many cases the policies and information about the pandemic are region-dependent. Developing applications for under-resourced languages is challenging, due to the lack of data and the limited user base (Hovy and Spruit, 2016). Nevertheless, we need to overcome language barriers and to provide contextualized information with respect to local policies, circumstances and statistics. Theano is debunking myths and conspiracy theories that are prevalent in Greece, such as the negative effects that masks have in children or the involvement of the Greek church in COVID-19 policies. We have not added information about fake news that have spread abroad and do not interest the Greek public (e.g., drinking disinfectant to stop COVID-19). Therefore, it is essential to develop localized, native CAs.

In this work, we present Theano, a Greek speak-

[1] WHO Florence
[2] CDC Clara
[3] UNICEF, WHO/Europe HealthBuddy+
[4] Jennifer

Proceedings of the 1st Workshop on NLP for Positive Impact, pages 36–46
Bangkok, Thailand (online), August 5, 2021.

ing CA for COVID-19. Theano is a multipurpose CA, aiming to inform and support the Greek population. Specifically, Theano provides up-to-date localized statistics about the pandemic and expert guidelines. Furthermore, Theano debunks common myths about the use of masks, the need for vaccination, etc. Besides informing users, Theano can also support them, by helping them to self-assess the severity of their symptoms and direct them to the best avenues for receiving expert help. We make Theano available through a user-friendly web interface as a chatbot and through a Twilio telephone number as a voice assistant. The virtual assistant has already conversed with different users in more than 170 different conversations. Theano is continuously improved based on user feedback, by retraining the model using user conversations and including frequently requested features and improvements. Code is available as open-source[5]

2 Background Work

From a technical standpoint, CAs are systems that integrate multiple components in order to understand the user's query (Natural Language Understanding – NLU), isolate spans of interest in the input phrases (Entity Extraction) and select an appropriate action or response based on the input (Dialogue Management). Initial NLU systems were based on rule-based systems that use elaborate grammars (Allen, 1988; Dowding et al., 1993) and statistical language modeling (Suen, 1979), while recent research focuses on neural approaches, i.e., deep belief networks (Sarikaya et al., 2014), Recurrent Neural Networks (RNNs) (Yao et al., 2013) and Transformer (Vaswani et al., 2017) models (Liu et al., 2019; Dong et al., 2019; Bunk et al., 2020). Similarly, research for Entity Extraction (or Named Entity Recognition) systems, has moved from rule-based approaches and elaborate feature engineering (Mikheev et al., 1999; Collins and Singer, 1999) to approaches based on Conditional Random Fields (Lafferty et al., 2001) and neural networks (Chiu and Nichols, 2016; Devlin et al., 2019). Dialogue Management approaches include hierarchical plan-based systems (Bohus and Rudnicky, 2009), Hierarchical RNNs (Serban et al., 2016) and Transformers (Vlasov et al., 2020). These components have been integrated in dialogue frameworks that provide a streamlined developer experience. Popular open-source dialogue frameworks include Deeppavlov (Burtsev et al., 2018) and Rasa (Bocklisch et al., 2017)

[5]GitLab Repository

3 Conversation Design

Theano aims to provide a first line of support for end users during the pandemic. Our design choices are based on two key goals: a) keeping users well-informed about the current status of the pandemic in order to enable them to make good health choices and b) reducing panic by helping users self-assess their symptoms and directing them to first-line health-care providers. This objective has also been suggested by McKillop et al. (2020) and Følstad et al. (2018).

On the one hand, Theano provides general information about COVID-19. There is access to the number of COVID-19 new cases and deaths in Greece, other countries, and worldwide. Moreover, she knows the availability of Intensive Care Units, as well as the number of people that have been vaccinated on a specific date and in total in Greece. We have also included myth busters concerning the usage of masks and other conspiracy theories, e.g., that masks delay the development of children's lungs. There is a wide range of Frequently Asked Questions about COVID-19 supported, from how it started, ways of transmission and protection to how to wash hands or whether one should be wearing gloves in public. [6].

On the other hand, Theano can list the common COVID-19 symptoms and in case the user experiences symptoms, through a mixed initiative conversation, she starts a diagnostic survey. In all stages of the dialogue, she clearly states that she is not a doctor and the user should speak with the local authorities if they continue having symptoms. She can also find pharmacies that are open in the area that the user requests. In addition, Theano can advise users who have been in contact with a COVID-19 patient, i.e., she suggests that they get tested and informs them where they can obtain free tests provided by local authorities.

To better facilitate the fulfilment of the two goals mentioned earlier, namely, being informative, and also keeping users calm, we have created a relevant Persona for Theano. The importance of analytical design of the Persona is analyzed by Pearl (2016). Theano has the persona of a support agent that is honest, polite, and direct, but at the same time friendly. The core design principles we followed

[6]See Section 5 for our data sources.

are:

Engagement. We want Theano to be part of the daily life of users, so she has to be interesting and not only respond to questions. Ruane et al. (2019) highlight the importance of engagement when dealing with precarious topics. Theano tries to keep the users interested in the conversation at all dialogue stages, by suggesting new and relevant conversation topics. Theano is also ready to chitchat, which helps keeping certain users better engaged. Moreover, chitchatting includes general questions about Theano, e.g. age, favourite color and music, holidays, hobbies, weather, languages, so that the users can get to know the Persona in-depth and have an alternative from the COVID-related topics. As shown in Fig. 3, and will be discussed in the following, chitchat has actually been found to be one of Theano's most popular features.

Consistency. We want users to get the information they ask for, fast. Theano has short responses and doesn't contradict herself by giving conflicting information. We want the user to trust Theano. Short responses are also preferable for allowing spoken communication with Theano (on the phone). Longer responses on the phone tend to quickly tire users. This objective has been proposed by Bickmore and Giorgino (2004).

Clarity. The topic that Theano is handling is serious, that is the reason why we try to present pieces of information in a clear and concise manner, that is easily understood by everyone. By being explicit in every stage of the dialogue, we also ensure that the user acknowledges the capabilities of the CA and does not expect anything more than what is offered about a sensitive medical topic like COVID-19 (Laranjo et al., 2018).

Empathy. Theano is handling questions that are serious and have an impact on people's lives, in a period of profound crisis. She tries to mitigate user fear, comprehends the worries that the users express and offers emotional support with her responses, which is very valuable during the pandemic, as supported by Miner et al. (2020), De Gennaro et al. (2020) and Rashkin et al. (2019). For example:

USER : I am positive. What can I do?

THEANO : Since you know you are positive, it is important to stay calm and not panic. You should stay in contact with your doctor and the local authorities. In case your symptoms worsen you should go to the hospital. I think that it's all going to be okay. Try to stay calm.

4 System Description

Fig. 1 shows the architecture of Theano. The user's query is passed through a preprocessing pipeline that normalizes the raw text. Then, textual features are extracted from the raw text and are fed to Entity Extraction and the Intent Classification modules. Extracted entities are augmented with the output of a rule-based module based on External Lookup Tables. The state tracker saves the recognized intent and the extracted entities and passes them to the Dialogue Management module, which determines an appropriate response based on the user's query. All intermediate states are logged into an external database. Theano is implemented using the Rasa open-source dialogue framework, which provides a clean way to implement our dialogue pipeline.

In detail, for pre-processing, we use an in-house spell-checker based on a convolutional sequence to sequence architecture. The spell checker is trained on various synthetically corrupted Greek texts and can correct spelling and accenting errors for small Greek phrases. Online conversations in Greek often contain Greek words written in Latin characters (also known as Greeklish). Therefore, we also include as a preprocessing step a state-machine based Greeklish to Greek translator. The clean text is finally tokenized on whitespaces. During the Featurization step, we extract Bag of Words and N-gram features for the input tokens.

Entity extraction is performed using a Conditional Random Field (CRF) Named Entity Recognition (NER) module (Lafferty et al., 2001; Bocklisch et al., 2017). Additionally, we use Duckling[7], which provides a regex Lookup Table for time and date entities and aggregate the extracted entities with the CRF outputs. For example, for the message "What pharmacies will be open in Athens tomorrow morning at 8?", the CRF will extract "Athens" for the entity "city" and Duckling will extract the correct date and time string.

Intents are organized in a hierarchy, where high-level intents are recognized first (e.g., FAQ), and then fine-grained intents are extracted. This decision allows easily scaling up the dialogue system to a large number of intents with limited training data. Therefore, intent recognition is performed using a hierarchy of Dual Intent Entity Transformer (DIET) (Bunk et al., 2020) classifiers. DIET is

[7]Duckling Github repository

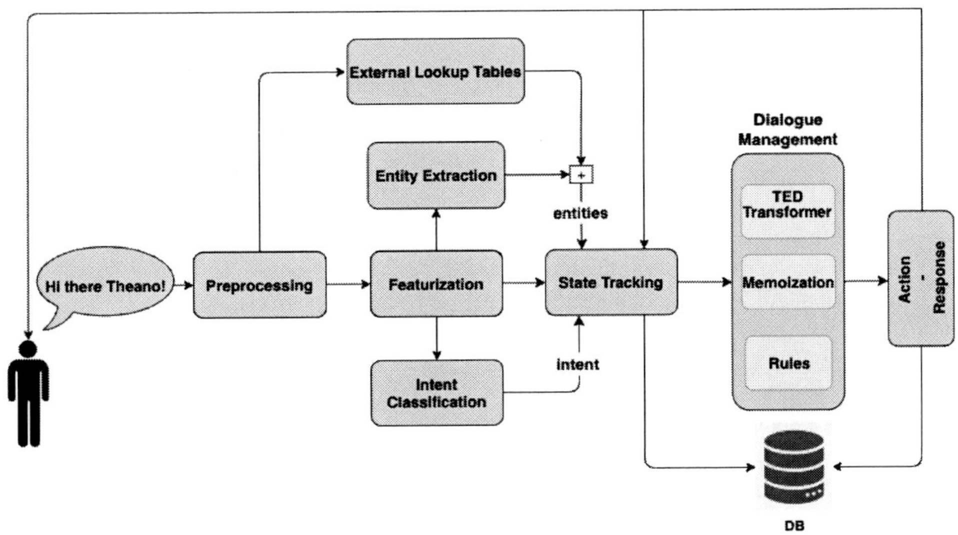

Figure 1: Architecture overview of Theano. The key components are the Preprocessing and Featurization steps, the Entity Extraction, the Intent Classification, and the Dialogue Management.

a Transformer based architecture that operates on Bag of Words features. The sparse features are embedded using a feedforward layer and then encoded using a 2-layer Transformer encoder with relative positional embeddings in the attention layers (Shaw et al., 2018). The first DIET classifier classifies coarse-grained intent classes, and then the input is routed to the second level of classifiers (i.e. response selectors). The output is the fine-grained recognized intent and the respective classifier confidence. An intent is considered to be recognized if the confidence level exceeds a specified threshold, otherwise a fallback strategy is adopted (e.g. "I did not understand your question. Can you rephrase?").

For dialogue management, we use three policies with different levels of complexity and priority. First, we use a Rule-based policy that explicitly maps a small, selected set of important intents to the desired actions or responses. Then, we fall back to a memoization policy that retrieves identical user inputs from past conversations. If the rule-based policy and the memoization policy do not produce a response, we use TED policy (Vlasov et al., 2020), a Transformer-based classifier for dialogue act classification. TED receives the user inputs, recognized intents, and extracted entities across a fixed history window, and outputs the appropriate response with respect to the user input.

It is important that detailed statistics and logs of past conversations are kept, in order to continu-

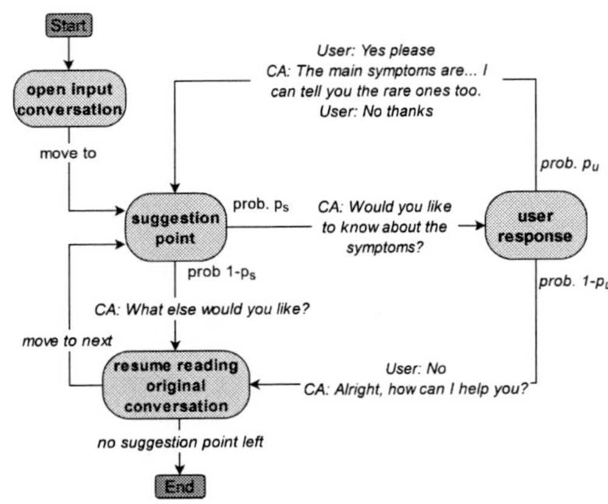

Figure 2: Overview of the synthetic data generator

ously improve Theano's performance. To this end, we track all conversations, and anonymized versions of the user inputs, recognized intents, and extracted entities are saved into a database. Thus, we can evaluate past system performance and improve the dialogue stories using expert knowledge from linguists.

4.1 Smart suggestions

An early test release of Theano showed us that users are typically unaware of the themes that the CA covers; consequently, they used to ask questions that Theano could not respond to while ignoring many of her functionalities. The dialogue flow did not allow transitioning between themes because the dialogue was limited to start with a question from the user, an exchange of messages on the topic, and, in the end, the CA would "What else can I do for you?". At that point, we realized that this question, which is at the end of every sub-conversation, is also what we call a suggestion point: a point where the bot could possibly say "I know about Y too, would you like me to tell you?". Suggestion Y should not be a random topic but something new to the conversation. Another question is how often the CA should suggest something; there is not an easy answer to this. We have experimented with the value of p_s, the probability of the CA making a suggestion upon reaching a suggestion point.

To implement this feature, we have to augment the training data of the TED policy with examples of conversations driven - at least partially - by the CA's suggestions. Due to the large amount of possible suggestions, instead of manually generating example conversations, we opt for a synthetic data generation process. During this process, we augment existing conversations in our training set with one or more additional turns that are driven by Theano's suggestions.

Fig. 2 shows the process of generating the augmented conversation samples. The input is an existing conversation with one or more suggestion points as well as p_s and p_u. The latter is used to model how willing a user is to accept a suggestion.

When the generator reaches a suggestion point, a suggestion loop begins. Firstly, it has to decide whether to suggest something from a topic previously not discussed (with probability p_s) or to leave the suggestion point unaltered, i.e., a generic prompt. If the generator makes a suggestion, then the proposed topic is either rejected or accepted by the simulated user with probability p_u. If the user rejects the suggestion, then the script adds the user's refusal and proceeds to the rest of the conversation. Otherwise, if the user accepts the suggestion, the generator appends a sub-conversation on the selected topic, which is followed by another suggestion point. The aforementioned procedure keeps repeating until either no suggestion is made or the user has chosen to disagree.

5 Integrations

Data Sources: Table 1 shows the data sources we have integrated into our backend to obtain the latest COVID-19 statistics, suggestions and facts. We prefer to use official or trusted sources, e.g., CDC, WHO, NPHO etc. Our main sources for statistics are the Covid API, OWiD and Nyrro's public data. Covid API and OWiD are trusted sources for global COVID-19 related statistics, while Nyrro's data is an individual's effort to aggregate latest COVID-19 statistics about Greece. Nyrro's is not an official source, but we opt to use it, because it is more up to date than OWiD and easier to access programmatically than statistics provided by Greek official sources (i.e. NPHO). Nevertheless we continuously cross-check the accuracy of Nyrro's statistics with the official sources, both manually and through regression tests. For COVID-19 related facts and expert suggestions, our main sources are the FAQs provided by ECDC, CDC, WHO and NPHO. Finally, in order to locate open pharmacies near the user's location, we utilize vrisko.gr, a site that provides information about the location and open hours of businesses through an API.

Data Source	Extracted Information
Covid API[8]	Foreign #cases , #deaths statistics
Nyrro's public domain[9]	Greek #cases, #deaths, ICU availability statistics
European Centre of Disease Control (ECDC)[10]	FAQs, diagnostic form
Centre of Disease Control (CDC)[11]	FAQs
Our World in Data (OWiD)[12]	Vaccine progress
Vrisko.gr[13]	Pharmacy locations, open hours
World Health Organization (WHO)[14]	FAQs, mask facts
National Public Health Organization (NPHO)[15]	Greek FAQs, mask facts

Table 1: Data sources for COVID-19 stats and facts.

Voice and Chat bot: In addition to the described chat functionality, Theano is also available as a voice bot. We integrate Google Automatic Speech Recognition (ASR) and Text to Speech (TTS) services for the Greek language. We use a master service, which receives voice input through websockets, routes the intermediate outputs to the appropriate microservices and then streams the voice response to the user. Overall, Theano is available through the following channels:

Web chat: Sends textual input to the master service

[7]Covid API

[8]Nyrros' Spreadsheet

[9]ECDC FAQ on Covid-19

[10]CDC FAQ on Covid-19

[11]OWiD Github repository

[12]Pharmacies on duty through Vrisko

[13]WHO FAQ on Covid-19

[14]NPHO FAQ on Covid-19

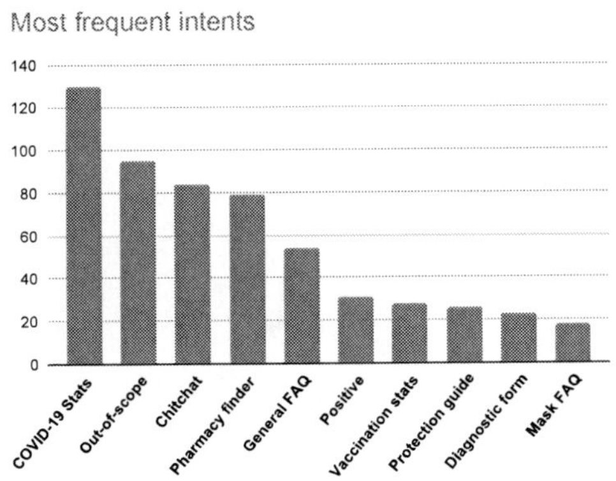

Figure 3: 10 most frequent intents asked by users in April 2021

text endopoint.
Twilio: Allows consuming voice streams from the telephone network. It receives the phone traffic, and forwards it to the master service websocket.
Web-based Voice bot: Connects directly to the master service, using websockets.

6 System Evaluation

We have constructed a training set that consists of 3719 real and synthetic conversations, which is constantly evolving based on real-world usage. Our dataset includes 37 core intents at the first level of the intent hierarchy. Four of these intents, i.e. Chitchat, General FAQ, Mask FAQ and Out-of-scope, extend to a second level in the hierarchy with 13, 31, 13 and 10 sub-intents respectively.

Fig. 3 shows the ten most frequent questions asked by users during a release in April 2021. There is a preference in the COVID-19 statistics and the pharmacy finder features, with the out-of-scope response selector as a close second. The latter includes topics that Theano does not cover, for example, lockdown updates or hospital operating hours; instead of resulting in a fallback action, in this case, Theano redirects the user to the appropriate website. An interesting fact is the tendency of users to chit-chatting.

We train DIET classifier for the 37 core intents for 10 epochs with batch size 32. We use the default values provided by Rasa for all other hyperparameters. Similarly we train separate classifiers for the sub-intent categories of Chitchat, Mask FAQ, General FAQ and Out of Scope for 25, 60, 50 and 50 epochs respectively. This yields an overall intent recognition accuracy of $92.2\% \pm 0.002$ for the core 37 intents and $92.0\% \pm 0.002$ for the 67 sub-intents during 5-fold cross-validation. The respective F1 scores are $92.1\% \pm 0.008$ and $91.8\% \pm 0.016$.

However, these proportions fall down to 86% when the system interacts with real users. During inference, if classifier confidence is small (i.e. less than 0.5), or the classifier is unsure (i.e. confidence for top two intents close – less than 0.1 difference) we choose the intent Fallback action.

For the dialogue manager, we configure memoization policy to memorize a window of 5 dialogue turns. TED classifier is configured with a history window of 10 turns and we set the output dimension to 64. We use default values for all other hyperparameters. TED is trained for 8 epochs with batch size 16, yielding 95.3% test accuracy. During inference we choose the fallback response if the output confidence of TED is less than 0.4.

Additionally to the test accuracy, we measure intent classification accuracy when the system is used by real users in the wild. Fig. 4 shows the confusion matrices over two user evaluation periods. The first user evaluation was performed in December 2020 in tandem with the first release of Theano, when we received 101 conversations. The second evaluation was completed in April 2021 with the second release of Theano, when we received 73 conversations. All the incoming data have been annotated by linguists. One thing to notice is that Theano was updated with more intents during the second release. Included intents are selected based on user feedback and the current developments. While more intents are introduced, the overall NLU performance is improved (79.5% accuracy in December 2020 versus 86.7% recognition accuracy in April). Finally we observe in both evaluation periods, most misclassified intents are successfully captured by the fallback strategy.

6.1 Qualitative comparison with other CAs

Table 2 shows the main features of Clara, Jennifer, and Theano. We examine five main functionalities that at least one of the CAs supports, or partially supports, which means that even if it does not provide an interactive response, it redirects the user to an appropriate website.

The main purpose of Clara is to provide self checking. The chatbot has a specific purpose, i.e. symptom self-checking. Clara does not allow for arbitrary textual input, instead allows users to se-

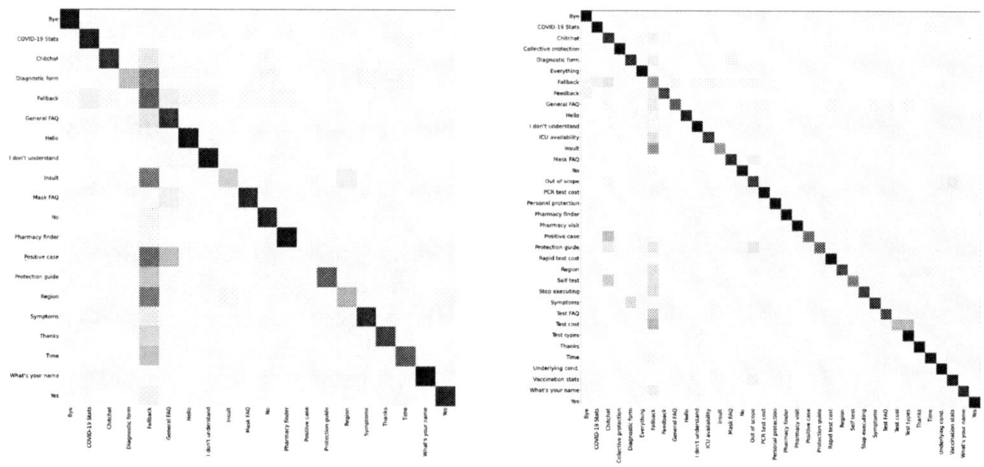

Figure 4: Confusion matrices for intent recognition in real conversations over two periods of user evaluation, i.e. December 2020 (left) and April 2021 (right).

	Theano	Jennifer	Clara
Language	GR	EN	EN
Voice interface	✓	✗	✗
COVID-19 statistics	✓	✓	✗
Diagnostic Form	✓	✗	✓
Treatment details	✗	✓	✗
Ways of protection	✓	✓	✓
Vaccine information	✓*	✓	✗
Chitchat	✓	✓	✗

Table 2: Comparison of supported features of Clara, Jennifer and Theano. ✗: not supported, ✓: supported, ✓*: partially supported

lect one query among a set of fixed choices. The purpose of this decision is to have a clear understanding of the symptoms, assess them, consult the user according to the responses, and give instructions about the ways of protection. The diagnostic forms have similar elements both in Theano and Clara, as both of them follow the same methodology. In particular, Theano and Clara present the main symptoms and ask the user which symptoms they experience. They then proceed with the more rare ones and finally advise the user per the best avenues of medical care they should seek.

Jennifer and Theano have similar functionalities, but the responses have different goals, apart from the common purpose of accurately informing the users. Jennifer's responses are longer, and at the end, she redirects the user to her sources, whereas Theano focuses more on user engagement by giving smaller, condensed answers, unless the user asks for details. Furthermore, Jennifer handles questions that she cannot reply with a diplomatic way by apologizing and suggesting that her developers will add this feature in the future. In comparison, Theano tries to overcome the fallback, by suggesting the topics that she is aware of, without explaining why she could not respond to the specific question. Jennifer offers general information about vaccines, for example which antiviral drugs are used, something that Theano is not capable of. Theano's goal is the dissemination of information that the users understand, without using specialized medical vocabulary. Both Jennifer and Theano cover similar chitchat topics; they give information about themselves (e.g., age, location, functionalities) and their interests (e.g., hobbies). The only difference is the content of their responses because Jennifer has a robotic persona, whereas Theano is anthropomorphic. To be more precise, a robotic persona means that the CA does not incorporate human-like elements, while a more anthropomorphic one imitates human characteristics (e.g., Theano has a favourite holiday island). From our evaluation, we present the responses that the two CAs have in the same question.

Conversation example with Theano:

USER : Do you have any hobbies?

THEANO : Sure. I love listening to music.

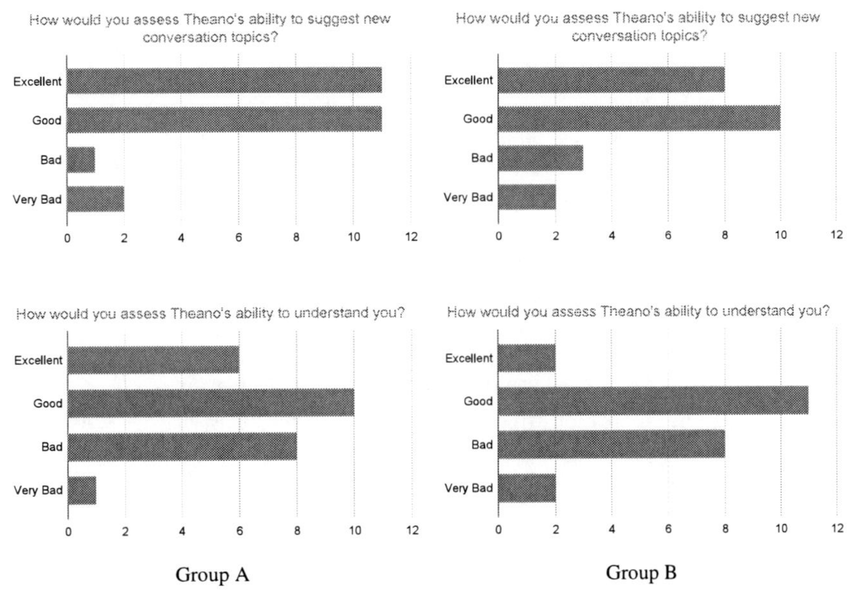

Figure 5: User assessment during A/B testing of the smart suggestion feature. We ask users to provide an assessment of Theano's comprehension ability and about the new conversation suggestion feature. For Group A we suggest new topics with $p_s = 0.2$, while for Group B with $p_s = 0.8$.

USER : What kind of music do you like?
THEANO : I prefer alternative Greek music.
USER : Where are you?
THEANO : I live in Athens.

Conversation example with Jennifer:

USER : Do you have any hobbies?
JENNIFER : understanding people - what they think and how they feel
USER : Where are you?
JENNIFER : I live in the cloud - my address would be something like: 128.0.0.0

While Jennifer and Clara are specialized chatbots for information dissemination and symptom self-checking respectively, Theano includes both functionalities. The role of Theano is not limited to the dissemination of accurate information concerning COVID-19, but also to provide a holistic support to the user by being empathetic, engaging, clear, and consistent. Jennifer and Clara are available for English-speaking users, while Theano is available in Greek. Finally, Theano includes a voice interface, whereas users can only interact with Jennifer and Clara via chat.

6.2 Smart Suggestion - A/B testing

An A/B test with real users was performed to evaluate the new smart suggestion feature, and specifically the optimal suggestion probability p_s. During the A/B test, users interacted with two versions of Theano. The first version, presented to Group A, was configured with $p_s = 0.2$ (few suggestions), while the second version, presented to Group B, was configured with $p_s = 0.8$ (lots of suggestions). Seventy three individuals aged 15-65 participated in the A/B test, and the system divided them into groups randomly (36 in Group A and 37 in Group B). At the end of the interaction, the users completed a survey. In Fig. 5 we present user assessments for two survey questions regarding the new suggestion feature and Theano's overall comprehension ability.

Users prefer the CA suggestions to be less intrusive, as, in Group A, the Excellent to Bad and Very Bad ratio is greater than the one from Group B. Also, the normalized sum of Bad and Very Bad counts is less than the respective sum from Group B. A remarkable observation is that the assessment of Theano's comprehension ability is worse in Group B than in Group A. Although the similarity between the two groups is noteworthy, Group A has overall better reviews. This fact indicates that deeper, CA-driven conversations may be more prone to intent recognition errors. With a higher p_s we increase the engagement, but it appears to negatively affect how much the user feels understood by the CA. This suggests that the optimal value for p_s is somewhere between 0.2 and 0.8, with the purpose of engaging the user without losing the mutual understanding between user and CA.

Furthermore, the average number of conversation turns was measured as a proxy to assess user engagement, which is 10.74 and 13.06 average turns for Group A and B respectively. These figures indicate that conversations last longer when the CA directs the user by making suggestions frequently, even though this may upset users that want to have better control of the conversation.

7 Conclusions and Future Work

We present Theano, a CA for COVID-19 information dissemination and symptom self-checking in Greek. We believe, Theano is a valuable contribution to the list of digital tools for battling COVID-19, as it provides a feature-rich and scalable support system tailored to the needs of our user-base. Theano needs to be constantly updated with new intents and conversation topics without sacrificing NLU performance, in order to keep up with the latest developments. We show that this is possible; in the second iteration, we double the number of supported intents and even improve the intent recognition performance in the real-world user evaluation. We also propose a simple smart suggestion feature, in order to improve user engagement and interactively show Theano's capabilities to users. During our A/B testing, we receive encouraging -though not conclusive- results, that this can improve user engagement, as the use of this feature leads to higher number of conversation turns.

In the future, we want to keep improving Theano's abilities by continuously adding intents based on our users needs. We also want to introduce a reinforcement learning based smart suggestion module, for open domain smart suggestions. Finally, we want to develop a large scale deployment of Theano and reach a wider user base.

Acknowledgements

- We want to thank the reviewers for their constructive feedback and our user-base for helping us improve Theano.
- This research has been co-financed by the European Regional Development Fund of the European Union and Greek national funds through the Operational Program Competitiveness, Entrepreneurship and Innovation, under the call RESEARCH – CREATE – INNOVATE (project safety4all with code:T1EDK-04248).

References

James Allen. 1988. *Natural language understanding*. Benjamin-Cummings Publishing Co., Inc.

Timothy Bickmore and Toni Giorgino. 2004. Some novel aspects of health communication from a dialogue systems perspective. In *AAAI Fall Symposium on Dialogue Systems for Health Communication*, pages 275–291.

Tom Bocklisch, Joey Faulkner, Nick Pawlowski, and Alan Nichol. 2017. Rasa: Open source language understanding and dialogue management. *CoRR*, abs/1712.05181.

Dan Bohus and Alexander I Rudnicky. 2009. The ravenclaw dialog management framework: Architecture and systems. *Computer Speech & Language*, 23(3):332–361.

Tanja Bunk, Daksh Varshneya, Vladimir Vlasov, and Alan Nichol. 2020. Diet: Lightweight language understanding for dialogue systems.

Mikhail Burtsev, Alexander Seliverstov, Rafael Airapetyan, Mikhail Arkhipov, Dilyara Baymurzina, Nickolay Bushkov, Olga Gureenkova, Taras Khakhulin, Yurii Kuratov, Denis Kuznetsov, et al. 2018. Deeppavlov: Open-source library for dialogue systems. In *Proceedings of ACL 2018, System Demonstrations*, pages 122–127.

Gillian Cameron, David Cameron, Gavin Megaw, Raymond Bond, Maurice Mulvenna, Siobhan O'Neill, Cherie Armour, and Michael McTear. 2017. Towards a chatbot for digital counselling. In *Proceedings of the 31st International BCS Human Computer Interaction Conference (HCI 2017) 31*, pages 1–7.

Gillian Cameron, David Cameron, Gavin Megaw, Raymond Bond, Maurice Mulvenna, Siobhan O'Neill, Cherie Armour, and Michael McTear. 2018. Assessing the usability of a chatbot for mental health care. In *International Conference on Internet Science*, pages 121–132. Springer.

Jason PC Chiu and Eric Nichols. 2016. Named entity recognition with bidirectional lstm-cnns. *Transactions of the Association for Computational Linguistics*, 4:357–370.

Michael Collins and Yoram Singer. 1999. Unsupervised models for named entity classification. In *1999 Joint SIGDAT Conference on Empirical Methods in Natural Language Processing and Very Large Corpora*.

Mauro De Gennaro, Eva G Krumhuber, and Gale Lucas. 2020. Effectiveness of an empathic chatbot in combating adverse effects of social exclusion on mood. *Frontiers in psychology*, 10:3061.

Jacob Devlin, Ming-Wei Chang, Kenton Lee, and Kristina Toutanova. 2019. Bert: Pre-training of deep bidirectional transformers for language understanding. In *Proceedings of the 2019 Conference of the North American Chapter of the Association for Computational Linguistics: Human Language Technologies, Volume 1 (Long and Short Papers)*, pages 4171–4186.

Li Dong, Nan Yang, Wenhui Wang, Furu Wei, Xiaodong Liu, Yu Wang, Jianfeng Gao, Ming Zhou, and Hsiao-Wuen Hon. 2019. Unified Language Model Pre-training for Natural Language Understanding and Generation. In *33rd Conference on Neural Information Processing Systems (NeurIPS 2019)*.

John Dowding, Jean Mark Gawron, Douglas Appelt, John Bear, Lynn Cherny, Robert C Moore, and Douglas B Moran. 1993. Gemini: A natural language system for spoken-language understanding. In *31st Annual Meeting of the Association for Computational Linguistics*, pages 54–61.

Asbjørn Følstad, Petter Bae Brandtzæg, Tom Feltwell, Effie LC Law, Manfred Tscheligi, and Ewa A Luger. 2018. Sig: chatbots for social good. In *Extended Abstracts of the 2018 CHI Conference on Human Factors in Computing Systems*, pages 1–4.

Christine Grové. 2020. Co-developing a mental health and wellbeing chatbot with and for young people. *Frontiers in Psychiatry*, 11:1664.

Ankur Gupta, Yash Varun, Prarthana Das, Nithya Muttineni, Parth Srivastava, Hamim Zafar, Tanmoy Chakraborty, and Swaprava Nath. 2021. Truthbot: An automated conversational tool for intent learning, curated information presenting, and fake news alerting. *arXiv preprint arXiv:2102.00509*.

Alastair van Heerden, Xolani Ntinga, and Khanya Vilakazi. 2017. The potential of conversational agents to provide a rapid hiv counseling and testing services. In *2017 international conference on the frontiers and advances in data science (FADS)*, pages 80–85. IEEE.

Dirk Hovy and Shannon L Spruit. 2016. The social impact of natural language processing. In *Proceedings of the 54th Annual Meeting of the Association for Computational Linguistics (Volume 2: Short Papers)*, pages 591–598.

John D. Lafferty, Andrew McCallum, and Fernando C. N. Pereira. 2001. Conditional random fields: Probabilistic models for segmenting and labeling sequence data. In *Proceedings of the Eighteenth International Conference on Machine Learning*, ICML '01, page 282–289, San Francisco, CA, USA. Morgan Kaufmann Publishers Inc.

Liliana Laranjo, Adam G Dunn, Huong Ly Tong, Ahmet Baki Kocaballi, Jessica Chen, Rabia Bashir, Didi Surian, Blanca Gallego, Farah Magrabi, Annie YS Lau, et al. 2018. Conversational agents in healthcare: a systematic review. *Journal of the American Medical Informatics Association*, 25(9):1248–1258.

Yunyao Li, Tyrone Grandison, Patricia Silveyra, Ali Douraghy, Xinyu Guan, Thomas Kieselbach, Chengkai Li, and Haiqi Zhang. 2020. Jennifer for COVID-19: An NLP-powered chatbot built for the people and by the people to combat misinformation. In *Proceedings of the 1st Workshop on NLP for COVID-19 at ACL 2020*, Online. Association for Computational Linguistics.

Xiaodong Liu, Pengcheng He, Weizhu Chen, and Jianfeng Gao. 2019. Multi-task deep neural networks for natural language understanding. In *Proceedings of the 57th Annual Meeting of the Association for Computational Linguistics*, pages 4487–4496.

Mollie McKillop, Brett R South, Anita Preininger, Mitch Mason, and Gretchen Purcell Jackson. 2020. Leveraging conversational technology to answer common covid-19 questions. *Journal of the American Medical Informatics Association*.

Andrei Mikheev, Marc Moens, and Claire Grover. 1999. Named entity recognition without gazetteers. In *Ninth Conference of the European Chapter of the Association for Computational Linguistics*.

Adam S Miner, Liliana Laranjo, and A Baki Kocaballi. 2020. Chatbots in the fight against the covid-19 pandemic. *NPJ digital medicine*, 3(1):1–4.

Cathy Pearl. 2016. *Designing voice user interfaces: principles of conversational experiences*. " O'Reilly Media, Inc.".

Hannah Rashkin, Eric Michael Smith, Margaret Li, and Y-Lan Boureau. 2019. Towards empathetic open-domain conversation models: A new benchmark and dataset. In *Proceedings of the 57th Annual Meeting of the Association for Computational Linguistics*, pages 5370–5381, Florence, Italy. Association for Computational Linguistics.

Elayne Ruane, Abeba Birhane, and Anthony Ventresque. 2019. Conversational ai: Social and ethical considerations. In *AICS*, pages 104–115.

Ruhi Sarikaya, Geoffrey E Hinton, and Anoop Deoras. 2014. Application of deep belief networks for natural language understanding. *IEEE/ACM Transactions on Audio, Speech, and Language Processing*, 22(4):778–784.

Iulian Serban, Alessandro Sordoni, Yoshua Bengio, Aaron Courville, and Joelle Pineau. 2016. Building end-to-end dialogue systems using generative hierarchical neural network models. In *Proceedings of the AAAI Conference on Artificial Intelligence*, volume 30.

Peter Shaw, Jakob Uszkoreit, and Ashish Vaswani. 2018. Self-attention with relative position representations. In *Proceedings of the 2018 Conference of the North American Chapter of the Association for Computational Linguistics: Human Language Technologies, Volume 2 (Short Papers)*, pages 464–468, New Orleans, Louisiana. Association for Computational Linguistics.

Ching Y Suen. 1979. N-gram statistics for natural language understanding and text processing. *IEEE transactions on pattern analysis and machine intelligence*, pages 164–172.

Ashish Vaswani, Noam Shazeer, Niki Parmar, Jakob Uszkoreit, Llion Jones, Aidan N Gomez, Ł ukasz Kaiser, and Illia Polosukhin. 2017. Attention is all you need. In *Advances in Neural Information Processing Systems*, volume 30. Curran Associates, Inc.

Vladimir Vlasov, Johannes E. M. Mosig, and Alan Nichol. 2020. Dialogue transformers.

Xuewei Wang, Weiyan Shi, Richard Kim, Yoojung Oh, Sijia Yang, Jingwen Zhang, and Zhou Yu. 2019. Persuasion for good: Towards a personalized persuasive dialogue system for social good. In *Proceedings of the 57th Annual Meeting of the Association for Computational Linguistics*, pages 5635–5649.

Kaisheng Yao, Geoffrey Zweig, Mei-Yuh Hwang, Yangyang Shi, and Dong Yu. 2013. Recurrent neural networks for language understanding. In *Interspeech*, pages 2524–2528.

Are we human, or are we users? The role of natural language processing in human-centric news recommenders that nudge users to diverse content

Myrthe Reuver[1*] Nicolas Mattis [1*] Marijn Sax[2*]
Suzan Verberne[3] Nava Tintarev[5] Natali Helberger[2] Judith Moeller[2]
Sanne Vrijenhoek[2] Antske Fokkens[1,4] Wouter van Atteveldt[1]
* The first three authors contributed equally, and are shared first authors.
[1] Vrije Universiteit Amsterdam [2]University of Amsterdam [3]Leiden University
[4]Eindhoven University of Technology [5]Maastricht University
{myrthe.reuver,n.m.mattis}@vu.nl, M.Sax@uva.nl

Abstract

In this position paper, we present a research agenda and ideas for facilitating exposure to diverse viewpoints in news recommendation. Recommending news from diverse viewpoints is important to prevent potential filter bubble effects in news consumption, and stimulate a healthy democratic debate. To account for the complexity that is inherent to humans as citizens in a democracy, we anticipate (among others) individual-level differences in acceptance of diversity. We connect this idea to techniques in Natural Language Processing, where distributional language models would allow us to place different users and news articles in a multidimensional space based on semantic content, where diversity is operationalized as distance and variance. In this way, we can model individual "latitudes of diversity" for different users, and thus personalize viewpoint diversity in support of a healthy public debate. In addition, we identify technical, ethical and conceptual issues related to our presented ideas. Our investigation describes how NLP can play a central role in diversifying news recommendations.

1 Introduction

Recommender systems are very present in our online experience. Services recommend movies in movie streaming platforms, possible purchases in online shops, and news articles on news sites. People increasingly live their lives *through* digital environments that recommend some items over others. Recommender systems thus have a significant influence on the lived experiences of people. Precisely because we can expect recommender systems to perform ever more (important) functions in the near future, it is essential to incorporate *the people they end up influencing* in our thinking about recommender systems.

We focus on one case in this paper: news recommender systems (NRS) such as news aggregators, online newspapers, or news widgets. We believe Natural Language Processing (NLP) should have a more prominent role in the development of NRS. These systems are an interesting case because the role of the media has historically always been understood as essential to democratic societies and democratic debate (Karppinen, 2013). Our central argument is that the users of NRS are not just collections of data points, but are democratic citizens, who perform more social roles than that of a consumer. We propose a research agenda to put the user *as a human being* at the centre of NLP and Computer Science research into recommender systems.

For a functioning democracy, we want users to come into contact with opinions, debates, or ideas they disagree with or even dislike. This implies that simply optimizing a news recommender system for user preference, as is common now, is not enough. The public value of diversity, in terms of a diversity of issues and opinions, is essential (Helberger, 2015, 2019). There already is work on the question of how opinion, sentiment, and argument diversity for news recommendation should be understood and captured by (evaluation) metrics (Vrijenhoek et al., 2021), or NLP tasks (Reuver et al., 2021). In this paper, we want to develop a different *additional* perspective. We propose that a turn to the user – i.e., democratic citizens reading news recommended by NRS – is needed. This paper explores challenges and opportunities for facilitating this with the help of NLP.

More specifically, we propose the notion of individual *latitutes of diversity* which can help make the diversity of news recommendations more meaningful by taking the user-as-a-human-being into account. Although the promotion of news diversity is desirable from societal perspective, not every user

Proceedings of the 1st Workshop on NLP for Positive Impact, pages 47–59
Bangkok, Thailand (online), August 5, 2021.

has a similar acceptance of diversity. Simply maximizing the diversity of news recommendations can therefore have serious backfire effects (Helberger et al., 2018; Taber and Lodge, 2006).

We combine perspectives from communication science, NLP, and ethics to develop this contribution. Building on theories from communication science, we explore how the notion of latitude of diversity can help facilitate engagement with diverse content. Work in the NLP field is used to suggest how NRS can capture viewpoint diversity in news articles *and* connect to individual users' latitudes of diversity. Lastly, we incorporate ethical reflections on the value and need of diversity, as well as on some of the risks of designing (data-intensive) personalized recommendation engines.

In our paper, these different fields and perspectives all contribute to answer one central question: *How do we nudge citizens towards actual engagement with diverse viewpoints in news recommender systems with NLP techniques, while treating the user as a complex human and democratic citizen?*

To answer this question, our paper is organized as follows. Section 2 introduces why viewpoint diversity in the news context is important for democracy, how NLP is connected, and why focusing on maximizing viewpoint diverse recommendations is not enough. Section 3 presents our ideas and discusses the current technical and conceptual challenges relevant for building a more user-centric news recommender. Section 4 explores some important ethical questions that should be considered before implementing our ideas. Lastly, we restate our argument in Section 5.

2 Background

We first provide some background literature for our idea for diverse news recommendation. Section 2.1 addresses why viewpoint news diversity is important from a democratic perspective. In Section 2.2, we introduce how viewpoint diversity is connected to NLP. We then discuss nudging theory and how it can inform news recommender design in Section 2.3. Lastly, we explain how our concept of "latitude of diversity" can help make news recommenders more user-centric in Section 2.4.

2.1 Why (viewpoint) diversity matters in the news context

The literature on the importance of news diversity for a democratic society describes various models of democracy to explain how different types of diversity are important to democracy. The general idea found in this literature is that *depending on one's conception* of democracy, different *kinds* of news diversity can be important (Bozdag and van den Hoven, 2015; Dahlberg, 2011; Helberger, 2019; Strömbäck, 2005). Examples of such models are the deliberative model of democracy (Habermas, 2006), which emphasizes democracy requires a rational debate in society of different opinions and ideas, and the agonistic model (Mouffe, 2005), which emphasizes the importance of facilitating civil but ongoing *clashes* between different political beliefs, ideologies, and emotions.

Regardless of the specific democratic theory one supports in the news diversity context, nearly all strands of democratic theory emphasize the importance of promoting viewpoint diversity in this context. For example, for both the deliberative democracy and agonistic democracy models, "encouraging encounters between conflicting ideas seems to be a shared goal" (Karppinen, 2013). Both require citizens of a democracy to have a diverse news diet in order to be informed about a diversity of viewpoints, because this can help citizens to understand (and sometimes even empathize) with (the viewpoints of) other citizens. Diverse viewpoints can also provide them with information to help them think and deliberate critically about issues that matter to them or society in general. Serving citizens with a diverse set of viewpoints can also help invigorate productive clashes of political opinion or ideology.

With 'viewpoint', these theoretical models usually mean different arguments, claims, or ideas about the same publicly debated topics. Examples of such topics are vaccines and immigration. As viewpoint diversity is an (almost) universally shared goal among different democratic theories, we do not choose or support one specific model of democracy in particular.

2.2 The connection with NLP

The focus on viewpoint diversity has as a central task the detection of viewpoints in news articles. In the NLP field, the detection of different claims (Levy et al., 2014), arguments (Stab and Gurevych, 2017), and stances (Mohammad et al., 2016) are established tasks that are related. Work on such tasks is often on topics publicly debated in a political context, such as vaccinations, abortion, and immigration. This makes them potentially useful for operationalization of the viewpoint concept.

Large-scale pre-trained language models (Devlin et al., 2019) are a recent development in NLP, and could be used to detect viewpoints. Reimers et al. (2019) use such methods for the NLP task claim detection. In this work such language models are also used to cluster similar claims and arguments, giving the opportunity to also detect *dissimilar* claims or arguments. See section 3.1.2 for more concrete and detailed ideas we have on the operationalization of viewpoints with NLP.

2.3 Nudging

Besides the detection of viewpoints, we also seek to incorporate nudge-like personalization features. The key insight from the nudging literature (Thaler and Sunstein, 2008) is that environments can be designed in a manner that takes heuristics and biases into account to steer behavior of the users of these environments. Such nudges could also be aimed at the individual person. The most famous example is the 'cafeteria example', where the healthy food options are placed in an easier to reach spot than the unhealthy options. As a result, more people choose the healthier options *without making the unhealthy options completely unavailable*. The same approach can be connected to the idea of a "healthy media diet", where "healthy" is connected to a healthy democracy and public debate.

Nudging has previously been incorporated in recommender systems. A 2021 systematic review by Jesse and Jannach (2021) reveals that of 87 nudging mechanisms identified in the literature, only a small subset was previously investigated in the context of recommender systems. These include using visuals to increase item salience, item re-ranking, and setting defaults. For news recommendation specifically, Gena et al. (2019) found that nudges based on giving users the idea certain items were popular were not effective, while negative framing (nudging users to consume certain news items because of limited availability) was. The authors argue that future work should address which types of nudges are ethically acceptable in the area of persuasive technologies.

2.4 Latitudes of diversity

We define *latitude of diversity* as an individual user's acceptance of diversity. Research shows that (groups of) individual users can differ considerably in the extent to which they are open towards and interested in diverse viewpoints (Kim and Pasek, 2020; Tintarev, 2017). We argue that considering individual users' latitudes of diversity increases the likelihood that a given user engages with diverse recommendations and potentially prevents unwanted side effects.

If individual latitudes of diversity are not considered, users who are not interested in or open towards diverse viewpoints might simply not select diverse recommendations. Moreover, recommending news that are too diverse can backfire (Helberger et al., 2018). Motivated reasoning literature suggests that people evaluate counter-attitudinal information more critically than attitude-congruent information (Taber and Lodge, 2006). Under some circumstances, this might go as far as that exposure to counter-attitudinal information causes people to actively counter-argue, resulting in even stronger attitudes and increased political polarisation (Bail et al., 2018; Nyhan and Reifler, 2010). Moreover, the exposure to diverse viewpoints has also been linked to decreased political participation (Kim and Kwak (2017), but also see Matthes et al. (2019)). Thus, more diversity is not always better.

A (drastically simplified) example may help to show the potential relevance of latitudes of diversity. Imagine a close-minded extremist and a very moderate open-minded person. The extremist is not at all open to most of the news stories that do not closely resemble their own worldview; such stories fall far outside their latitude of diversity. Presenting them with very moderate news stories may enrage them and turn them off from the news source(s) in question and engaging in the public debate. So, given their latitude of diversity, it makes sense to focus on recommendations that are slightly less extremist than the one they would choose themselves, but that are still close enough to what they would accept so that there is at least a possibility that they would interact with the recommendations. It would not make much sense to recommend overly diverse content to the extremist that they would never engage with to begin with. For the moderate and open-minded person, the far wider latitude of diversity means that much more diverse content can be recommended to them without there being a serious risk that they doesn't want to engage with the recommended content because it is too fringe for them.

Some methods and interventions that aim to diversify news consumption already exist (Bozdag and van den Hoven, 2015). However, they do not take individual latitudes of diversity into account. Moreover, news consumption choices do not exist in a vacuum, but depend on the nature and content of the information environment (Powell et al., 2020), as well as various characteristics of the user and the situation in which they make a selection (Meijer and Kormelink, 2020; Tintarev, 2017). As of now, news recommendation often fails to capture these individual and situational differences in news selection. Understanding and modelling users' individual latitude of diversity is one step towards alleviating this issue.

3 Ideas and challenges for user-centric diverse recommendation

Earlier solutions to diversity in NRS have focused on author or metadata-based diversity (Lu et al., 2020), or on optimizing for diversity without considering user interest and susceptibility (Vrijenhoek et al., 2021). We take the next step towards support of democratic values in NRS: putting the user central, and especially the individual's latitude of diversity. We aim to optimize not for user preference, but for the user's diversity range required to participate in a functioning democracy. This is a more nuanced and long-term goal than the short-term one of user preference. In order to answer our research question, we will discuss the different elements in this problem separately in the following subsections.

3.1 Representation and processing of news articles

The representation of news articles for a viewpoint-diverse and user-centric recommendation has several sub-problems. In good NLP fashion, we break the diverse recommendation pipeline up into several sub-tasks, which also helps us to think about the problem(s) and solutions related to these.

We identify four separate steps in our pipeline. First, identifying the different current issues (or topics) in the news. Second, identifying different viewpoints on these current issues expressed in the media content. Third, measuring diversity computationally. And lastly, measuring and providing different latitudes of diversity to different users.

In the following sections, we will discuss these different sub-tasks of the problem of how to represent content of a news recommender system in order to create a diverse recommender. One particular challenge to the news domain is the cold start problem (news items are added every day, and the newest do not yet have user interaction data useful for a recommendation algorithm). A related issue specific for viewpoint-diverse recommendation is the constant appearance of new topics and notable entities in the news, and thus also new perspectives and viewpoints on these entities and topics that need to be detected. We address these issues in the following sections when they come up in our pipeline.

3.1.1 Identifying current issues or topics in the news

Before we can identify what different perspectives or viewpoints are debated in the news, we need to automatically identify (contentious) political debates in large collections of news texts. Such debates are for instance ones on immigration, or vaccination. Commonly, only one or a handful recurring contentious debates are discussed in current work on arguments and debates in the news. Some such topics used as case-studies are the benefits and dangers of vaccination (Morante et al., 2020) and the ethics of abortion (Draws et al., 2021).

One option for identifying topics is a rule-based method with pre-defined lists or gazetteers of known contentious, newsworthy topics, for instance websites listing (political) debates topics, as done by Draws et al. (2021) and Roy and Goldwasser (2020), and using these lists either for further manual annotation of a training set used to train a classifying machine learning model, or using heuristics and rules to identify these topics in news articles. Another option is manual annotation of (journalistic) topics already being distinguished in the (online) news room by editors or journalists, as used by Lu et al. (2020), who use features such as website sections (e.g."sports", "politics" or more fine-grained: "U.S. elections") and journalistic tags (e.g. "opinion") to represent news articles for a diverse recommender.

One challenge here is the above-mentioned appearance of new topics in the news. One potentially useful technique for this is zero- or one-shot learning. In such an approach, the model learns to generalize from one or several example topic how to identify all kinds of different topics (or, in the next step, viewpoints) not encountered in the training data. This option has been explored for topic and stance detection in Allaway and McKeown (2020).

Current state of the art text classification relies

on vector space representations of texts. Traditional vector space models and neural language models such as Doc2vec (Le and Mikolov, 2014), the Universal Sentence Encoder (Cer et al., 2018), and sentence-BERT (Reimers and Gurevych, 2019) semantically represent documents (sentences) in a multi-dimensional space. We argue that vector space representations could also be useful when considering different users with different latitudes of diversity for different topics or viewpoints. It means modelling not only articles in a vector space, but also users.

3.1.2 Automatically identifying different viewpoints

We define a viewpoint as a public argument or claim in a public debate on an issue. For instance, concerning the topic of immigration a citizen can have different viewpoints, claims, and ideas.

Most of the current work on politically related debates in news articles exclusively uses English-language data, specifically: news articles news outlets based in the United States. The U.S. political context and also publicly debated issues make perspectives and viewpoints easily translatable to identifying two opposing broad political groups, and this is often what happens in such papers: left-wing (i.e. the Democratic party) and right-wing (the Republican party) viewpoints are detected and extracted, as in Roy and Goldwasser (2020). However, not every political climate has such a polarized and two-party political system, so such an approach might not fit every language or context. Nuanced concept from political science such as framing and agenda setting have also been analysed with NLP beyond the U.S context, e.g., in Russian news media (Field et al., 2018).

There are several related NLP tasks and solutions to identifying different viewpoints on (politically contentious) issues in news texts. Names for such tasks are stance detection (Hanselowski et al., 2018), argument mining (Stab and Gurevych, 2017), and perspective detection (Morante et al., 2020; van Son et al., 2016). All these tasks focus on capturing an opinion on issues, events, or entities, which make them useful for identifying viewpoints for a recommender system that supports democratic values such as deliberation. In Reuver et al. (2021), several of these aformentioned NLP tasks and their usefulness for this goal are discussed in detail. For instance, a 'stance' can be useful for operationalizing the idea of a 'viewpoint', since stances often related to a particular opinion on a contentious issue (e.g. is the text pro, against, or neutral towards immigration?). This is inherently related to the idea of debates in society between different viewpoints on these contentious topics, implicitly or explicitly expressed in news articles.

Both unsupervised and supervised methods are used for identifying viewpoints. The most commonly used unsupervised approach is Topic Modelling, as used by Draws et al. (2021) and Mulder et al. (2021) to not only identify different topics, but also different perspectives and (sub)topics. An unsupervised approach is useful for a cold-start problem, but also potentially poses validation issues (do we know what the model is measuring? Is it actually measuring a coherent topic or viewpoint?). Most relevant NLP tasks (stance detection, claim detection) are thereby addressed with *supervised* methods. This means the models are trained at detecting viewpoints by examples in their training data, which are often manually annotated. Thus there is by definition a finite set of different viewpoints that the model can detect (the annotated ones).

Useful datasets for training models for detecting viewpoints consist of textdata on topics that are in public debate and the news, also annotated for the opinion on these topics that is expressed in the text unit (sentence, paragraph, or article). This is the case for the sentential argument mining corpus (Stab et al., 2018), which consists of English sentences on eight controversial topics, such as abortion and minimum wage, annotated for stance in three classes: pro, con, and neutral towards the topic. There are also established datasets that are more fine-grained, such as the MPQA Corpus (Deng and Wiebe, 2015): English news texts annotated for negative or positive sentiment towards targets (such as events or persons), but also more fine-grained annotation of opinions, beliefs, and judgements. Some datasets focus on stances, claims, or arguments on one topic, such as climate change (Luo et al., 2020; Varini et al., 2020) or vaccination (Morante et al., 2020).

Detecting new stances on new topics that are not in the training data could provide a challenge for supervised models. Like with new topic identification discussed above, few-shot learning has recently been used for complex semantics-related NLP tasks such as topic and stance detection and summarization, and allows language models to generalize beyond their training data (Allaway and McKeown, 2020; Schick and Schütze, 2020).

Do note that all mentioned NLP tasks and datasets would operationalize the idea of a viewpoint differently (e.g. either as an argument, claim, stance, or sentiment on a topic). Different tasks also often use different types of text: social media texts, online discussion boards, or news articles (see for a discussion Reuver et al. (2021)), and even within these tasks there are many completely different approaches in method and annotation. Selecting one of these frameworks, datasets, or tasks requires careful reflection on what aspect(s) of a viewpoint is central to a certain recommender, context, or even specific debate, and how NLP can best support this idea.

3.1.3 Defining, capturing, and evaluating diversity

After identifying topics and viewpoints in news texts, the next challenge for our approach becomes measuring, capturing and evaluating for a *diversity* of these viewpoints or ideas. This is needed for supporting a healthy democratic debate.

There is no shortage of work in recommender systems on different metrics related to diversity, from "unexpectedness" and "serendipity" to "coverage" (Zhou et al., 2010). These metrics assess the score of recommendation sets, and can be used to optimize and assess certain recommender systems on their performance beyond simply click accuracy. However, none of these beyond-accuracy metrics are informed by theories or models of democracy, and implicitly or explicitly still aim for user preference rather than a larger-scale societal goal.

An exception are the metrics in Vrijenhoek et al. (2021), who explicitly connect different diversity metrics for the evaluation and optimization of news recommender systems to goals and ideas in democratic models. Metrics from this study can be used to measure or optimize for different aspects related to diversity and different models of democracy. These metrics concern the representation of minority voices, whether the recommendations activate users to take action, and the degree of fragmentation (difference) between different users in news recommender systems. Implementing these metrics requires NLP methods. For instance, the "Activation" metric can be operationalized in terms of articles' emotional valence and arousal, because emotional content is more likely to elicit concrete actions from readers (Vrijenhoek et al., 2021). This requires NLP models to automatically measure whether the chosen texts contain more or less activating content than in the pool of available texts. NLP offers methods to measure sentiment and activation in text, though whether such models correctly and reliably operationalize such social science concepts has recently been questioned (van Atteveldt et al., 2021).

The metrics from Vrijenhoek et al. (2021) that measure "representation" and "alternative voices" in news texts require measuring different viewpoints and ideas, of especially marginalized groups. We run into the same challenges outlined above: the appearance of new topics, viewpoints, and opinion groups in news media. We need to further scrutinise the use and implementation of these evaluation metrics connected to models of democracy. Especially so, since consistent and nuanced evaluation metrics would help further advance recent news recommendation attempts that combine public and journalistic values like diversity with user preferences.

As highlighted above, an approach based on vector space models could aid diversification, and do so in a way that can ensure individual users are not alienated by suggestions too different from their own preferences. Such a vector space approach can do this because the idea of "distance" in a vector space. This means we can calculate relative distance between articles, viewpoints, and topics, and the optimal distance for individual users. Vector space models allow the use of similarity metrics such as cosine similarity to find (dis)similar content. This allows us to compute the distance between a user representation (based on history or personae) and news articles, and find *similar* or *dissimilar* viewpoints or opinions, such as in Reimers et al. (2019). It also means an optimal distance for individual users could be found, where "maximally distant viewpoints" could be interpreted as "(a diverse set of) different viewpoints".

3.1.4 Measuring different latitudes of diversity

In our case, there is also the challenge of connecting our technical implementation for news items to the individual user's latitude of diversity, which is again linked to our goal of supporting public diversity values and democratic debate. This aspect also has related challenges, such as the difficulty of technically identifying which news articles fall into the narrow latitude of diversity people are susceptible to in (news)texts.

The envisioned algorithm will recommend articles within the user's latitude of diversity, with this latitude's width changing with user's comfort, context, as well as interest (clickability). The model would optimize for the articles at the edges of this latitude (a maximally diverse set of viewpoint that is still within the user's latitude of diversity).

An added bonus of such an approach is the explainability to users. Users will perhaps be able to see their specific place in the multidimensional news landscape, or adjust the values of their latitude, though this might be counter-productive for our goal of promoting engagement with viewpoints the user likes less.

3.2 The User

In terms of user modelling, determining users' individual latitudes of diversity requires understanding not only what counts as diverse information to a given user, but also if and to what extent that user is open to engaging with diverse news recommendations at a given point in time (see also Section 2.4). This introduces three interrelated challenges which we address in this section.

3.2.1 Data availability for user profiles

In section 3.1, we outlined several promising approaches for how NLP techniques can help represent news articles and their level of diversity. However, linking article representations to individual users also requires modelling these users' past consumption and situational information needs. In many cases, this may necessitate the creation and maintenance of personalised user profiles that capture users' reading histories as well as preferences of style, sources and content. However, since most news consumption takes place anonymously (Raza and Ding, 2020), session-based, and stretches across various mediums and platforms (Bruns, 2019), meaningful information for creating user profiles is often not available in the NRS domain. Thus, a first challenge in user modelling is filling in those blanks.

One way to achieve this are collaborative filtering approaches where missing data is estimated based on other users with a (seemingly) similar reading behaviour. However, this approach is limited by both the quality and quantity of user data available. It also leaves little room to capture users' situational reading goals, which might vary considerably between reading sessions. What further complicates the matter, is that while news consumption is often measured in terms of clicks and exposure time, in reality it includes various other reading practices (e.g. checking and scanning) that are harder to capture (Meijer and Kormelink, 2020; Costera Meijer and Groot Kormelink, 2015).

An alternative strategy could be to use *algorithmic recommender personae*, which are "preconfigured and anthropomorphized types of recommendation algorithms" (p. 4) that users can choose from to explicitly express their preferred recommendation logic in a certain situation and for specific goals. (Harambam et al., 2018). This would grant users more control over the recommendation algorithm (Harambam et al., 2018), and allow for meaningful user modelling in the absence of personalised user profiles. However, there is a natural tension between granting users control over the type of content that they want to consume, and nudging them towards specific news selections (see also section 4).

3.2.2 Individual-level differences

To maximise the likelihood of engagement with diverse news, methods taking into account individual latitudes of diversity should determine which content is acceptable for a given reader at a given point in time. Thereby, situations where introducing too much diversity limits user satisfaction (Bryanov et al., 2020) could be prevented.

In addition to the extent to which they value diverse viewpoints, users also differ in how they process them. Especially when it comes to political content, selective exposure research shows that attitudes affect information processing in various biased ways (Stroud, 2017). For example, Hart et al. (2009) show that people exhibit a moderate preference for information whose views align with their own across a variety of contexts. In contrast, counter-attitudinal information is often evaluated more critically (Taber and Lodge, 2006). Therefore, NRS users with strongly-held attitudes are likely to exhibit confirmation bias in their news selections. Moreover, selective exposure indicates potential backfire effects when users are exposed to dissimilar opinion. This includes not only decreased user satisfaction, but also increased attitude polarisation (Bail et al., 2018; Helberger and Wojcieszak, 2018; Nyhan and Reifler, 2010; Taber and Lodge, 2006).

In sum, news recommenders that aim to contribute to pro-social democratic outcomes and mitigate potential backfire effects need to accommodate individual-level differences (see also (Rieger et al., 2020)). Modelling users' latitude of diversity is therefore an important objective of diverse NRS. To this end, news recommenders could learn from past user behaviour either implicitly, or through explicit feedback options that allow users to express when they consider an article to be too far out of their comfort zone. What remains open however, is to what extent NRS could also deliberately facilitate drift, whereby individual users become more open towards diverse viewpoints over time.

3.2.3 Situational differences

A further complication for user modelling stems from the fact that many news selection predictors are highly situational. Whereas attitudes and diversity values can be considered comparatively stable, news consumption is also shaped by a variety of additional situational factors (Hasebrink and Popp, 2006; Raza and Ding, 2020). For example, qualitative research shows that individual news-selections are guided by different goals that can range from general surveillance to more specific goals such as gaining new perspectives or acquiring fodder for conversation (Meijer and Kormelink, 2020).

Research into context-aware recommendation might help to better capture such differences. As of now, context-aware news recommendation is largely limited to location, time of day, or device used (Asikin and Wörndl, 2014; De Pessemier et al., 2016; Lommatzsch et al., 2017), but there have also been efforts to capture more complex constructs such as emotions (Mizgajski and Morzy, 2019). Further work into this direction could help better capture users' situational information needs. If users employ them continuously – a notion that (Harambam et al., 2019) call into question – the aforementioned personae might also be a promising way to tap into those situational differences.

4 Ethical considerations

4.1 Ethics of Nudging towards Diverse News Consumption

Thus far we have explored how the user as a human being can be put more at the center of news recommender systems by developing the idea of latitudes of diversity, which builds on NLP research and methods. However, this proposed research direction also comes with potential risks.

First, our proposed approach implies that the providers of NRS must get to know their users better. In practice, this requires collecting (more) user data and building profiles. By doing so, NRS providers strengthen their position of power in relation to their users. This power can, of course, be used to *only* try to build better, more diverse NRS. But with this promise of user empowerment also comes an inevitable risk of user manipulation. There is a growing literature which addresses the *manipulative* potential of data-driven digital environments which try to nudge users towards certain ends or outcomes (Yeung, 2017; Lanzing, 2019; Susser et al., 2018, 2019; Sax, 2021). When digital environments use user data to learn about (patterns of behavior of) their users and run experiments which, through feedback loops, can inform subtle (personalized) tweaks to the digital environment, one is dealing with a subtle but important line between user empowerment and user manipulation. It is important to ask whose interests are being served by nudging strategies.

This question is as relevant as ever in the (online) news sector. The commercialization of the news has been discussed elaborately for decades (e.g. (McManus, 2009; Baldasty, 1992; Girija, 2019) and will remain important as private platforms such as Google and Facebook try (and succeed) to capture the news industry. In such a commercialized news context, one cannot simply assume that (an increased) collection of user data and user profiling tools for purposes of personalized nudging strategies will only be used to benefit the news consumer. The very same data and profiling tools that can be used for increasing exposure to news diversity can, at the very same time, can also be *mis*used in pursuit of commercial or political ends, without the knowledge of the user and/or their ability to object. The difficult line between empowerment and manipulation is underlined by the challenges news organization face in navigating the digital news economy. As a study by Bodó (2018) makes clear, different actors *within* one and the same news organization have to engage in a difficult process of mutual sense-making and negotiation to decide how a NRS should be implemented and what the NRS should aim to optimize.

The second potential risk is to reduce the news readers' autonomy. In general, it is important to note that Thaler and Sunstein's suggestion that nudging is a policy and design principle without any serious drawbacks has been met with a wide range of criticisms. Many authors point out that nudging strategies can in fact fail to respect the autonomy of citizens (Bovens, 2009; Yeung, 2012; Saghai, 2013; Engelen and Nys, 2020). If we understand autonomy as the capacity to critically deliberate about one's own intentions, preferences, values, and available options in order to make decisions one can consider one's own (Sax, 2021), our nudging-inspired proposal raises questions. We do, after all, suggest to try to subtly steer news readers' behaviors based on what is important *from a societal perspective*. Are we not thereby limiting the autonomy of the news reader? One important consideration is not only *whether* choice is influenced, but also, equally important, *how* choice is influenced. For example, when a news organization is transparent about its attempt and/or used strategies to nudge news readers, those news readers can incorporate this information in their decision-making on whether – and if so: how – to use the news platform. Being respectful of the news readers' autonomy can thus co-exist with attempts to shape behavior for public values (Susser et al., 2019). Still, nudging strategies usually aren't *either* fully transparent *or* completely opaque in digital environments, so questions concerning the autonomy of news readers will remain.

Lastly, there might be viewpoints that should not be recommended at all, because they are, for instance, explicitly anti-democratic or incite hate and violence. Determining which viewpoints should be excluded from recommendations, or receive a flag and/or warning for users, is challenging and requires a separate analysis. For now, we just want to flag that the existence of this difficult challenge.

4.2 Ethical issues with language models

An additional consideration concerns the methods and data used to facilitate this recommendation. The role of NLP, and vector space models, in this problem is not necessarily a "plug-and-play" approach where we can take an already pre-trained model and simply plug it into our recommendation pipeline. Pre-trained language models can introduce bias, hate speech, and language not representative of real-life language use in the model by its training data based on a large, but in terms of diversity very limited set of internet texts (Bender et al., 2021). Diversity for news recommendation is therefore not only important for the recommendation output, but also for the texts in the language model input. Additionally, data practices of NLP currently do not consist of careful consideration of the exact contents and purposes of datasets (Paullada et al., 2020), further complicating how to ensure distributional language models trained on large datasets contain diverse and representative language.

For diverse news recommendation, these data biases are important to consider. When detecting contentious topics and viewpoints in political debates, such biases potentially leading to models only detecting certain viewpoints are especially unwelcome. We do not purport to solve these issues, but we do want to highlight them.

5 Conclusion

In this paper, we presented an important objective for societal impact of NLP: (viewpoint) diversity in news recommendation to support a healthy democratic debate. Going further than previous work, we connect diversity in news recommendation to democratic theory and to findings in communication science on individual user differences in acceptance of diversity. We conclude that to foster a healthy democratic public debate, we should detect viewpoints, but also detect individual *latitudes of diversity*. NLP can play a pivotal role in these tasks: vector space models would allow us to place different users (or user representations) and news articles in a multidimensional space, where diversity is operationalized as distance and variance. Thereby, we could personalize different users' latitudes of diversity, and accordingly deliver diverse recommendations that support a healthy public debate while still keeping the user satisfied. However, we also point out several technical, conceptual, and ethical problems that show this objective needs more than the "plug and play" of NLP solutions, but rather requires further research and careful reflection.

Acknowledgments

This research is funded through Open Competition Digitalization Humanities and Social Science grant nr 406.D1.19.073 awarded by the Netherlands Organization of Scientific Research (NWO). We would like to thank the anonymous reviewers whose detailed comments helped improve the paper. All opinions and remaining errors are our own.

References

Emily Allaway and Kathleen McKeown. 2020. Zero-shot stance detection: A dataset and model using generalized topic representations. *EMNLP Findings 2020.*

Yonata Andrelo Asikin and Wolfgang Wörndl. 2014. Stories around you: Location-based serendipitous recommendation of news articles. In *UMAP Workshops*. Citeseer.

Wouter van Atteveldt, Mariken ACG van der Velden, and Mark Boukes. 2021. The validity of sentiment analysis: Comparing manual annotation, crowd-coding, dictionary approaches, and machine learning algorithms. *Communication Methods and Measures*, pages 1–20.

Christopher A Bail, Lisa P Argyle, Taylor W Brown, John P Bumpus, Haohan Chen, MB Fallin Hunzaker, Jaemin Lee, Marcus Mann, Friedolin Merhout, and Alexander Volfovsky. 2018. Exposure to opposing views on social media can increase political polarization. *Proceedings of the National Academy of Sciences*, 115(37):9216–9221.

Gerald J Baldasty. 1992. *The commercialization of news in the nineteenth century.* Univ of Wisconsin Press.

Emily M Bender, Timnit Gebru, Angelina McMillan-Major, and Shmargaret Shmitchell. 2021. On the Dangers of Stochastic Parrots: Can Language Models Be Too Big? In *Proceedings of the 2021 ACM Conference on Fairness, Accountability, and Transparency*, pages 610–623.

Balázs Bodó. 2018. Means, not an end (of the world)– the customization of news personalization by european news media. In *Prepared for the Algorithms, Automation, and News Conference, Munich*, pages 22–23.

Luc Bovens. 2009. The ethics of nudge. In *Preference change*, pages 207–219. Springer.

Engin Bozdag and Jeroen van den Hoven. 2015. Breaking the filter bubble: democracy and design. *Ethics and Information Technology*, 17(4):249–265.

Axel Bruns. 2019. *Are filter bubbles real?* John Wiley & Sons.

Kirill Bryanov, Brian K Watson, Raymond J Pingree, and Martina Santia. 2020. Effects of partisan personalization in a news portal experiment. *Public Opinion Quarterly*, 84(S1):216–235.

Daniel Cer, Yinfei Yang, Sheng-yi Kong, Nan Hua, Nicole Limtiaco, Rhomni St John, Noah Constant, Mario Guajardo-Cespedes, Steve Yuan, Chris Tar, et al. 2018. Universal sentence encoder for english. In *Proceedings of the 2018 Conference on Empirical Methods in Natural Language Processing: System Demonstrations*, pages 169–174.

Irene Costera Meijer and Tim Groot Kormelink. 2015. Checking, sharing, clicking and linking: Changing patterns of news use between 2004 and 2014. *Digital Journalism*, 3(5):664–679.

Lincoln Dahlberg. 2011. Re-constructing digital democracy: An outline of four 'positions'. *New media & society*, 13(6):855–872.

Toon De Pessemier, Cédric Courtois, Kris Vanhecke, Kristin Van Damme, Luc Martens, and Lieven De Marez. 2016. A user-centric evaluation of context-aware recommendations for a mobile news service. *Multimedia Tools and Applications*, 75(6):3323–3351.

Lingjia Deng and Janyce Wiebe. 2015. Mpqa 3.0: An entity/event-level sentiment corpus. In *Proceedings of the 2015 conference of the North American chapter of the association for computational linguistics: human language technologies*, pages 1323–1328.

Jacob Devlin, Ming-Wei Chang, Kenton Lee, and Kristina Toutanova. 2019. BERT: Pre-training of deep bidirectional transformers for language understanding. In *Proceedings of the 2019 Conference of the North American Chapter of the Association for Computational Linguistics: Human Language Technologies, Volume 1 (Long and Short Papers)*, pages 4171–4186, Minneapolis, Minnesota. Association for Computational Linguistics.

Tim Draws, Jody Liu, and Nava Tintarev. 2021. Helping users discover perspectives: Enhancing opinion mining with joint topic models. *2020 International Conference on Data Mining Workshops (ICDMW)*. Publisher: IEEE.

Bart Engelen and Thomas Nys. 2020. Nudging and autonomy: Analyzing and alleviating the worries. *Review of Philosophy and Psychology*, 11(1):137–156.

Anjalie Field, Doron Kliger, Shuly Wintner, Jennifer Pan, Dan Jurafsky, and Yulia Tsvetkov. 2018. Framing and agenda-setting in Russian news: a computational analysis of intricate political strategies. In *Proceedings of the 2018 Conference on Empirical Methods in Natural Language Processing*, pages 3570–3580, Brussels, Belgium. Association for Computational Linguistics.

Cristina Gena, Pierluigi Grillo, Antonio Lieto, Claudio Mattutino, and Fabiana Vernero. 2019. When personalization is not an option: An in-the-wild study on persuasive news recommendation. *Information*, 10(10).

Sreekala Girija. 2019. Political economy of media entrepreneurship: Commercialization and commodification in a digital news media enterprise. *Journal of Media Management and Entrepreneurship (JMME)*, 1(1):27–39.

Jürgen Habermas. 2006. Political communication in media society: Does democracy still enjoy an epistemic dimension? the impact of normative theory on empirical research. *Communication theory*, 16(4):411–426.

Andreas Hanselowski, PVS Avinesh, Benjamin Schiller, Felix Caspelherr, Debanjan Chaudhuri, Christian M Meyer, and Iryna Gurevych. 2018. A retrospective analysis of the fake news challenge stance-detection task. In *Proceedings of the 27th International Conference on Computational Linguistics*, pages 1859–1874.

Jaron Harambam, Dimitrios Bountouridis, Mykola Makhortykh, and Joris Van Hoboken. 2019. Designing for the better by taking users into account: A qualitative evaluation of user control mechanisms in (news) recommender systems. In *Proceedings of the 13th ACM Conference on Recommender Systems*, pages 69–77.

Jaron Harambam, Natali Helberger, and Joris van Hoboken. 2018. Democratizing algorithmic news recommenders: how to materialize voice in a technologically saturated media ecosystem. *Philosophical Transactions of the Royal Society A: Mathematical, Physical and Engineering Sciences*, 376(2133):20180088.

William Hart, Dolores Albarracín, Alice H Eagly, Inge Brechan, Matthew J Lindberg, and Lisa Merrill. 2009. Feeling validated versus being correct: a meta-analysis of selective exposure to information. *Psychological bulletin*, 135(4):555.

Uwe Hasebrink and Jutta Popp. 2006. Media repertoires as a result of selective media use. a conceptual approach to the analysis of patterns of exposure. *Communications*, 31(3):369–387.

Natali Helberger. 2015. Public service media— merely facilitating or actively stimulating diverse media choices? public service media at the crossroad. *International Journal of Communication*, 9:17.

Natali Helberger. 2019. On the democratic role of news recommenders. *Digital Journalism*, 7(8):993–1012.

Natali Helberger, Kari Karppinen, and Lucia D'acunto. 2018. Exposure diversity as a design principle for recommender systems. *Information, Communication & Society*, 21(2):191–207.

Natali Helberger and Magdalena Wojcieszak. 2018. Exposure diversity. In Philip Michael Napoli, editor, *Mediated Communication*, volume 7, chapter 28, pages 535–560. Walter de Gruyter GmbH & Co KG.

Mathias Jesse and Dietmar Jannach. 2021. Digital nudging with recommender systems: Survey and future directions. *Computers in Human Behavior Reports*, 3:100052.

Kari Karppinen. 2013. *Rethinking media pluralism*. Fordham University Press.

Dam Hee Kim and Nojin Kwak. 2017. Media diversity policies for the public: Empirical evidence examining exposure diversity and democratic citizenship. *Journal of Broadcasting & Electronic Media*, 61(4):682–702.

Dam Hee Kim and Josh Pasek. 2020. Explaining the diversity deficit: Value-trait consistency in news exposure and democratic citizenship. *Communication Research*, 47(1):29–54.

Marjolein Lanzing. 2019. "strongly recommended" revisiting decisional privacy to judge hypernudging in self-tracking technologies. *Philosophy & Technology*, 32(3):549–568.

Quoc Le and Tomas Mikolov. 2014. Distributed representations of sentences and documents. In *International conference on machine learning*, pages 1188–1196. PMLR.

Ran Levy, Yonatan Bilu, Daniel Hershcovich, Ehud Aharoni, and Noam Slonim. 2014. Context dependent claim detection. In *Proceedings of COLING 2014, the 25th International Conference on Computational Linguistics: Technical Papers*, pages 1489–1500.

Andreas Lommatzsch, Benjamin Kille, and Sahin Albayrak. 2017. Incorporating context and trends in news recommender systems. In *Proceedings of the international conference on web intelligence*, pages 1062–1068.

Feng Lu, Anca Dumitrache, and David Graus. 2020. Beyond optimizing for clicks: Incorporating editorial values in news recommendation. In *Proceedings of the 28th ACM Conference on User Modeling, Adaptation and Personalization*, UMAP '20, page 145–153, New York, NY, USA. Association for Computing Machinery.

Yiwei Luo, Dallas Card, and Dan Jurafsky. 2020. Desmog: Detecting stance in media on global warming. In *Proceedings of the 2020 Conference on Empirical Methods in Natural Language Processing: Findings*, pages 3296–3315.

Jörg Matthes, Johannes Knoll, Sebastián Valenzuela, David Nicolas Hopmann, and Christian Von Sikorski. 2019. A meta-analysis of the effects of cross-cutting exposure on political participation. *Political Communication*, 36(4):523–542.

John H McManus. 2009. The commercialization of news. *The handbook of journalism studies*, pages 218–233.

Irene Costera Meijer and Tim Groot Kormelink. 2020. *Changing News Use: Unchanged News Experiences?* Routledge.

Jan Mizgajski and Mikołaj Morzy. 2019. Affective recommender systems in online news industry: how emotions influence reading choices. *User Modeling and User-Adapted Interaction*, 29(2):345–379.

Saif Mohammad, Svetlana Kiritchenko, Parinaz Sobhani, Xiaodan Zhu, and Colin Cherry. 2016. Semeval-2016 task 6: Detecting stance in tweets. In *Proceedings of the 10th International Workshop on Semantic Evaluation (SemEval-2016)*, pages 31–41.

Roser Morante, Chantal Van Son, Isa Maks, and Piek Vossen. 2020. Annotating perspectives on vaccination. In *Proceedings of The 12th Language Resources and Evaluation Conference*, pages 4964–4973.

Chantal Mouffe. 2005. *The return of the political*, volume 8. Verso.

Mats Mulder, Oana Inel, Jasper Oosterman, and Nava Tintarev. 2021. Operationalizing framing to support multiperspective recommendations of opinion pieces. In *Proceedings of the 2021 ACM Conference on Fairness, Accountability, and Transparency*, pages 478–488.

Brendan Nyhan and Jason Reifler. 2010. When corrections fail: The persistence of political misperceptions. *Political Behavior*, 32(2):303–330.

Amandalynne Paullada, Inioluwa Deborah Raji, Emily M Bender, Emily Denton, and Alex Hanna. 2020. Data and its (dis) contents: A survey of dataset development and use in machine learning research.

Thomas E Powell, Michael Hameleers, and Toni GLA van der Meer. 2020. Selection in a snapshot? the contribution of visuals to the selection and avoidance of political news in information-rich media settings. *The International Journal of Press/Politics*, page 1940161220966730.

Shaina Raza and Chen Ding. 2020. A survey on news recommender system–dealing with timeliness, dynamic user interest and content quality, and effects of recommendation on news readers. *arXiv preprint arXiv:2009.04964*.

Nils Reimers and Iryna Gurevych. 2019. Sentence-bert: Sentence embeddings using siamese bert-networks. In *Proceedings of the 2019 Conference on Empirical Methods in Natural Language Processing and the 9th International Joint Conference on Natural Language Processing (EMNLP-IJCNLP)*, pages 3973–3983.

Nils Reimers, Benjamin Schiller, Tilman Beck, Johannes Daxenberger, Christian Stab, and Iryna Gurevych. 2019. Classification and clustering of arguments with contextualized word embeddings. In *Proceedings of the 57th Annual Meeting of the Association for Computational Linguistics*, pages 567–578.

Myrthe Reuver, Antske Fokkens, and Suzan Verberne. 2021. No nlp task should be an island: Multi-disciplinarity for diversity in news recommender systems. In *Proceedings of the EACL Hackashop on News Media Content Analysis and Automated Report Generation*. Association for Computational Linguistics.

Alisa Rieger, Mariët Theune, and Nava Tintarev. 2020. Toward natural language mitigation strategies for cognitive biases in recommender systems. In *2nd Workshop on Interactive Natural Language Technologyfor Explainable Artificial Intelligence 2020*. Association for Computational Linguistics (ACL).

Shamik Roy and Dan Goldwasser. 2020. Weakly supervised learning of nuanced frames for analyzing polarization in news media. In *Proceedings of the 2020 Conference on Empirical Methods in Natural Language Processing (EMNLP)*, pages 7698–7716.

Yashar Saghai. 2013. Salvaging the concept of nudge. *Journal of medical ethics*, 39(8):487–493.

Marijn Sax. 2021. Optimization of what? for-profit health apps as manipulative digital environments. *Ethics and Information Technology*, pages 1–17.

Timo Schick and Hinrich Schütze. 2020. Few-shot text generation with pattern-exploiting training. *arXiv preprint arXiv:2012.11926*.

Chantal van Son, Tommaso Caselli, Antske Fokkens, Isa Maks, Roser Morante, Lora Aroyo, and Piek Vossen. 2016. Grasp: A multilayered annotation scheme for perspectives. In *Proceedings of the Tenth International Conference on Language Resources and Evaluation (LREC'16)*, pages 1177–1184.

Christian Stab, Johannes Daxenberger, Chris Stahlhut, Tristan Miller, Benjamin Schiller, Christopher Tauchmann, Steffen Eger, and Iryna Gurevych. 2018. Argumentext: Searching for arguments in heterogeneous sources. In *Proceedings of the 2018 conference of the North American chapter of the association for computational linguistics: demonstrations*, pages 21–25.

Christian Stab and Iryna Gurevych. 2017. Parsing argumentation structures in persuasive essays. *Computational Linguistics*, 43(3):619–659.

Jesper Strömbäck. 2005. In search of a standard: Four models of democracy and their normative implications for journalism. *Journalism studies*, 6(3):331–345.

Natalie Jomini Stroud. 2017. Selective exposure theories. In *The Oxford handbook of political communication*.

Daniel Susser, Beate Roessler, and Helen Nissenbaum. 2018. Online manipulation: Hidden influences in a digital world. *Georgetown Law Technology Review*, 4(1):1–45.

Daniel Susser, Beate Roessler, and Helen Nissenbaum. 2019. Technology, autonomy, and manipulation. *Internet Policy Review*, 8(2).

Charles S Taber and Milton Lodge. 2006. Motivated skepticism in the evaluation of political beliefs. *American journal of political science*, 50(3):755–769.

Richard H Thaler and Cass R Sunstein. 2008. *Nudge: Improving decisions about health, wealth, and happiness*. Yale University Press.

Nava Tintarev. 2017. Presenting diversity aware recommendations. In *FATREC Workshop on Responsible Recommendation Proceedings*.

Francesco Saverio Varini, Jordan Boyd-Graber, Massimiliano Ciaramita, and Markus Leippold. 2020. Climatext: A dataset for climate change topic detection. In *Proceedings of the Tackling Climate Change with Machine Learning workshop, co-located at NeurIPS*.

Sanne Vrijenhoek, Mesut Kaya, Nadia Metoui, Judith Möller, Daan Odijk, and Natali Helberger. 2021. Recommenders with a mission: assessing diversity in news recommendations. In *SIGIR Conference on Human Information Interaction and Retrieval (CHIIR) Proceedings*.

Karen Yeung. 2012. Nudge as fudge. *Mod. L. Rev.*, 75:122.

Karen Yeung. 2017. 'hypernudge': Big data as a mode of regulation by design. *Information, Communication & Society*, 20(1):118–136.

Tao Zhou, Zoltán Kuscsik, Jian-Guo Liu, Matúš Medo, Joseph Rushton Wakeling, and Yi-Cheng Zhang. 2010. Solving the apparent diversity-accuracy dilemma of recommender systems. *Proceedings of the National Academy of Sciences*, 107(10):4511–4515.

Automatic Sentence Simplification in Low Resource Settings for Urdu

Yusra Anees and Sadaf Abdul Rauf
Fatima Jinnah Women University,Pakistan
(yusra.anees96,sadaf.abdulrauf)@gmail.com

Abstract

To build automated simplification systems, corpora of complex sentences and their simplified versions is the first step to understand sentence complexity and enable the development of automatic text simplification systems. We present a lexical and syntactically simplified Urdu simplification corpus with a detailed analysis of the various simplification operations and human evaluation of corpus quality. We further analyze our corpora using text readability measures and present a comparison of the original, lexical simplified and syntactically simplified corpora. In addition, we compare our corpus with other existing simplification corpora by building simplification systems and evaluating these systems using BLEU and SARI scores. Our system achieves the highest BLEU score and comparable SARI score in comparison to other systems. We release our simplification corpora for the benefit of the research community.

1 Introduction

Complex Sentences are always hard to understand for humans as well as automated applications. Complexity of a sentence often hinders proper communication of the intended meaning and hence a bottleneck in the learning pipeline. It has been found that students having problems with language often find it difficult to excel academically (Kyle, 2016). Research in the last decade has largely focused on complexity level identification of texts so that readability of such sentences can be enhanced to facilitate learning for students as per their learning grade.

Simplified sentences have specially been proved useful for producing understandable content for foreign speakers (Paetzold and Specia, 2016), language learners, children and people with lower literacy (Aluísio and Gasperin, 2010; Max, 2006; Petersen and Ostendorf, 2007). They are also recommended for cognitive and reading impairments like dyslexia (Rello et al., 2013), disorder of autism spectrum and aphasia (Carroll et al., 1999). On the other end, they are also valuable for many natural language processing (NLP) applications like semantic role labeling (Vickrey and Koller, 2008), machine translation (Oliveira et al., 2010) and relation extraction (Jonnalagadda et al., 2009) etc.

Generally, literary works have a higher difficulty level as compared to daily life language. This is specifically true for Urdu for which this gap is increasing day by day, literary texts often include complex words and composite sentence structure (Alison and Mushta,2004). Over the time with English taking over as official language and phenomenon of code mixing and switching becoming prevalent, the natives are inclined to use simpler language and often find it difficult to understand the level of Urdu used in traditional literature. Thus, a need arises for simplified versions of the classic works of the language to preserve the gems of literature and also to familiarize younger generation with such works.

Urdu is an international language having large quantity of educational and reading material and many new language learners. But unfortunately, sentence simplification is an unexplored area. Recently, Anees et al. (2020) present a small simplification corpus and Qasmi et al. (2020) present a simplification system using word embedding together with a set of morphological features to generate simplifications without parallel simplification data. It is the need of the day to ad-

Proceedings of the 1st Workshop on NLP for Positive Impact, pages 60–70
Bangkok, Thailand (online), August 5, 2021. ©2021 Association for Computational Linguistics

dress this issue and come up with effective complexity reduction and readability enhancement measures.

To be able to study complexity and simplicity parameters for any language, the first step is to have a corpus containing complex sentences and their simplified versions. Such sentence aligned texts are known as simplification parallel corpus and have been prepared for many languages, for example for English there exist simple Wikipedia corpus, PWKP (Zhu et al., 2010), Newsela (Xu et al., 2015), Onestop (Vajjala and Lucic, 2018) and SimPA (Scarton et al., 2018). Sentence simplification corpora for other languages include Ancora (Taulé et al., 2008), ERNESTA (Barbu et al., 2015), CLEAR (Grabar and Cardon, 2018) etc.

To enable research on automatic text simplification systems and text readability for Urdu, development of a simplification corpus providing enough complex sentences and their corresponding simple versions is imperative. We developed one such corpus for the high school students and simplified (lexically and syntactically) short stories from a renowned author. We have considered three-levels in our simplification process: Original, lexical and syntactic simplification. In Lexical Simplification (LS), complex words are replaced with simple and easy words. Whereas, Syntactic Simplification (SS) may result in an entirely new but simpler sentence.

We show the effectiveness of our corpora by human evaluation as well as comparing our corpus with other existing simplification corpora by building simplification systems. For automatic evaluation, we use BLEU (Papineni et al., 2001), an adequacy metric and SARI, simplification metric. Our system achieves the highest BLEU score and comparable SARI score in comparison to other systems. Lexical analysis and metric scores for each corpus, i.e. original, lexically simplified and syntactically simplified show correlation with human evaluations.

2 Literature review

Sentence simplification has been an active topic of research since the last decade. Many approaches have been proposed to develop the simplification corpora. Xu et al. (2015) present the first human built English simplification corpus, Newsela. It provides articles, re-written with 4 levels of readability for children of different ages. Brunato et al. (2015) report an Italian simplification corpus made using three-levels: local coherence, global coherence and lexical/syntax. Syntax and lexical simplification is done by reordering, insert, split, merge, transformation and delete. These simplification operations are also followed by (Tonelli et al., 2016; Brunato et al., 2016).

Vajjala and Lucic (2018) provide simplified version of texts taken from websites in three-levels elementary, intermediate and advanced. (Scarton et al., 2018) is a public administration domain corpus produced using syntactically and lexical simplification on around 1000 sentences. Other simplification corpora include (Grabar and Cardon, 2018) for French. Štajner et al. (2019) present an automatic lexical simplifier for Spanish by using synonyms and paraphrases from existing resources. The training corpus is from news and general literature consisting of 764 sentences. These are simplified using the six simplification rules defined in (Mitkov and Štajner, 2014).

For Urdu since no prior work exists on the topic, we follow the simplification schemes defined in the research literature and used the most frequent evaluation metrics to lay the ground work for future research.

3 Corpus Development

We gathered data from Urdu library [1] which has a huge collection of Urdu classic literary works. We chose 69 short, philosophical and thought-provoking stories based on daily life. These stories are written by Ashfaq Ahmad and published in the form of book. It uses complex sentence structure with typical Urdu literature vocabulary which is not very easy. We simplified the sentences using lexical and syntactic methods. Online Urdu Lughat [2] (dictionary) was used to find simpler synonyms.

All the sentences used in our corpus are available online. Initially we consulted language professionals to properly identify complex sentences in literature. Complex sen-

[1] http://www.udb.gov.pk/

[2] http://www.urdulibrary.org/

tences are further processed for removal of irrelevant characters and words to avoid ambiguities in data set. Rules for lexical simplification and syntactic simplification were defined after thorough literature review and discussion with language experts. Simplified corpora are rechecked by language experts to remove any anomalies. Our corpus creation methodology is consistent with the recent works like (Štajner et al., 2019; Scarton et al., 2018; Katsuta and Yamamoto, 2018; Grabar and Cardon, 2018; Brunato et al., 2016, 2015) who also simplified using basic lexical simplification operations and (Yatskar et al., 2010) for syntactic simplification. Since our corpus is composed of short stories, each sentence is linked to the previous and whole theme of stories is based on daily life emotions. The corpus is available at [3].

3.1 Simplification Annotation Scheme

Sentence simplification was performed using two techniques: lexical and syntactic substitution. LS uses lexical operations and SS uses syntactical operations. Most productive simplification operations according to literature including insertion, deletion, splitting, merging, substitution, deletion and reordering are used to produce the simpler sentences. During the corpus development process, we were also able to make a complex: simple word and paraphrase dictionary based on the simplifications applied on our text. Below we explain each of these operations with corresponding examples for a clear understanding of the operations.

3.1.1 Lexical Substitution

Lexical simplification operations include word and phrase replacement. LS replaces complex words in corpus by their simple synonyms or the complex phrase with its suitable analog.

Word level: Word level substitution is the case when a single word or compound word is replaced by the corresponding simple word(s).Rello et al. (2013) reported that dyslexic individuals understand more frequently used words better than their less frequent counterparts. We chose the most frequent synonyms for simplification, for example, for the sentence in example below, with lexical simplification, (e.g."عہدے"«position» is replaced with "نوکری" «Job» and " شربک حپات " is replaced with"بیوی" «wife).

- ***Original.*** کہ شریک حیات کی موت پر آنسو نہ بہانے والا حرکت قلب بند ہو جانے پر اس دار فانی سے کوچ کر گیا ہے۔
- ***English.*** That the spouse who did not shed tears over the death of his spouse has escaped from his ordeal when the heart stopped beating.
- ***Simplified.*** کہ بیوی کی موت پر آنسو نہ بہانے والا دل کی دڑھکن بند ہو جانے پراس دنیا سے چلا گیا ہے۔
- ***English.*** The spouse who did not shed tears over the death of his spouse has died due to heartbeat stoppage.

Phrase level: Is the case when a group of words is replaced by a simple word or two words. Similarly, the complex phrase can also be replaced by the meaning of that phrase. For example in the following the phrase "اس کی روح پرواز کر گئی" « his soul flew »is replaced by "فوت ہو گئے" « died ».

- ***Original.*** ابھی وہ مسجد کی سیڑھیاں چڑھ ھی رھا تھا کہ اس کی حرکت قلب بند ھو گئی اور مسجد کے باھر ھی اس کی روح پرواز کر گئی۔
- ***English.*** As he was mounting the stairs of the mosque, his heart stopped and his soul flew, just outside the mosque.
- ***Simplified.*** ابھی وہ مسجد میں داخل ھو رھا تھا کہ اس کی دڑھکن رک گئی اور مسجد کے باھر ھی وہ فوت ھو گئے۔
- ***English.*** As he was entering the mosque his heart stopped and he died outside the mosque.

3.1.2 Syntactical Substitution:

"Syntactic simplification is the process of reducing the grammatical complexity of a text, while retaining its information content and meaning" (Siddharthan, 2006). It involves removal of phrases or words such that main context and meaning of sentence remains same. Syntactic simplification changes the order of words grammatically, and inserts new words

[3] https://github.com/umauh/Urdu-Sentence-Simplfication

to reduce the complexity. Merging and splitting of sentence are also used to reduce the complexity which is frequently used by (Zhu et al., 2010).

Deletion: Deals with removing extra information in a complex sentence to make it short, simple and clear to understand. A simple sentence normally has lesser numbers of words for conveying the important and content information. Often sentences use multiple adjectives which make the text complex and lengthy (Brunato et al., 2016) without conveying any meaningful information. For instance in the following sentence the phrases "وجہ یہ ھے کہ" « The reason is that», "پڑوس میں رہ کر" « living in your neighborhood », "ھاتھوں پل پل" « every moment » are redundant and thus deleted.

- ***Original.*** فوزیہ وجہ یہ ھے کہ میں نے پڑوس میں رہ کر تمہیں بچپن ھی سے اپنی سوتیلی ماں کے ھاتھوں پل پل دکھ جھیلتے اور اذیتیں اٹھاتے ھوئے دیکھا۔ ھے
- ***English.*** Fauzia the reason is that living in your neighborhood, I have seen you suffering every moment from your childhood at the hands of your stepmother.
- ***Simplified.*** فوزیہ میں نے تمہیں بچپن سے اپنی سوتیلی ماں سے دکھ سہتے ھوئے دیکھا ھے۔
- ***English.*** Fauzia I have seen you suffer from your stepmother since childhood.

Insertion: It is interesting that in the syntactically simplification process there is an insertion operation. Such operation is sometimes referred to as an 'elaboration' process, which is not simplification itself but helps improving text understanding. The simplified sentence may also be longer than its original sentence due to the insertion of meaning or some words which make the meaning of the original sentence clearer. Sometimes, it is difficult to predict the meaning of words or the text which requires supportive information for making it easy to understand. We have used the insertion operation for 9.12% sentences to clarify the meaning. For example, in the following sentence inserting "سے ملیں گی" « as well as get »made the meaning of the sentence complete.

- ***Original.*** تب مجھے تنخواہ بھی ملے گی اور ٹپس الگ۔
- ***English.*** Then I will get paid and tips aside.
- ***Simplified.*** تب تنخواہ بھی ملے گی اور ٹپس الگ سے ملیں گی۔
- ***English.*** Then I will get salary and tips will be given separately.

Reordering: This operation is carried out by changing the order of some words or phrases, e.g. changing the order of the clause in the original sentence to form a newer but simpler sentence (Brunato et al., 2016). In Urdu, reordering eliminates the complexity of sentence making it easier to understand, like in the example below changing order of the "میں سب سے بڑا ھوں" « I am the biggest » made the sentence easy to understand.

- ***Original.*** میں بھٹکے ھوئے مسافروں کو راستہ دکھاتا ھوں میں سب سے بڑا ھوں۔
- ***English.*** I guide lost passengers to the right path, I am superior to all.
- ***Simplified.*** میں سب سے بڑا ھوں کیونکہ میں بھٹکے ھوئے مسافروں کو راستہ دکھاتا ھوں۔
- ***English.*** I am the biggest because I guide the stray travelers.

Merging and Splitting: These operations are antithetical to each other in the simplification process. Merging is specifically used to join two or more sentences into one simplified sentence. It is commonly carried out by insertion of one or two suitable words or by placing suitable conjunction between both sentences. On the other hand, splitting is an operation through which one sentence is split into two or more sentences to make a simplified sentence (Gonzalez-Dios et al., 2018). For example in the following sentence merge and split make the sentence quite simple.

Merge.

- ***Original.*** دیکھتے ھی دیکھتے بچوں کا صفحہ پھٹ گیا۔ اور پھر وہ دونوں لڑ پڑے۔
- ***English.*** As you watch, the children's page tears. And then they both fought

- ***Simplified.*** صفحہ پھٹ گیا اوروہ دونوں لڑ پڑے۔
- ***English.*** The page tore and they both fought.

Split

- ***Original.*** لیکن خیال رہے اسٹیج کے سامنے سبھی سوٹ بوٹ والے لوگوں کو بٹھانا اور مزدور پیشہ لوگوں کو نعرے لگانے اور تالیاں بجانے کے لئے پیچھے کھڑے کر دینا۔
- ***English.*** But be careful to place all the well dressed and suited people in front of the stage and make the working class people stand at back to clap and shout slogans.
- ***Simplified.*** لیکن اسٹیج کے سامنے سب امیر لوگوں کو بٹھانا - غریب لوگوں کو نعرے لگانے کے لئے پیچھے کھڑے کر دینا۔
- ***English.*** Seat all the rich people in front of the stage - Make the poor people stand behind to shout slogans.

3.2 Complex:Simple Lexicon

During the course of our simplification, we were able to develop a complex:simple word and phrase lexicon. Our lexicon has 490 dictionary entries, with 270 word-level and 220 phrase-level entries. For example, "تعارف" «introduction» has been translated to "نام" «name», "فکر مند" «concerned» to "پریشان" «upset» and "فصیح و بلیغ" «rhetorical» to "صاف تفصیل سے" «clearly». Similarly, around 220 phrases have been translated into simpler versions. For example, "سوٹ بوٹ والے لوگ" has been converted into "امیر لوگ", "سمبھل کر" to "حالت پر قابو پا کر" and "اس دار فانی سے کوچ کر گیا ہے" to "فوت ہو گیا". Context of a sentence is strictly followed in translation so that meaning of a sentence remains same. List of deleted words and inserted phrases has also been embedded into the corpus.

4 Human Evaluation

For evaluating the quality and simplicity of our corpus, we performed human evaluation which were done by two native Urdu speakers of 35 to 42 year with good grasp on the language.

We evaluated the sentences for adequacy, fluency and simplicity. The annotators were asked to rank the sentence pairs for the three parameters based on the questions given in Table 1. Q1 measures fluency of the sentence, Q2 is based on the adequacy of the sentence which is concerned with meaning preservation, and Q3 measures simplicity. We have the evaluation scheme used by (Sulem et al., 2018).We have made slight modification in Q2 and Q3 w.r.t to our simplification scheme as in Table 1, since our corpus has two levels of simplification in which lexical simplification is carried out by words and phrase transformation so in our case, complexity of words can not be ignored in human evaluation. Possible answers to these questions shown in Table 1 are : 1 is for "no", 2 is for "may-be" and 3 is for "yes". We used 3-scale criteria as (Sulem et al., 2018; Toutanova et al., 2016) prefer 3-scales over 5-scales. We measured inter annotator agreement using Cohen's kappa score which is reported in Table 2.

Human Evaluation Questions	
Fluency	Is the simplified sentence grammatical?
Adequacy	Does the Simplified sentence address the same information, compared to the original?
Simplicity	Is the simplified sentence simpler than the Original.?

Criteria	
1	No
2	May be
3	Yes

Table 1: Human evaluation questions and the criteria

	Fluency	Adequacy	Simplicity	Average
LS	0.76(0.31)	0.91(0.50)	0.8(0.41)	0.82(0.40)
SS	0.85(0.76)	0.78(0.45)	0.9(0.70)	0.84(0.63)

Table 2: Inter-annotator agreement score(Cohen's Kappa score) over human evaluation and Avg Human score carried out on Inter-annotator agreement score.

5 Simplification Statistics

We have produced a corpus of 1220 simplified sentences by simplifying 610 sentences, both lexical and syntactical. These are simplified using two level simplification process. Figure 1 presents the statistics of our simplification procedure. After an in depth analysis of language and content, we have approximately 58.8% sentences which were simplified using

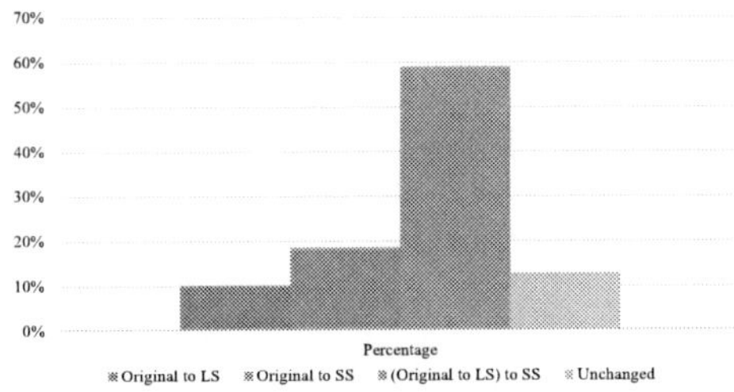

Figure 1: Percentages of each simplification level, LS indicates Lexical simplification and SS indication Syntactic simplification

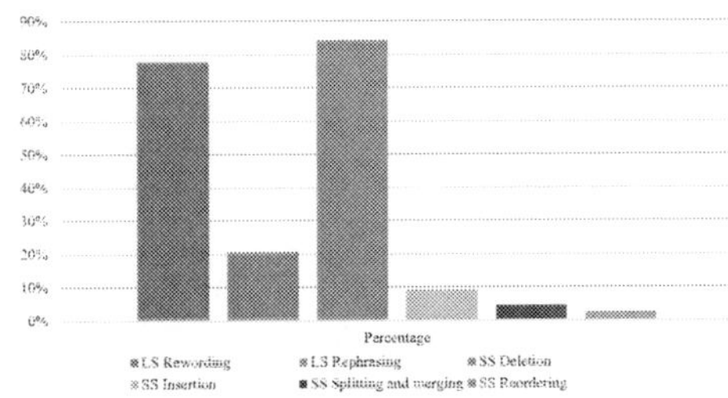

Figure 2: the percentage of each operation applied. LS indicates Lexical simplification and SS indication Syntactic simplification

three-level simplification, original to LS then Lexical simplification to syntactic simplification. On the other hand, 10% sentences were not very complex and only LS was sufficient to produce the final simplified version, whereas 18.3% sentences could only be simplified by SS. Around 12.7% sentences were simple enough not to require simplification of any form.

Figure 2 also summarizes the percentage of each of the simplification operation. Rewording is the most significant operation followed in Lexical Simplification through which 77.61% of simplification was accomplished. Same trend was observed by (Coster and Kauchak, 2011) where they report 65% rewording operations for English. In case of Syntactic Simplification, deletion was found to be the most frequent operation accounting to 84% of cases, this is also in line with results from previous researches (Coster and Kauchak, 2011; Brunato et al., 2016; Gonzalez-Dios et al., 2018). Insertion, split and merge and reordering follow with 9.12%, 4.24% and 2.14% usage respectively.

Figure 3 shows the data statistics found in the corpus, which depicts the average characters and words per sentence in the form of graph. Total numbers of words are lesser in lexical and syntactically simplified sentences as compared to original sentences. Average words per sentence in original sentence, Lexical simplified sentence and syntactically simplified sentence are 13.87, 13.51 and 10.33 respectively. This corpus can be specifically useful for developing automatic Sentence simplification as well as for improving many NLP tasks like text summarizing (Siddharthan, 2014), machine translation (MT) (Štajner and Popovic, 2016) and generation of questions (Heilman and Smith, 2010).

6 Text Simplification model

We used phrase based MT to build Automatic Text simplification models as has been commonly done in the literature. We divided our corpora into three parallel groups: (1) original to simplified lexical corpus, with 641 pairs of sentences with 31 sentences from the news domain, (2) lexical to syntactic simplified corpus with 661 sentences pair with 51 sentences added from kids stories and (3) (Original-Lexical-Syntactic) the concatenation of the both first and second group with the 1,302 sentences pair in which original appears two times as source data and lexical and syntactic level corpora as the target data. Each group is divided into 3 parts to build the PB-SMT models on random selection as 55% of sentences for training, 25% of sentences pairs for tuning and 20% of sentences pairs for testing.

Moses toolkit (Koehn et al., 2007) was used to train the simplification models separately.The models were evaluated using the EASSE toolkit and obtained the BLEU score 66.41 for first group of data, 40.18 for second group and 54.28 for concatenation of both data as shown in the Table 3. Our corpus may not be sufficient to build powerful models for simplifying sentences, but it is useful to test the generalization of the model for simplification of sentences.

Table 4 shows the simplified sentences from the model; first row sentences are simplified by Original to the lexical simplification system; second row is by Lexical to syntactic sim-

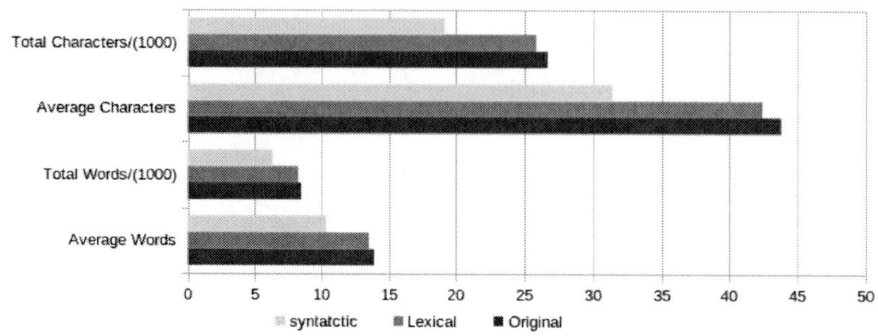

Figure 3: Average words and character per level in the corpus

Corpus	sentences pair	BLEU	SARI
Original to Lexical	641	70.437	37.382
Lexical to Syntactic	661	44.387	21.862
Original-lexical-Syntactic	1,302	53.615	28.333

Table 3: BLEU and SARI score of Urdu Systems

plification system; and the last row is simplified by Original-lexical-syntactic. The system has successfully replaced the complex word with a common word in the target sentences. The first system replaced نگاهیں <look> with نظر<look>. The second system performed a deletion operation in simplification, but the output sentence still needs to be corrected in comparison to the reference sentence. Increasing corpus size can improve the system output. In the last sentence, The system has simplified the sentence via both lexical and syntactically. The system has replaced the complex word حقارت<contempt> with کمتر <Inferior> and deleted کی the same as in reference sentence.

System	Sentence
1	
Input	اُسے چاروں طرف نگاهیں دوڑائی
Output	اُسے چاروں طرف نظر دوڑائی
Reference	اُسے چاروں طرف نظر دوڑائی (She looked around)
2	
Input	اس نے اپنے بچوں کی پرورش اور دیکھ بھال میں کوئی کمی نہیں آنے دئ ۔
Output	اس نے اپنے بچوں کی پرورش اور دیکھ بھال میں کمی نہیں آنے دئ ۔
Reference	اس نے اپنے بچوں کی پرورش میں کوئی کمی نہیں آنے دئ۔ (She did not allow her children's upbringing to diminish.)
3	
Input	وہ همیں حقارت کی نظروں سے دیکھتے هیں۔
Output	وہ همیں کمتر نظروں سے دیکھتے هیں۔
Reference	وہ همیں کمتر نظروں سے دیکھتے هیں۔ (They look down on us.)

Table 4: Output example of each Urdu system mentioned in Table 3

7 Comparison of Systems

In order to establish a comparison of our prepared corpus with corpora of other languages, we built systems using various corpora including OneStopEnglish (Vajjala and Lucic, 2018), SimPA (Scarton et al., 2018), and PWKP (Hwang et al., 2015) corpus which are in English language, and Simpliki (Tonelli et al., 2016) and PaCCSS-It (Brunato et al., 2016) which are Italian simplification corpora. We translated these corpora to Urdu using google translate randomly selected 1,302 pairs of sentences. Automatic translations of the Turk corpus (Xu et al., 2015) were used as test set. Tables 5 and 6show the metrics scores and output of these systems. The system build on simUR (our created corpora) showed an excellent BLEU score. The SARI score of all systems is between 24 and 29. SARI score of SimUr is 26.036. Paccss-it obtained the best SARI score which is 29.441 but obtained the lowest BLEU score. The simplification of Paccss-it corpus is based on few additional operations such as verbal features, sentence type and this corpus original level is also more complex than our corpus. The lowest SARI score is obtained by the simPA-ls that are 24.738 where this corpus is based solely on lexical simplification but has obtained a higher BLUE score.

8 Discussion and Analysis

Table 5 shows that simUr got a better BLEU score as compared to other systems. However, the SARI score for the system is average. If scores of simUr are compared with other systems, it shows that the corpus level of this system is intermediate because the values of this system are nearer to OneStopEnglish (Ele-Adv) corpus level. We can therefore conclude from the result that if the small corpus is to be built, then it should be complex on an advanced level as the paCCSS-It corpus. The paCCSS-It system achieved the highest SARI score, since it includes complex sentences in comparison with our corpus. The more complicated the corpus, the more vocabulary it will cover.

Because of the short dataset the PBSMT works well on lexical substitution. As Table 6 shows some simple sentences by all systems built on different corpora. simUr is the only system that has substituted the complex word حیثیت سے <As> with simple word طور پر <As> in the first sentence. simUr has simplified the sentence with a lexical operation, but the reference sentence is simplified with a syntactic operation. In second sentence, simUR has replaced the word لمبے لمبے <long long> with the بڑے بڑے <Big big> , PaCCSS-IT system has replaced ظاہر <appears> with شاید <Probably> and simPA-ls replaced طرف <side> with چاروں <All four>. In the reference sentence, لمبے لمبے شے <long long things> is replaced with پھیلی ہوئی چیز <Spread out>. In all these changes, the replacement of the simUr system is more similar in the sense of the original word based on the context of the Urdu language.

9 Summary

We have done experimentation through the supervised method using the Moses toolkit (Koehn et al., 2007) on our corpus. Three systems are constructed using the corpus; the first is based on a simplified lexical corpus, the second system is based on the syntactically simplified corpus, and the third system is based on the lexical and syntactic corpus. The lexical system achieved an excellent score of BLEU and SARI as compared to the other two systems.

Corpus	Sub-levels	BLEU	SARI
SimUR		50.736	26.036
Wiki		49.653	27.244
PaCCSS-IT		46.287	29.441
SimPA	*SS-sim*	46.19	28.854
	SS-LS-sim	49.276	27.351
	LS-sim	52.066	24.738
OneStopEnglish	*Ele-adv*	49.822	27.018
	Adv-ini	49.741	27.678
	Adv-ele	48.612	27.943
Simpitiki		50.523	25.835

Table 5: BLEU and SARI score of all systems

No.	System	Sentence
1	Input	یہ جمہوریہ چیک میں بوھیمیا سوئٹزرلینڈ کی حیثیت سے جاری ہے۔
simUR	Output	یہ جمہوریہ چیک میں بوھیمیا سوئٹزرلینڈ کی طور پر جاری ہے۔
paCCSS-IT	Output	جمہوریہ چیک میں بوھیمیا سوئٹزرلینڈ کی حیثیت سے جاری ہے۔
Wiki	Output	• جمہوریہ چیک میں بوھیمیا سوئٹزرلینڈ کی حیثیت سے جاری ہے۔
SimPA-ss	Output	یہ جمہوریہ چیک میں بوھیمیا سوئٹزرلینڈ کی حیثیت سے جاری ہے۔
SimPA-ls	Output	یہ جمہوریہ چیک میں بوھیمیا سوئٹزرلینڈ کی حیثیت سے جاری ہے۔
SimPA-ss-ls	Output	یہ جمہوریہ چیک میں بوھیمیا سوئٹزرلینڈ کی حیثیت سے جاری ہے۔
Adv-Ele1	Output	یہ جمہوریہ چیک میں بوھیمیا سوئٹزرلینڈ کی حیثیت سے جاری ہے۔
Adv-ini	Output	یہ جمہوریہ چیک میں بوھیمیا سوئٹزرلینڈ کی حیثیت سے حرارت چھوڑ ہے۔
ele-Adv	Output	یہ جمہوریہ چیک میں بوھیمیا سوئٹزرلینڈ کی حیثیت سے آگے ہے۔
	Reference	اسے اب بھی جمہوریہ چیک میں بوھیمیا سوئٹزرلینڈ کہا جاتا ہے۔ (It is still called Bohemia Switzerland in the Czech Republic.)
2	Output	وائجر 2 امیجوں میں اوفیلیا لمبے لمبے شے کے طور پر ظاہر ہوتا ہے ، اہم محور یورینس کی طرف اشارہ کرتا ہے۔
simUR	Output	وائجر 2 امیجوں میں اوفیلیا بڑے بڑے شے کے طور پر ظاہر ہوتا ہے ، اہم محور یورینس کی طرف اشارہ کرتا ہے۔
PaCCSS-IT	Output	وائجر 1 امیجوں میں اوفیلیا لمبے لمبے شے کے طور پر شاید ہوتا ہے ، اہم محور یورینس کی طرف اشارہ کرتا ہے۔
Wiki	Output	وائجر 2 امیجوں میں اوفیلیا لمبے لمبے شے کے طور پر ظاہر ہوتا ہے ، اہم محور یورینس کی طرف اشارہ کرتا ہے۔
simPA-ss	Output	وائجر 2 امیجوں میں اوفیلیا لمبے لمبے شے کے طور پر ظاہر ہوتا ؛ ، اہم محور یورینس کی طرف اشارہ کرتا ہے۔
simPA-ls	Output	وائجر 2 امیجوں میں اوفیلیا لمبے لمبے شے کے طور پر ظاہر ہوتا ہے ، اہم محور یورینس کی چاروں اشارہ کرتا ہے۔
simPA-ss-ls	Output	وائجر 2 امیجوں میں اوفیلیا لمبے لمبے شے کے طور پر ظاہر ہوتا ہے ، اہم محور یورینس کی طرف اشارہ کرتا ہے۔
Adv-Ele	Output	وائجر 2 امیجوں میں اوفیلیا لمبے لمبے شے کے طور پر ظاہر ہوتا ہے ، کریم اہم محور یورینس کی طرف اشارہ کرتی ہے۔
Adv-ini	Output	وائجر 2 امیجوں میں اوفیلیا لمبے لمبے شے کے طور پر ظاہر ہوتا ہے ، اہم محور یورینس کی طرف اشارہ کرتا ہے۔
Ele-Adv	Output	وائجر 2 امیجوں میں اوفیلیا لمبے لمبے شے کے طور پر ظاہر ہوتا ہے ، اہم محور یورینس کی طرف اشارہ کرتا ہے۔
	Reference	وائجر 2 تصویروں میں اوفیلیا ایک پھیلی ہوئی چیز کے طور پر ظاہر ہوتا ہے۔ ایک پھیلی ہوئی چیز بڑی محور تھی۔ یہ یورینس کی طرف اشارہ کرتا ہے۔ (Ophelia appears in the Voyager 2 images as a spreading object. A spreading object was a big axis. It refers to Uranus.)

Table 6: comparison of output of all systems

We compared our corpus with other available simplification corpus by construction system through PBMT. All systems are trained on the same size of the corpus. These systems are test on the Turk corpus (Xu et al., 2015). For preparing other corpora, we translated all corpora to Urdu language via google translate.

Although the best score of BLEU is achieved by the system build on our simUr corpora as shown in table 5; however, the simUr system got a comparable SARI score. PaCCSS-It achieved the best SARI score. The simplification of this corpus is based on few additional operations such as verbal features and sentence type of PaCCSS-It, so it is also complex than simUr corpora. A PBMT system on Wiki corpus achieves almost similar levels of BLEU as SimUR. This shows that good simplification systems can be built for Urdu even with such small amounts of parallel corpus for lexical simplification.

10 Conclusion

We have introduced the first monolingual parallel Urdu corpus for sentence simplification using text from a famous writer's book. The corpus is the basic requirement for developing an automatic simplification system and has a multitude of applications in NLP. Our corpus contains 1220 simple sentences based on 610 complex sentences along with their simpler versions lexical and syntactic. This simplification is carried out by using simplification operations including substitution, deletion, insertion and reordering of words and phrases. We also built simplification systems using our corpus and have taken an initiative towards Urdu simplification systems.

References

Sandra Maria Aluísio and Caroline Gasperin. 2010. Fostering digital inclusion and accessibility: the porsimples project for simplification of portuguese texts. In *Proceedings of the NAACL HLT 2010 Young Investigators Workshop on Computational Approaches to Languages of the Americas*, pages 46–53. Association for Computational Linguistics.

Yusra Anees, Sadaf Abdul Rauf, Nauman Iqbal, and Abdul Basit Siddiqi. 2020. Developing a monolingual sentence simplification corpus for Urdu. In *Proceedings of the The Fourth Widening Natural Language Processing Workshop*, pages 92–95, Seattle, USA. Association for Computational Linguistics.

Eduard Barbu, M Teresa Martín-Valdivia, Eugenio Martínez-Cámara, and L Alfonso Ureña-López. 2015. Language technologies applied to document simplification for helping autistic people. *Expert Systems with Applications*, 42(12):5076–5086.

Dominique Brunato, Andrea Cimino, Felice Dell'Orletta, and Giulia Venturi. 2016. Paccss-it: A parallel corpus of complex-simple sentences for automatic text simplification. In *Proceedings of the 2016 Conference on Empirical Methods in Natural Language Processing*, pages 351–361.

Dominique Brunato, Felice Dell'Orletta, Giulia Venturi, and Simonetta Montemagni. 2015. Design and annotation of the first italian corpus for text simplification. In *Proceedings of The 9th Linguistic Annotation Workshop*, pages 31–41.

John Carroll, Guido Minnen, Darren Pearce, Yvonne Canning, Siobhan Devlin, and John Tait. 1999. Simplifying text for language-impaired readers. In *Ninth Conference of the European Chapter of the Association for Computational Linguistics*.

William Coster and David Kauchak. 2011. Simple english wikipedia: a new text simplification task. In *Proceedings of the 49th Annual Meeting of the Association for Computational Linguistics: Human Language Technologies: Short papers-Volume 2*, pages 665–669. Association for Computational Linguistics.

Itziar Gonzalez-Dios, María Jesús Aranzabe, and Arantza Díaz de Ilarraza. 2018. The corpus of basque simplified texts (cbst). *Language Resources and Evaluation*, 52(1):217–247.

Natalia Grabar and Rémi Cardon. 2018. CLEAR – simple corpus for medical French. In *Proceedings of the 1st Workshop on Automatic Text Adaptation (ATA)*, pages 3–9, Tilburg, the Netherlands. Association for Computational Linguistics.

Michael Heilman and Noah A Smith. 2010. Extracting simplified statements for factual question generation. In *Proceedings of QG2010: The Third Workshop on Question Generation*, volume 11.

William Hwang, Hannaneh Hajishirzi, Mari Ostendorf, and Wei Wu. 2015. Aligning sentences from standard Wikipedia to Simple Wikipedia. In *Proceedings of the 2015 Conference of the North American Chapter of the Association for Computational Linguistics: Human Language Technologies*, pages 211–217, Denver, Colorado. Association for Computational Linguistics.

Siddhartha Jonnalagadda, Luis Tari, Jörg Hakenberg, Chitta Baral, and Graciela Gonzalez. 2009. Towards effective sentence simplification for automatic processing of biomedical text. In *Proceedings of Human Language Technologies: The 2009 Annual Conference of the North American Chapter of the Association for Computational Linguistics, Companion Volume: Short Papers*, pages 177–180. Association for Computational Linguistics.

Akihiro Katsuta and Kazuhide Yamamoto. 2018. Crowdsourced corpus of sentence simplification with core vocabulary. In *Proceedings of the Eleventh International Confer-*

ence on Language Resources and Evaluation (LREC-2018).

Philipp Koehn, Hieu Hoang, Alexandra Birch, Chris Callison-Burch, Marcello Federico, Nicola Bertoldi, Brooke Cowan, Wade Shen, Christine Moran, Richard Zens, et al. 2007. Moses: Open source toolkit for statistical machine translation. In *Proceedings of the 45th annual meeting of the association for computational linguistics companion volume proceedings of the demo and poster sessions*, pages 177–180.

Kristopher Kyle. 2016. Measuring syntactic development in l2 writing: Fine grained indices of syntactic complexity and usage-based indices of syntactic sophistication.

Aurélien Max. 2006. Writing for language-impaired readers. In *International Conference on Intelligent Text Processing and Computational Linguistics*, pages 567–570. Springer.

Ruslan Mitkov and Sanja Štajner. 2014. The fewer, the better? a contrastive study about ways to simplify. In *Proceedings of the Workshop on Automatic Text Simplification-Methods and Applications in the Multilingual Society (ATS-MA 2014)*, pages 30–40.

Francisco Oliveira, Fai Wong, and Iok-Sai Hong. 2010. Systematic processing of long sentences in rule based portuguese-chinese machine translation. In *International Conference on Intelligent Text Processing and Computational Linguistics*, pages 417–426. Springer.

Gustavo Paetzold and Lucia Specia. 2016. Understanding the lexical simplification needs of non-native speakers of english. In *Proceedings of COLING 2016, the 26th International Conference on Computational Linguistics: Technical Papers*, pages 717–727.

K Papineni, S Roukos, T Ward, and W Zhu. 2001. Bleu: a method for automatic evaluation of machine translation, 2001. *URL http://www1. cs. columbia. edu/nlp/sgd/bleu. pdf*.

Sarah Elizabeth Petersen and Mari Ostendorf. 2007. *Natural Language Processing Tools for Reading Level Assessment and Text Simplification for Bilingual Education.* Citeseer.

Namoos Hayat Qasmi, Haris Bin Zia, Awais Athar, and Agha Ali Raza. 2020. Simplifyur: Unsupervised lexical text simplification for urdu. In *Proceedings of The 12th Language Resources and Evaluation Conference*, pages 3484–3489.

Luz Rello, Ricardo Baeza-Yates, Laura Dempere-Marco, and Horacio Saggion. 2013. Frequent words improve readability and short words improve understandability for people with dyslexia. In *IFIP Conference on Human-Computer Interaction*, pages 203–219. Springer.

Carolina Scarton, Gustavo Paetzold, and Lucia Specia. 2018. Simpa: A sentence-level simplification corpus for the public administration domain. In *Proceedings of the Eleventh International Conference on Language Resources and Evaluation (LREC-2018).*

Advaith Siddharthan. 2006. Syntactic simplification and text cohesion. *Research on Language and Computation*, 4(1):77–109.

Advaith Siddharthan. 2014. A survey of research on text simplification. *ITL-International Journal of Applied Linguistics*, 165(2):259–298.

Sanja Štajner and Maja Popovic. 2016. Can text simplification help machine translation? In *Proceedings of the 19th Annual Conference of the European Association for Machine Translation*, pages 230–242.

Sanja Štajner, Horacio Saggion, and Simone Paolo Ponzetto. 2019. Improving lexical coverage of text simplification systems for spanish. *Expert Systems with Applications*, 118:80–91.

Elior Sulem, Omri Abend, and Ari Rappoport. 2018. Semantic structural evaluation for text simplification. *arXiv preprint arXiv:1810.05022.*

Mariona Taulé, Maria Antònia Martí, and Marta Recasens. 2008. Ancora: Multilevel annotated corpora for catalan and spanish. In *Lrec*.

Sara Tonelli, Alessio Palmero Aprosio, and Francesca Saltori. 2016. Simpitiki: a simplification corpus for italian. *Proc. of CLiC-it.*

Kristina Toutanova, Chris Brockett, Ke M Tran, and Saleema Amershi. 2016. A dataset and evaluation metrics for abstractive compression of sentences and short paragraphs.

Sowmya Vajjala and Ivana Lucic. 2018. Onestopenglish corpus: A new corpus for automatic readability assessment and text simplification.

David Vickrey and Daphne Koller. 2008. Sentence simplification for semantic role labeling. In *Proceedings of ACL-08: HLT*, pages 344–352.

Wei Xu, Chris Callison-Burch, and Courtney Napoles. 2015. Problems in current text simplification research: New data can help. *Transactions of the Association of Computational Linguistics*, 3(1):283–297.

Mark Yatskar, Bo Pang, Cristian Danescu-Niculescu-Mizil, and Lillian Lee. 2010. For the sake of simplicity: Unsupervised extraction of lexical simplifications from wikipedia. In *Human Language Technologies: The 2010 Annual Conference of the North American Chapter of the Association for Computational Linguistics*, pages 365–368. Association for Computational Linguistics.

Zhemin Zhu, Delphine Bernhard, and Iryna Gurevych. 2010. A monolingual tree-based translation model for sentence simplification. In *Proceedings of the 23rd international conference on computational linguistics*, pages 1353–1361. Association for Computational Linguistics.

Challenges for Information Extraction from Dialogue in Criminal Law

Jenny Hong
Stanford University
jennyhong@cs.stanford.edu

Catalin Voss
Stanford University
catalin@cs.stanford.edu

Christopher D. Manning
Stanford University
manning@cs.stanford.edu

Abstract

Information extraction and question answering have the potential to introduce a new paradigm for how machine learning is applied to criminal law. Existing approaches generally use tabular data for predictive metrics. An alternative approach is needed for matters of equitable justice, where individuals are judged on a case-by-case basis, in a process involving verbal or written discussion and interpretation of case factors. Such discussions are individualized, but they nonetheless rely on underlying facts. Information extraction can play an important role in surfacing these facts, which are still important to understand. We analyze unsupervised, weakly supervised, and pre-trained models' ability to extract such factual information from the free-form dialogue of California parole hearings. With a few exceptions, most F1 scores are below 0.85. We use this opportunity to highlight some opportunities for further research for information extraction and question answering. We encourage new developments in NLP to enable analysis and review of legal cases to be done in a post-hoc, not predictive, manner.

1 Introduction

Our criminal justice system struggles to balance "the value of treating like cases alike, and the value of treating each case individually." (Bell et al., 2021) In criminal law, machine learning has been proposed as a tool to improve consistency in decision making, but to date, research efforts have primarily focused on *codified justice* – processes that make a determination given a limited set of case factors and using specifiable rules, such as a risk assessment used for a probation classification. However, various legal contexts balance a standard of codified justice with a standard of *equitable justice*, which requires decision-makers to apply moral principles to individuals' unique situations.

How can natural language processing aid equitable justice? Equitable justice centers human discretion and the uniqueness of each individual, but nonetheless is based on factual information. The facts of each case are typically discussed and interpreted through dialogue. Often, the dialogue produces transcripts, which are available as public records. Usually, the sheer length of transcribed conversational text all but prohibits any meaningful form of quantitative review, because of the immense effort involved in manually annotating case factors. NLP methods for information extraction over speech can assist in identifying the underlying facts of a case from hearing transcripts. The factors can then be used in statistical analyses of a decision-making process to (a) provide historical understanding over case records that are otherwise locked away in a filing cabinet, and (b) identify specific outlier cases for reconsideration of fair and equitable decision-making where human capacity for review is constrained. By applying information extraction post-hoc rather than filling in a data table or computing a risk score at the time of a hearing, the decision-maker retains full autonomy in conducting a legal process using their own discretion. In this role, information extraction supplements, but never fully supplants, the need for dialogue and transcripts. A broad set of stakeholders can then contribute to identifying the factors that may be relevant in comparing cases.[1]

We present a case study of the capabilities of information extraction methods for dialogue and identify areas for further research in the criminal law context. We have obtained a nearly complete dataset of 35,105 parole hearing transcripts from the State of California for individuals serving life sentences between 2007 and 2019. The California

[1] Bell et al. (2021) describes this approach in the context of the parole system in California. We provide a discussion of the ethical implications of our work in Section 9.

Proceedings of the 1st Workshop on NLP for Positive Impact, pages 71–81
Bangkok, Thailand (online), August 5, 2021.

parole hearing system serves as a useful case study because (1) California has one of the largest prison systems in the U.S., (2) the hearings are transcribed and available on the public record, (3) the hearings are relatively long (about 20,000 words) and illustrate the challenges of long dialogue, (4) human annotation of the hearings is expensive, and (5) the hearings are one continuous dialogue in a single sitting between a decision-maker and a parole candidate, with brief statements from the candidate's attorney. In comparison, criminal trials are much longer, present many forms of exhibits which are often not digitally available, and contain many additional complexities.

We have identified 11 case factors representative of the types of features (binary, multi-class, date, and numerical) that are relevant to the parole decision-making system and illustrate a range of challenges in information extraction. We evaluate three families of models on this task: (1) an unsupervised data programming paradigm (Ratner et al., 2016) extended to weak supervision, (2) pre-trained question answering models based on DistilBERT (Sanh et al., 2019) and Longformer (Beltagy et al., 2020), and (3) classification models based on BERT (Devlin et al., 2019) that are each fine-tuned to predict a single task.

Most models fall below an F1 score of 0.85 for most of the features. The different feature types challenge each of the models in different ways. Data programming remains a largely rule-based approach and works best when the keywords indicative of a label are clear, such as the penal code or a numerical education score. Pre-trained question answering models maintain or improve performance on most categories, except for boolean questions, which remains an area of active development. Surprisingly, all models perform poorly on extracting the risk assessment score, which relies on three simple keywords "low," "moderate," or "high."

Information extraction from long dialogues remains an open challenge, especially when the extraction tasks are not entity-based. We call on research in information extraction to move beyond entity-based tasks in order to tackle the range of tasks relevant for legal dialogue. We also emphasize the need for all methods to handle longer context windows. Long context windows are not merely a byproduct of underdeveloped retrieval methods; they are inherent to the level of personal detail required to apply equitable justice.

2 Related Work

2.1 Information Extraction and Question Answering

Information extraction spans a number of tasks, but neural approaches have concentrated on binary relation extraction. Many relation extraction tasks are performed on only the sentence level (Nguyen and Grishman, 2015; Adel et al., 2016; Levy et al., 2017; Karita et al., 2019; Luo et al., 2019), but techniques have emerged for cross-sentence or even document-level relation extraction (Yao et al., 2019). Compared to information extraction, question answering allows for a greater range of tasks, represented by the diversity of question formulations (Rajpurkar et al., 2016) and is an alternative approach to the task of creating parole hearing annotations.

For both information extraction and question answering, current top-performing models are pre-trained large language models (Devlin et al., 2019; Radford et al., 2019) that have been fine-tuned on specific tasks, such as question answering.

Applications to dialogue focus on entity-based tasks like argument extraction (Swanson et al., 2015), named entity recognition (Chen and Choi, 2016; Choi and Chen, 2018; Bowden et al., 2018), relation extraction (Yu et al., 2020), and task-based extraction (Fang et al., 2018; Finch et al., 2020; Liang et al., 2020). Dialogue-like settings are relatively new for question answering. CoQA (Reddy et al., 2019) aims to answer questions over a written text in an abstractive way, but it is only conversational in that multiple questions can be asked of the same source text sequentially. FriendsQA (Yang and Choi, 2019) answers extractive questions about a multiparty dialogue. The questions are considered to be asked of the dialogue, by a third party outside the dialogue. Like FriendsQA, DREAM (Sun et al., 2019) also uses a dialogue as its source text, but its answers are multiple-choice.

2.2 Machine Learning for Criminal Law

Machine learning in law has mainly relied on tabular data, and mostly for prediction, e.g., policing (Ferguson, 2017; Barrett, 2017; Goel et al., 2016), pre-trial detention (Kleinberg et al., 2018a), sentencing (Elek et al., 2015). Retrospectively, past human (and algorithmic) decisions can be analyzed through the lens of algorithmic fairness, which seeks to understand the way machine learning models or human decisions systematically encode bias

```
Somebody actually took the time to count
up all your 115s and make a list of them
for me, and they covered the gambit,
but I am very surprised that you're
not a gang member.  We've got attempted
murder here in '01, deadly weapon in
'02, battery with a deadly weapon in '05,
pruno, '06, mutual combat, '06, deadly
weapon, '06, battery of peace officer,
'06.  And that seems to be sort of the
general way your life goes.  You picked
up a couple of these in 2013.
```

Figure 1: Example of a section of a hearing during which the deputy commissioner discusses the recent disciplinary history (recorded on Form "115") of the candidate. This occurs about halfway into a 50-page hearing. One extraction task is to identify the date of the most recent disciplinary writeup.

(Dwork et al., 2012; Barocas et al., 2017; Corbett-Davies et al., 2017; Corbett-Davies and Goel, 2018; Kleinberg et al., 2018b; Ho and Xiang, 2020).

Within natural language processing, computational linguistics has been used to scale up lexical analyses of various contexts, such as policing (Voigt et al., 2017) and judicial decisions (Danescu-Niculescu-Mizil et al., 2012). Lexical features can also be used in downstream analysis (Altenburger and Ho, 2019). Relational information extraction has been applied in the context of using named entities (e.g. attorneys, law firms, judges, districts, and parties of a case) as features for downstream risk analysis for intellectual property litigation (Surdeanu et al., 2011). However, both extractive and abstractive question answering are still largely unexplored in legal texts.

3 Data

Our text corpus consists of 35,105 parole hearing transcripts, averaging 18,499 words each, covering 15,852 unique individuals from 2007–2019 parsed from PDF documents. Each hearing is attended by a presiding and a deputy parole commissioner, the parole candidate, and typically an attorney for the candidate. Often, hearings also include a district attorney representative from the county of the commitment offense, who makes a statement, and a victim or their next-of-kin, who may make a statement. Some hearings are attended by visitors who do not participate in the dialogue. The majority of the conversation occurs between the parole candidate, their attorney, and the presiding commissioner.

3.1 Feature Selection

We selected 11 features from a set of case factors identified in discussion with legal scholars[2], former parole candidates, advocacy groups including appellate attorneys, representatives from the California Governor's office, and the Parole Board.

Four features are binary: `off_mur1` ("Do the controlling offenses include first-degree murder?"), `proggang` ("While in prison, did the parole candidate participate in gang-related programming?"), `da_opp` ("Did the district attorney attend the hearing and oppose parole?"), and `job_offer` ("Does the parole candidate have an offer letter for a job post-release?").

Two features are multi-class: `edu_level` ("What is the parole candidate's education level?"), which falls into one of five categories: "no high school or GED," "high school or GED or CHSPD," "some college courses," "college degree," or "other"; and `risk_assess` ("What is the risk score assigned by the psychological evaluation?"), which also has five categories: low, low/moderate, moderate, moderate/high, and high.

Three features are dates. Various dates are mentioned in the course of a parole hearing. Two that are usually stated at the start of the hearing are the MEPD (minimum eligible parole date) and the date that the parole candidate was received into the California Department of Corrections and Rehabilitation (CDCR). Discussing disciplinary writeups that occurred in prison is another key part of the hearing, and we use `last_writeup` to denote the year of the most recent such writeup.

Finally, two features are numerical. One is `yrserved`, the number of years the parole candidate has served in state prison. Another is `tabe`, a measure of educational attainment that corresponds roughly to grade levels (10.5 corresponds to finishing half of 10th grade, where 12.9, corresponding to high school completion, is the highest score).

The context window, or section of dialogue required to identify a feature, varies greatly. Figure 1 shows an example of a context window for the `last_writeup` task. In other hearings, the context window may be longer, e.g., the commissioner may decide to focus on the "mutual combat" in 2006 and speak about the single incident in depth before returning to the list of Forms 115.

[2]All 11 features are identified as more than marginally predictive in Bell (2019) and Young et al. (2015)'s studies of California parole hearings.

Feature	Num. Train	Num. Val.
off_murl	16,201	1,867
proggang	563	48
da_opp	1,173	106
job_offer	1,173	106
edu_level	1,174	106
risk_assess	1,173	106
mepd	1,174	106
last_writeup	563	48
year_received	10,866	1,261
tabe	367	36
yrserved	982	94

Table 1: Training and validation split sizes for each feature.

3.2 Annotation

We collected annotations over a subset of transcripts from three sources. CDCR provided the controlling offense for 26,780 transcripts, which yields `off_murl`. We scraped CDCR's "Inmate Locator" website to obtain `year_received` for each parole candidate. Bell (2019) provided human labels for 426 juvenile lifer parole hearings for a superset of the 11 factors.

We manually labeled 827 transcripts with 118 features with a team of 11 research assistants who were trained and supervised by a legal expert. Through the process of annotation, we narrowed down the 118 proposed fields through multiple rounds of annotations and inter-rater reliability evaluations. The first round of annotations included all 11 features. Subsequent rounds dropped `tabe` and `proggang`.

We split data into training and validation sets by sampling at the transcript level. We withheld an additional portion of the data in a separate test split that is not uncovered for the present work in progress. A subset of training transcripts was designated "development" and used for inspection during model development, in particular for developing human intuition for writing label functions.

Because not all features are covered by all label sources, the amount of labeled data varies by feature across the splits. Table 1 includes the number of examples in each group.

4 Human Performance

To compute a human performance baseline for the reliability with which the selected features can be extracted from transcripts, we use Cohen's κ coefficients. Because the overlap of annotators varies by feature, we compute a mean κ-statistic per feature, weighted by the number of documents that overlapped between the annotators . For the kth feature and two labelers i, j, $i \neq j$, let $\kappa_k(i,j) = \frac{p_0 - p_e}{1-p_e}$, where p_0 is the relative observed agreement among labelers i and j and p_e is the probability of chance agreement under the observed data available for the labelers and let $N_k(i,j)$ be the number of documents for which i and j overlap on feature k. Table 2 reports the statistic

$$\hat{\kappa}_k = \frac{\sum_{i \neq j} N_k(i,j) \cdot \kappa_k(i,j)}{\sum_{i \neq j} N_k(i,j)}.$$

Feature	Human $\hat{\kappa}$ IRR
off_murl	0.94
proggang	0.93
da_opp	0.99
job_offer	0.77
edu_level	0.92
risk_assess	0.80
mepd	0.61
last_writeup	0.69

Table 2: Inter-rater reliability $\hat{\kappa}$ score of human annotators for each feature

5 Extraction Models

5.1 Weakly Supervised Models

Labeling features for parole hearings is burdensome; each hearing takes about one hour to annotate per person. An alternative approach is to generate a noisy but larger dataset using data programming (Ratner et al., 2016). Data programming improves on purely rule-based methods by learning to automatically weight rules, also known as labeling functions, to produce a probabilistic label. When combined, multiple labeling functions $\lambda_1, \ldots, \lambda_n$ can comprise a high-quality estimate of a single label y. For example, for the task of classifying whether a candidate has a count of first-degree murder, λ_1 can be an indicator of whether the phrase "first degree" appears in the first ten conversational turns. Or, a labeling function might instead relying on neural sentiment analysis models. We wrote a set of labeling functions for each extraction task. We also wrote a retrieval heuristic that selects a number of conversational turns from the transcripts over which labeling functions are run.

We use two strategies to produce an estimate $\hat{y}$ from multiple labeling functions. **Snorkel** MeTaL proposes an unsupervised method (Ratner et al., 2018). Supervised methods can also be used, e.g. using linear or logistic regression to learn a weighting of the labeling functions to produce an estimate. In our case, we use logistic regression for the binary variables, where learning a prior makes sense, and prior-free constrained least squares regression for all other variables. We call this method weakly supervised labeling functions, or **WSLF**.

5.2 Pre-Trained Language Models

Data programming generalizes the knowledge of domain experts; pre-trained language models generalize the knowledge of a large English corpus.

We first use models fine-tuned for question answering, which allows us to use a single model for a wide range of features. We study two question answering models: DistilBERT (Sanh et al., 2019) fine-tuned on SQuAD (Rajpurkar et al., 2016) and Longformer (Beltagy et al., 2020) fine-tuned on SQuAD 2.0 (Lee et al., 2020). We call these two models **QA1** and **QA2**, respectively. Through QA1, we hope to understand the overall performance gain, if any, from pre-training. Through QA2, we hope to understand any advantages of using a model with a longer context window (4,096 tokens) that can handle unanswerable questions, which are common in this corpus.

Our second approach is to model each task as a classification task and to fine-tune a language model for each task. We first fine-tune the base BERT model (Devlin et al., 2019) on all parole hearing text, including unlabeled documents. We then train a classifier layer on the labels produced in data generation, because of how limited human labels are. We train a separate model for each task (as opposed to a single multi-head multi-task model), i.e. there is one model to predict the binary feataure `off_mur1`, another one to predict the binary feature `proggang`, and so on. We call this approach task fine-tuned, or **Task-FT**.

6 Results

Table 3 reports the average F1 score across all classes. Binary and multi-class features have natural F1 score interpretations. Date features are quantized into years, and both numerical features have natural quantizations. The TABE score is already quantized to the nearest tenth of a point, and the years served rounded to the nearest year.

Because Snorkel, WSLF, and Task-FT models are trained for a given class, their results are given in the space of the label of the task, whether that is a binary label or a date, for example. However, both QA1 and QA2 models are extractive question answering models, i.e. the answers returned are taken from the text of the hearing. In some cases, the text needs additional processing to be transformed into a label. The transformation may be human intervention, such as in the case of `edu_level`, where the extractive answer "ninth grade" and needs to be translated into a categorical answer "no high school or GED." In other cases, such as with dates, the transformation can be partially or fully automated, such as by parsing answers like "March the 6th, 2019" into the MEPD year, 2019, using tools such as SUTime (Chang and Manning, 2012).

Overall, WSLF does well on most classification tasks, though it is beaten by QA2 on `risk_assess` and by the more powerful classifier Task-FT on `off_mur1`. QA2 is strongest on dates and generally outperforms QA1. Task-FT performs best on a variety of tasks, but surprisingly, it does not always improve over WSLF and Snorkel, even though its training process uses the very labels produced by the data programming methods, but augmented with even more information, the underlying text itself.

7 Discussion

Our case study on extracting features from parole hearings illustrates many outstanding challenges in question answering, information extraction, and text classification. Addressing these challenges is key to using NLP for positive impact in criminal law. The tasks posed by the parole dataset do not fall neatly into relation extraction, which has been the focus of neural information extraction. For legal domain tasks, human labels are scarce and expensive, which raises the question of whether weak supervision may be a more efficient allocation of labels than direct supervision. Legal hearings are long and don't fit neatly into the context window size of a neural model, which raises questions about how neural question answering systems can address this task. We answer the questions in turn.

Can weakly supervised methods be successfully used to reduce the cost of data annotation? Data programming provides the opportunity to produce a large number of labels, but it still comes

Binary Features	Snorkel	WSLF	QA1	QA2	Task-FT	Avg. # Words
off_murl	0.78	0.74	0.76*	0.78*	**0.80**	974
proggang	0.66	**0.87**	0.42*	0.53*	0.64	13,270
da_opp	**0.83**	**0.83**	0.73*	0.76*	**0.83**	5,219
job_offer	0.52	**0.63**	0.58*	0.53*	0.46	9,973
Multi-class Features	**Snorkel**	**WSLF**	**QA1**	**QA2**	**Task-FT**	**Avg. # Words**
edu_level	0.37	**0.41**	0.13*	0.30*	0.34	12,990
risk_assess	0.48	0.51	0.46	**0.53**	0.51	12,326
Dates	**Snorkel**	**WSLF**	**QA1**	**QA2**	**Task-FT**	**Avg. # Words**
mepd	0.74	0.83	0.79	0.79	**0.87**	2,405
last_writeup	0.27	0.03	0.35	**0.42**	0.24	4,811
year_received	0.47	0.01	0.73	**0.76**	0.15	1,700
Numerical	**Snorkel**	**WSLF**	**QA1**	**QA2**	**Task-FT**	**Avg. # Words**
tabe	0.87	0.88	0.87	0.90	**0.94**	972
yrserved	**0.28**	0.08	**0.28**	0.20	0.13	18,603

Table 3: F1 scores of information extraction models and the average number of words in the context windows that were the input text for each model. Scores with * in the QA columns required manual intervention to convert the extractive answer into a binary or multi-class label.

at the cost of requiring experts to translate domain knowledge into programs for each task. Rather than spending one hour labeling one document, an expert may spend dozens of hours designing labeling functions for a single task, e.g. "Does the parole candidate have a job offer?" Once designed, labeling functions are usually computationally light. In producing a final model, adding even weak supervision can improve performance, as seen by improvements of weakly supervised learning functions (WSLF) over the unsupervised Snorkel approach. But unsupervised and weakly supervised techniques mainly perform well only when the tasks can be framed as classification, or when the extractive procedure is relatively simple, such as finding a one-digit decimal TABE score. Reserving some human labels to supervise a WSLF approach outperforms the unsupervised Snorkel method.

Can neural question answering successfully address parole hearings? Neural question answering systems have the flexibility of handling a large range of question formulations and feature types. Compared to other models, this flexibility improves the performance on date features, but surprisingly, on only one additional task, `risk_assess`.

Boolean questions remain an outstanding challenge. Reading comprehension datasets like CoQA (Reddy et al., 2019) and BoolQ (Clark et al., 2019) include such questions but leave a substantial performance gap for future work. The reliance on manual conversion of some answers to binary or multi-class labels is problematic.

In general, including on date features, the most common failure mode for QA1 and QA2 is to return an incorrect answer of a correct type. For example, for `yrserved`, the models frequently returned any number they found in the context passage, such as the sentence (e.g. "15 years to life") or any other time range (e.g. "It was around two years I was part of that gang.")

How big a problem is document length? Long context windows continue to challenge all models present, especially neural models. Although developing retrieval models for dialogue can help narrow the context window for downstream question answering applications, an even bigger challenge is the fact that even with an ideal retrieval model, the "correct" context window can still be long. In conversation, speakers are free to go on tangents. More importantly, in the case of legal hearings, speakers elaborate on case factors, attending to detail (as they should), which can greatly prolong a hearing. For example, in discussions of the psychological risk score, both data generation methods and neural question answering systems fail to identify the sentence and keyword containing "low," "moderate," or "high." We suspect that this is because discussions of all risk factors are usually several thousand words long. The score can be mentioned at the very beginning or very end, but often it is tucked away somewhere in the middle.

8 Conclusion

Parole hearing transcripts go into a great amount of detail in discussing numerous case factors centered around a single named entity, an incarcerated individual who has reached their parole eligibility date. The lack of relational structure and long format of these hearings makes information extraction from transcripts very challenging using several very different approaches from modern NLP.

We estimate that an F1 score of 0.80–0.85 across a broad set of features would provide the ability to conduct meaningful downstream research on a hearing-driven decision-making process like parole. To flag individual cases for reconsideration, we believe that the bar likely lies even higher, since misclassifications often cause outliers. The performance of present models approaches the level at which we can provide useful automatic extraction tools to parole stakeholders for some features, especially certain binary ones. However, for other, seemingly simple medium- and high-cardinality tasks, much work remains.

We plan to conduct future experiments to provide more transparency to model performance. The opaque nature of NLP modeling perplexes our legal collaborators: "How can you identify whether a candidate has participated in gang-related rehabilitation programming but not pick out the risk assessment score from a choice of three words?"

The largest challenge moving forward remains natural language understanding in the face of document length. Of course, length is not the only problem and other artifacts of spoken dialogue cause challenges, including interruptions, corrections, and colloquial speech. Improved retrieval techniques or even summarization methods can help assess the extent to which document length remains a challenge and possibly mitigate its impact. However, there is no getting around the level of detail that is regarded as due process.

One solution is to incorporate the hierarchical nature of dialogue (Asher and Vieu, 2005). Within a discussion about risk assessment, a parole commissioner may ask about various sub-factors, such as mental illness, or behavior toward other individuals in prison. We suspect that the word "low," "moderate," or "high" can appear in any of those sub-topics without referring to the risk score. We hope to conduct further research to assess the need for and viability of a hierarchical model. Conversely, an extractive model sometimes picks up on risk-related words in the sub-topics, rather than returning to the higher level question of the risk scores.

Common sense knowledge will also play a role in solving this challenge. In one section of a hearing, the commissioner says, "And, uh, I note that you – you have both a high school diploma and GED, is that correct?" Over the course of the next eight thousand words, the parole candidate describes his life, from playing sports in high school, to having a child, to the chaos of teenage co-parenting, to night school, to getting married, and to moving cities to protect his children. Later on, the commissioner revisits the record and says, "You've taken some college classes," which the candidate himself failed to mention. In addition to understanding the topics and sub-topics in which education occurs, the `edu_level` task benefits from real-life knowledge about educational levels. The WSLF model performs well because of tailored labeling functions that encode information about "high school" and "college."

Finally, cross-sentence reference resolution remains important. In Figure 1, the question of the most recent Form 115 can be answered in a short context window. Yet, extracting the answer requires resolving the reference of "these" in " You picked up a couple of these in 2013."

While the amount of attention to personal detail in these hearings presents the biggest challenge to our extraction models, individualized attention is also precisely what defines *equitable justice*. We hope that the NLP community will take up this challenge.

9 Ethical Implications

Our work raises ethical questions about the use of NLP in criminal law. We argue that machine learning can have a positive impact in a decision-making process like parole when it is applied as a review tool. NLP can provide transparency into millions of pages of hearing dialogue that would otherwise remain inaccessible for any form of analysis. It is possible to use information aggregation as part of a toolkit that centers human discretionary judgment and uses technology to promote consistency, reconciling our desire for a human-led decision-making process with the reality that human discretion introduces inconsistencies and systemic biases. The analysis of the present work falls under the umbrella of the "Recon Approach" (Bell et al., 2021) and serves the purposes of conducting *reconnaissance* at the systemic level and creating an opportunity for *reconsideration* of individual cases.

The dual use objection. Perhaps the most prominent objection to the Recon Approach is analogous to the "dual use" argument for sentencing (Leins et al., 2020). While we have developed information aggregation tools for a review use case, what is there to stop someone turning that around and using these exact same features and for a codified justice use case?

In the California parole context, employing technology for a predictive, rule-based system requires legislative parole reform and an overhaul of California's approach to criminal data record keeping. As it is currently constructed, the Board of Parole Hearings operates with great discretion. Parole hearings are based only in part on data that is available before the hearing. For example, parole hearings often discuss mitigating pre-commitment factors such as the living circumstances of an individual at the time that the crime was committed, touching on topics such as childhood abuse, gang membership, or neighborhood crime. These data are often not even available in sentencing transcripts. Even for factors that are available in records before the hearing, such as a candidate's disciplinary conduct in prison, the data often only exists in archived handwritten reports that prison staff aggregate prior to the hearing. The data are read out in semi-structured form for the first time by the commissioner during the hearing. It is therefore not possible to extract a meaningful number of the features that are currently considered for a parole decision in California without first conducting a hearing. [3]

[3] A related question is why proponents of codified justice or social scientists do not ask commissioners to tabulate factors in a hearing as the input to an algorithm, preempting the need for NLP. (Bell et al., 2021) provides a response to this: First, many parole stakeholders greatly value the "human factors" of the parole process; neither the legislature nor the Parole Board believe that an entirely tabular approach is appropriate. Second, by asking the agency that is conducting the hearings to tabulate such data, we postulate that CDCR would provide reliable annotations for all relevant factors. However, sometimes the agency under scrutiny of a review process is not incentivized to provide key data in structured form. For example, the Parole Board in California refused to provide race data for its parole candidates until it faced repeated litigation. Finally, in order to identify systemic inequities, the Recon Approach relies on a broad set of stakeholders to propose factors of inquiry, and knowledge of which factors are relevant may only become available after the fact, such as when legislation changes years after a hearing.

The risk assessment path. A second ethical question is whether features extracted from hearing dialogue can be used as the input to a risk assessment algorithm before a decision is reached. While constructing a such a risk assessment algorithm is possible in theory, we believe that such an algorithm would be hard to construct and virtually meaningless in the context of parole. Unlike applications to sentencing (Chen et al., 2019; Hu et al., 2018; Zhong et al., 2018), the outcome variable for parole is unclear. Lifer recidivism is extremely low (under 3% in California) and it has not risen even as the parole grant rate has increased from 3% to over 20% in the past two decades (Committee on Revision of the Penal Code, 2020).

Impact on mass incarceration. Finally, a third common question about our work is whether it is possible to use automatically extracted factors for increased review of parole grants, thus increasing the rate at which grants are overturned and contributing to the cycle of mass incarceration. The existing parole review process in California makes additional denials and reversals of grants unlikely. Immediately after a parole hearing, two parole commissioners make a recommendation to grant or deny parole. In the next 120 days, the decision is reviewed by the Parole Board. Afterward, the Governor has 30 days to review the decision before it becomes final. In practice, all parole grants are reviewed, but both the Parole Board and the Governor's review unit say that they lack the resources to review many denials. If the decision is a grant, the candidate is released from prison and the outcome is final. However, if the decision is a denial, nothing changes; the parole candidate remains in prison. So what happens if a prisoner is denied parole, but the decision was in fact inconsistent with the parole decision process? It means there is very limited opportunity to reconsider the case, possibly leaving a prisoner incarcerated much longer than necessary. If an analysis based on features extracted using NLP can identify outlier cases, this is actionable. The Governor may request a review, the Parole Board may advance the date of a hearing, or an appeals attorney may petition a court. On the other hand, there exists no basis on which we should assume that either the Governor or the Parole Board would overturn more hearings when provided with more data about the parole process.

References

Heike Adel, Benjamin Roth, and Hinrich Schütze. 2016. Comparing convolutional neural networks to traditional models for slot filling. In *Proceedings of the 2016 Conference of the North American Chapter of the Association for Computational Linguistics: Human Language Technologies*, pages 828–838, San Diego, California. Association for Computational Linguistics.

Kristen M Altenburger and Daniel E Ho. 2019. Is yelp actually cleaning up the restaurant industry? a re-analysis on the relative usefulness of consumer reviews. In *The World Wide Web Conference*, pages 2543–2550.

Nicholas Asher and Laure Vieu. 2005. Subordinating and coordinating discourse relations. *Lingua*, 115(4):591–610.

Solon Barocas, Moritz Hardt, and Arvind Narayanan. 2017. Fairness in machine learning. *NeurIPS tutorial*, 1:2.

Lindsey Barrett. 2017. Reasonably suspicious algorithms: predictive policing at the United States border. *N.Y.U. Review of Law & Social Change*, 41:327.

Kristen Bell. 2019. A stone of hope: Legal and empirical analysis of California juvenile lifer parole decisions. *Harvard Civil Rights-Civil Liberties Law Review*, 54:455.

Kristen Bell, Jenny Hong, Nick McKeown, and Catalin Voss. 2021. The Recon Approach: A new direction for machine learning in criminal law. *Berkeley Technology Law Journal*, 37.

Iz Beltagy, Matthew E. Peters, and Arman Cohan. 2020. Longformer: The long-document transformer. *arXiv:2004.05150.*

Kevin Bowden, Jiaqi Wu, Shereen Oraby, Amita Misra, and Marilyn Walker. 2018. SlugNERDS: A named entity recognition tool for open domain dialogue systems. In *Proceedings of the Eleventh International Conference on Language Resources and Evaluation (LREC 2018)*, Miyazaki, Japan. European Language Resources Association (ELRA).

Angel X. Chang and Christopher Manning. 2012. SUTime: A library for recognizing and normalizing time expressions. In *Proceedings of the Eighth International Conference on Language Resources and Evaluation (LREC'12)*, pages 3735–3740, Istanbul, Turkey. European Language Resources Association (ELRA).

Huajie Chen, Deng Cai, Wei Dai, Zehui Dai, and Yadong Ding. 2019. Charge-based prison term prediction with deep gating network. In *Proceedings of the 2019 Conference on Empirical Methods in Natural Language Processing and the 9th International Joint Conference on Natural Language Processing (EMNLP-IJCNLP)*, pages 6362–6367, Hong Kong, China. Association for Computational Linguistics.

Yu-Hsin Chen and Jinho D. Choi. 2016. Character identification on multiparty conversation: Identifying mentions of characters in TV shows. In *Proceedings of the 17th Annual Meeting of the Special Interest Group on Discourse and Dialogue*, pages 90–100, Los Angeles. Association for Computational Linguistics.

Jinho D. Choi and Henry Y. Chen. 2018. SemEval 2018 task 4: Character identification on multiparty dialogues. In *Proceedings of The 12th International Workshop on Semantic Evaluation*, pages 57–64, New Orleans, Louisiana. Association for Computational Linguistics.

Christopher Clark, Kenton Lee, Ming-Wei Chang, Tom Kwiatkowski, Michael Collins, and Kristina Toutanova. 2019. BoolQ: Exploring the surprising difficulty of natural yes/no questions. In *Proceedings of the 2019 Conference of the North American Chapter of the Association for Computational Linguistics: Human Language Technologies, Volume 1 (Long and Short Papers)*, pages 2924–2936, Minneapolis, Minnesota. Association for Computational Linguistics.

Committee on Revision of the Penal Code. 2020. Parole release and penal code section 1170(d)(1) resentencing: Overview.

Sam Corbett-Davies and Sharad Goel. 2018. The measure and mismeasure of fairness: A critical review of fair machine learning. *arXiv:1808.00023.*

Sam Corbett-Davies, Emma Pierson, Avi Feller, Sharad Goel, and Aziz Huq. 2017. Algorithmic decision making and the cost of fairness. In *Proceedings of the 23rd ACM SIGKDD international conference on knowledge discovery and data mining*, pages 797–806.

Cristian Danescu-Niculescu-Mizil, Lillian Lee, Bo Pang, and Jon Kleinberg. 2012. Echoes of power: Language effects and power differences in social interaction. In *Proceedings of the 21st international conference on World Wide Web*, pages 699–708.

Jacob Devlin, Ming-Wei Chang, Kenton Lee, and Kristina Toutanova. 2019. BERT: Pre-training of deep bidirectional transformers for language understanding. In *Proceedings of the 2019 Conference of the North American Chapter of the Association for Computational Linguistics: Human Language Technologies, Volume 1 (Long and Short Papers)*, pages 4171–4186, Minneapolis, Minnesota. Association for Computational Linguistics.

Cynthia Dwork, Moritz Hardt, Toniann Pitassi, Omer Reingold, and Richard Zemel. 2012. Fairness through awareness. In *Proceedings of the 3rd innovations in theoretical computer science conference*, pages 214–226.

Jennifer K Elek, Roger K Warren, and Pamela M Casey. 2015. *Using risk and needs assessment information at sentencing: Observations from ten jurisdictions*. National Center for State Courts.

Hao Fang, Hao Cheng, Maarten Sap, Elizabeth Clark, Ari Holtzman, Yejin Choi, Noah A. Smith, and Mari Ostendorf. 2018. Sounding board: A user-centric and content-driven social chatbot. In *Proceedings of the 2018 Conference of the North American Chapter of the Association for Computational Linguistics: Demonstrations*, pages 96–100, New Orleans, Louisiana. Association for Computational Linguistics.

Andrew Guthrie Ferguson. 2017. Illuminating black data policing. *Ohio State Journal of Criminal Law*, 15:503.

Sarah E Finch, James D Finch, Ali Ahmadvand, Ingyu Choi, Xiangjue Dong, Ruixiang Qi, Harshita Sahijwani, Sergey Volokhin, Zihan Wang, Zihao Wang, and Jinho D Choi. 2020. Emora: An inquisitive social chatbot who cares for you. In *3rd Proceedings of Alexa Prize*.

Sharad Goel, Justin M Rao, and Ravi Shroff. 2016. Personalized risk assessments in the criminal justice system. *American Economic Review*, 106(5):119–23.

Daniel E Ho and Alice Xiang. 2020. Affirmative algorithms: The legal grounds for fairness as awareness. *University of Chicago Law Review Online*.

Zikun Hu, Xiang Li, Cunchao Tu, Zhiyuan Liu, and Maosong Sun. 2018. Few-shot charge prediction with discriminative legal attributes. In *Proceedings of the 27th International Conference on Computational Linguistics*, pages 487–498, Santa Fe, New Mexico, USA. Association for Computational Linguistics.

Shigeki Karita, Nanxin Chen, Tomoki Hayashi, Takaaki Hori, Hirofumi Inaguma, Ziyan Jiang, Masao Someki, Nelson Enrique Yalta Soplin, Ryuichi Yamamoto, Xiaofei Wang, Shinji Watanabe, Takenori Yoshimura, and Wangyou Zhang. 2019. A comparative study on transformer vs RNN in speech applications. pages 449–456. IEEE.

Jon Kleinberg, Himabindu Lakkaraju, Jure Leskovec, Jens Ludwig, and Sendhil Mullainathan. 2018a. Human decisions and machine predictions. *The Quarterly Journal of Economics*, 133(1):237–293.

Jon Kleinberg, Jens Ludwig, Sendhil Mullainathan, and Ashesh Rambachan. 2018b. Algorithmic fairness. In *AEA papers and proceedings*, volume 108, pages 22–27.

Gyeongbok Lee, Seung-won Hwang, and Hyunsouk Cho. 2020. SQuAD2-CR: Semi-supervised annotation for cause and rationales for unanswerability in SQuAD 2.0. In *Proceedings of the 12th Language Resources and Evaluation Conference*, pages 5425–5432, Marseille, France. European Language Resources Association.

Kobi Leins, Jey Han Lau, and Timothy Baldwin. 2020. Give me convenience and give her death: Who should decide what uses of NLP are appropriate, and on what basis? In *Proceedings of the 58th Annual Meeting of the Association for Computational Linguistics*, pages 2908–2913, Online. Association for Computational Linguistics.

Omer Levy, Minjoon Seo, Eunsol Choi, and Luke Zettlemoyer. 2017. Zero-shot relation extraction via reading comprehension. In *Proceedings of the 21st Conference on Computational Natural Language Learning (CoNLL 2017)*, pages 333–342, Vancouver, Canada. Association for Computational Linguistics.

Kaihui Liang, Austin Chau, Yu Li, Xueyuan Lu, Dian Yu, Mingyang Zhou, Ishan Jain, Sam Davidson, Josh Arnold, Minh Nguyen, and Zhou Yu. 2020. Gunrock 2.0: A user adaptive social conversational system. In *3rd Proceedings of Alexa Prize*.

Fan Luo, Ajay Nagesh, Rebecca Sharp, and Mihai Surdeanu. 2019. Semi-supervised teacher-student architecture for relation extraction. In *Proceedings of the Third Workshop on Structured Prediction for NLP*, pages 29–37, Minneapolis, Minnesota. Association for Computational Linguistics.

Thien Huu Nguyen and Ralph Grishman. 2015. Combining neural networks and log-linear models to improve relation extraction. arXiv:1511.05926.

Alec Radford, Jeff Wu, Rewon Child, David Luan, Dario Amodei, and Ilya Sutskever. 2019. Language models are unsupervised multitask learners. OpenAI.

Pranav Rajpurkar, Jian Zhang, Konstantin Lopyrev, and Percy Liang. 2016. SQuAD: 100,000+ questions for machine comprehension of text. In *Proceedings of the 2016 Conference on Empirical Methods in Natural Language Processing*, pages 2383–2392, Austin, Texas. Association for Computational Linguistics.

Alex Ratner, Braden Hancock, Jared Dunnmon, Roger Goldman, and Christopher Ré. 2018. Snorkel metal: Weak supervision for multi-task learning. In *Proceedings of the Second Workshop on Data Management for End-To-End Machine Learning*, pages 1–4.

Alexander Ratner, Christopher De Sa, Sen Wu, Daniel Selsam, and Christopher Ré. 2016. Data programming: Creating large training sets, quickly. *Advances in Neural Information Processing Systems*, 29:3567.

Siva Reddy, Danqi Chen, and Christopher D Manning. 2019. CoQA: A conversational question answering challenge. *Transactions of the Association for Computational Linguistics*, 7:249–266.

Victor Sanh, Lysandre Debut, Julien Chaumond, and Thomas Wolf. 2019. Distilbert, a distilled version of bert: smaller, faster, cheaper and lighter. arXiv:1910.01108. Version 4.

Kai Sun, Dian Yu, Jianshu Chen, Dong Yu, Yejin Choi, and Claire Cardie. 2019. DREAM: A challenge data set and models for dialogue-based reading comprehension. *Transactions of the Association for Computational Linguistics*, 7:217–231.

Mihai Surdeanu, Ramesh Nallapati, George Gregory, Joshua Walker, and Christopher D Manning. 2011. Risk analysis for intellectual property litigation. In *Proceedings of the 13th International Conference on Artificial Intelligence and Law*, pages 116–120.

Reid Swanson, Brian Ecker, and Marilyn Walker. 2015. Argument mining: Extracting arguments from online dialogue. In *Proceedings of the 16th Annual Meeting of the Special Interest Group on Discourse and Dialogue*, pages 217–226, Prague, Czech Republic. Association for Computational Linguistics.

Rob Voigt, Nicholas P Camp, Vinodkumar Prabhakaran, William L Hamilton, Rebecca C Hetey, Camilla M Griffiths, David Jurgens, Dan Jurafsky, and Jennifer L Eberhardt. 2017. Language from police body camera footage shows racial disparities in officer respect. *Proceedings of the National Academy of Sciences*, 114(25):6521–6526.

Zhengzhe Yang and Jinho D. Choi. 2019. FriendsQA: Open-domain question answering on TV show transcripts. In *Proceedings of the 20th Annual SIGdial Meeting on Discourse and Dialogue*, pages 188–197, Stockholm, Sweden. Association for Computational Linguistics.

Yuan Yao, Deming Ye, Peng Li, Xu Han, Yankai Lin, Zhenghao Liu, Zhiyuan Liu, Lixin Huang, Jie Zhou, and Maosong Sun. 2019. DocRED: A large-scale document-level relation extraction dataset. In *Proceedings of the 57th Annual Meeting of the Association for Computational Linguistics*, pages 764–777.

Kathryne M Young, Debbie A Mukamal, and Thomas Favre-Bulle. 2015. Predicting parole grants: An analysis of suitability hearings for California's lifer inmates. *Federal Sentencing Reporter*, 28:268.

Dian Yu, Kai Sun, Claire Cardie, and Dong Yu. 2020. Dialogue-based relation extraction. In *Proceedings of the 58th Annual Meeting of the Association for Computational Linguistics*, pages 4927–4940. Association for Computational Linguistics.

Haoxi Zhong, Zhipeng Guo, Cunchao Tu, Chaojun Xiao, Zhiyuan Liu, and Maosong Sun. 2018. Legal judgment prediction via topological learning. In *Proceedings of the 2018 Conference on Empirical Methods in Natural Language Processing*, pages 3540–3549, Brussels, Belgium. Association for Computational Linguistics.

Detecting Hashtag Hijacking for Hashtag Activism

Pooneh Mousavi
University of Texas at Dallas
pxm153230@utdallas.edu

Jessica Ouyang
University of Texas at Dallas
jessica.ouyang@utdallas.edu

Abstract

Social media has changed the way we engage in social activities. On Twitter, users can participate in social movements using hashtags such as #MeToo; this is known as hashtag activism. However, while these hashtags can help reshape social norms, they can also be used maliciously by spammers or troll communities for other purposes, such as signal boosting unrelated content, making a dent in a movement, or sharing hate speech. We present a Tweet-level hashtag hijacking detection framework focusing on hashtag activism. Our weakly-supervised framework uses bootstrapping to update itself as new Tweets are posted. Our experiments show that the system adapts to new topics in a social movement, as well as new hijacking strategies, maintaining strong performance over time.

1 Introduction

Social media has changed the way we live, trade, share news, and engage in social activities. Twitter is one of the most popular social networks, where users post short textual messages called "Tweets." A hashtag (#) before a particular keyword or phrase in a Tweet is used to categorize the Tweet, helping users find topics that are of interest to them.

One of the achievements of social media is reshaping and re-scaling engagement in social movements via *hashtag activism.* Yang (2016) defines hashtag activism as large numbers of social media posts using a common hashtagged phrase with a social or political claim. Some popular hashtag activism movements include "#MeToo," a movement against sexual harassment and assault, and "#BlackLivesMatter," which campaigns against violence and systemic racism towards African Americans. These hashtags help engage people in social movements by raising awareness on a larger scale and by giving opportunities for those with access limitations, like the physically challenged, to participate.

Unfortunately, hashtag activism is also a good target for spammers. *Hashtag hijacking* occurs when users "[use] a trending hashtag to promote topics that are substantially different from its recent context" (VanDam and Tan, 2016) or "to promote one's own social media agenda" (Darius and Stephany, 2019). While the detection of spam Tweets in general is an important issue, the detection of spam related to social movements is of even greater importance because it targets excluded or marginalized groups.

We present a weakly-supervised, bootstrapping framework to detect Tweet-level hashtag hijacking targeting specific social movements, using a combination of features based on the Tweet text, use of other hashtags, replies, and user profile. Our experiments focus on #MeToo, but our methodology can be applied to any hashtag. Prior work on hashtag hijacking has focused on general trending hashtags like #job or #android and could not adapt over time to attacker strategies; these approaches were unable to account for changes in hashtag use over time. Ours is the first self-updating approach to be developed for detecting hashtag hijacking at the Tweet level. Our main contributions are as follows:

- A new dataset of #MeToo Tweets from October 2017 through May 2020[1].
- A bootstrapping framework to detect hashtag hijacking that can adapt over time to hijackers' changing strategies.

2 Related Work

Hashtag hijacking is a relatively new problem, and there is little prior work on the task.

Previous studies have analyzed cases of political hashtag activism spamming ("hacktivism"), which

[1] https://github.com/poonehmousavi/Detecting-Hashtag-Hijacking-for-Hashtag-Activism

Proceedings of the 1st Workshop on NLP for Positive Impact, pages 82–92
Bangkok, Thailand (online), August 5, 2021.

often involves cyberbullying (Taylor, 2005; Hampson, 2012; Deseriis, 2017; Solomon, 2017), emphasizing the destructive role of spamming on political movements and protests and how it can change the direction and goals of the targeted movement. Lindgren (2019) identifies noise and trolling as the main challenges facing hashtag activism movements, and Kalbitzer et al. (2014) discusses on the harmful effects of excessive unwanted information on social media, which can even affect the physical condition of vulnerable users. Bode et al. (2015) evaluate the composition of political networks on Twitter; they find that hashtag "hashjacking (encroaching on opposition's keywords to inject contrary perspectives into a discourse stream)" to be one of the main types of strategic political communication on Twitter.

Few studies have investigated computation pipelines to detect hashtag hijacking. Prior work focuses exclusively on general trending hashtags and cannot adapt over time to attacker strategies.

Jain, Agarwal, and Pruthi (2015) proposed an unsupervised framework for detecting hashtag hijacking. They argued that hijacked Tweets use different words than do the more common relevant Tweets. Jain et al. grouped trending hashtags into general categories, such as *technology*, *entertainment*, and *politics*, and calculated words' TF-IDF scores at the category level. They then predicted whether or not a Tweet using a given hashtag was hijacked based on its word overlap with its category's word list. By using categories, rather than individual hashtags, Jain et al. were able to increase the amount of data for calculating their scores, and also to determine which categories of hashtags were more likely to be hijacked. In contrast, our goal is to focus on a specific hashtag associated with social activism.

Van Dam and Tan (2016) applied topic learning and time series analysis to the hijacking task for trending hashtags. They analyzed each hashtag's distribution of topics over time: if a hashtag's topic distribution in a one-day window differed significantly from its previous distribution, the hashtag was considered hijacked. Van Dam and Tan's approach operates at the level of hashtags and does not attempt to predict whether or not a specific Tweet is hijacked. Like Jain et al., they assume that a hashtag's topic distribution is constant over time, and that changes in topic indicate hijacking; in contrast, our work assumes that the topics associated with a social activism hashtag can shift over time.

Figure 1: Hijacked #MeToo Tweets. Usernames are masked to protect the privacy of the users.

Virnami et al. (2017) trained a fully supervised neural network to detect hashtag hijacking. They extracted Tweet-level features, such as the relatedness among hashtags used and information about the user account that posted the Tweet, and trained a feed-forward network to classify Tweets as hijacked or not. Like Jain et al. and Van Dam and Tan, Virnami et al. focused on trending hashtags; they used a manually-labeled dataset of ten thousand Tweets corresponding to the top ten trending hashtags. Like Jain et al., Virnami et al. treat hijacking as a general problem unrelated to any specific hashtag; their features are independent of the hashtags used in a Tweet, allowing them to train a single neural model on a much larger dataset than would be available for any individual hashtag.

Twitter spam detection is a related area of work. Rather than detecting unrelated Tweets that hijack a given hashtag, spam detection is a more general task: determine whether or not a Tweet is spam, regardless of the hashtags it uses. Most existing techniques for spam detection can be categorized into approaches that focus on user-level features to identify spammers (Wang, 2010; Yardi et al., 2010; Lee et al., 2010), those focus on Tweet-level features to identify spam Tweets ((Gao et al., 2012)), and hybrid approaches that use a combination of features based on both Tweet and user (Sedhai and Sun, 2018; Hu et al., 2014, 2013).

A related line of research is the relationship between spam Tweets and the hashtags they use; Sedhai and Sun (2017) analyzed hashtags in spam Tweets based on their frequency, position, orthography, and co-occurrence counts. It is important to emphasize the difference between *hijacked* and *spam* Tweets. Tweets are hijacked in terms of a specific hashtag; not all hijacked Tweets are spam. Figure 1 shows examples of hijacked #MeToo Tweets

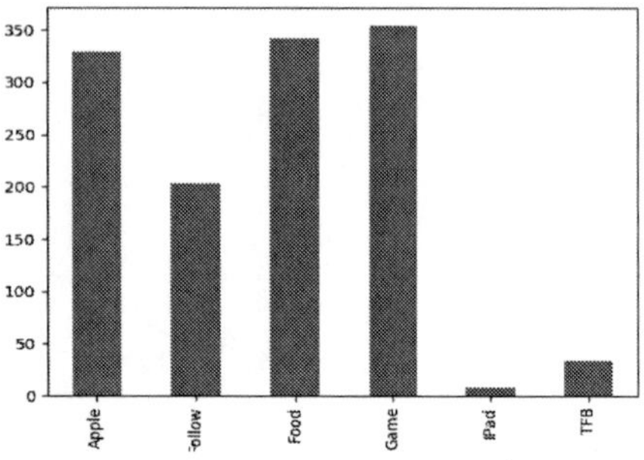

Figure 2: Tweet distribution over spam categories.

that are not spam in the general sense.

3 Data

We use data from #MeToo, a movement used by women to share their experiences with sexual harassment. The online #MeToo movement started in October 2017 with actress Alyssa Milano's Tweet about sexual abuse allegations against Harvey Weinstein. #MeToo has since become widespread and a target for hijackers to increase their own visibility and promote their products.

3.1 Data Collection

There is an enormous and continuously growing number of #MeToo Tweets, most of which are not hijacked. Thus, the first challenge addressed in our work is to collect enough hijacked Tweets for our seed set, before the Tweets are even labeled. We use the Twitter spam analysis of Sedhai and Sun (2017) to create a list of hashtags that are likely to occur in spam Tweets (Table 1). Using the Twitter API, we find Tweets containing both #Metoo and at least one of these spammy hashtags. After removing duplicates (Tweets containing multiple spammy hashtags), we are left with 1370 Tweets that are likely to be hijacked. Figure 2 shows the distribution of these Tweets over spam categories.

Note that, while a Tweet may hijack a hashtag without being spam — hijacking occurs when the hashtag is used to boost visibility for any unrelated topic, not just spam topics — a spam Tweet that uses the #MeToo hashtag is almost certainly hijacked. Thus, our collected spammy Tweets are likely to be cases of #MeToo hijacking, although they are not necessarily a representative sample of all hijacked #MeToo Tweets. From the 1370 collected Tweets, we randomly sample 100 for test set and use the rest for training and validation.

For non-hijacked Tweets, we collect 500 #MeToo Tweets from each month between October 2017, when the online #MeToo movement started, and November 2019. We remove retweets and replies, for a total of 12,892 Tweets. Since non-hijacked Tweets are much more common than hijacked Tweets, we expect most of this collection to be genuine #MeToo Tweets that capture the hashtag's use over the course of its lifespan. We randomly sample 1500 and 100 of these Tweets, evenly distributed over the 25 months, merge them with the potentially hijacked Tweets described above, and remove any duplicates, for a seed set of 2770 #MeToo Tweets for training and validation and 200 Tweets for testing; we expect roughly half of these seed Tweets to be hijacked.

3.2 Data Annotation

We use crowdsourcing on Amazon Mechanical Turk (AMT) to label our collected Tweets. #metoo was a popular tag before the movement and had a different meaning, but since the #MeToo movement has had such a large impact on popular culture, we assume in this work that anyone using the #MeToo hashtag after October 2017 would be aware of its new meaning. We consider anything related to the #MeToo, including criticism, to be non-hijacked; we ask workers to label Tweets as "related" (not hijacked) if they are relevant to the #MeToo movement, "unrelated" (hijacked) if they are irrelevant to #MeToo, or "hard to tell" if it is difficult to decide; details of the task are in Appendix A.

For each Tweet, we obtain labels from 7 AMT workers and take the majority vote among them; we break ties by randomly selecting one worker as the tie breaker. Ties happen when there are equal numbers of 'valid' and 'hijacked' votes, eg. 3 'hijacked,' 3 'valid,' and 1 'hard to tell.' Table 2 shows statistics for the distribution of data over the three labels, hijacked, non-hijacked (which we henceforth call *valid* for clarity), and hard to tell, as well as the inter-annotator agreement on the task.

3.3 Noisy Labels

On examining the AMT statistics in Table 2, we find that interannotator agreement is low: Fleiss's κ of 0.212 and 0.168 on the training and test sets, respectively. One possible cause for low agreement is that our AMT task asks workers to read and judge a single Tweet. Because the task takes very little time to do, workers may be tempted to answer randomly, without putting much effort into the task.

Category	Hashtags
TFB	#TFB, #TeamFollowBack, #FollowGain
Food	#food, #foodporn
Follow	#follow4follow, #followforfollow, #likeforlike, #like4like
Apple	#apple, #iphone
IPad	#ipad, #ipadgames
Game	#PS4live, #Gamer, #Gaming, #games, #GameNight, #VideoGames

Table 1: Spammy hashtags for collecting hijacked Tweets.

Dataset	Total	Valid	Hijacked	Hard to Tell	Agreement
AMT Training	2770	1867	830	73	0.212
Snorkel Training	2770	1603	1158	9	-
AMT Test	200	144	51	5	0.168
Expert Test	200	104	85	11	0.389
Expert Validation	200	117	74	9	0.450
Expert Live Samples	380	212	149	19	0.340

Table 2: Data annotation statistics. AMT Training and Test are produced by seven workers on Amazon Mechanical Turk. Snorkel Training is the final training data that we use to train our model; Expert Test, Validation, and Live Samples are produced using two expert annotators (Section 3.3). The Agreement column shows Fleiss's κ for AMT and Cohen's κ for Expert.

To address the issue of low agreement and questionable annotator trustworthiness, we turn to expert annotations. We train six expert annotators, graduate students from our university's computer science department. For the relatively small test and validation sets, we relabel the entire set using these expert annotators. We assign two annotators to each Tweet; for ties, we ask a third annotator to label the Tweet and break the tie. As shown in Table 2, the expert annotators achieve higher inter-annotator agreement, and the relabeled test set is more balanced between *hijacked* and *valid.*

As the training set is much larger, using expert annotators to label the whole dataset would be time-consuming and expensive. Therefore, we need an approach to reduce the noise or lessen its effect on the existing AMT-labeled data, rather than re-annotating it entirely. We use Snorkel (Ratner et al., 2017), a framework for building and managing training datasets. The Snorkel framework takes user-defined labeling functions, learns weights for each of these functions, and generates the final label using a weighted vote among the functions. We use three different types of labeling functions: a keyword-based function, a model-based function, and crowdworker-based functions.

- **Keyword-based.** Labels Tweets containing any hashtag from Table 1 as *hijacked.*
- **Model-based.** We use feature-based submodular optimization Wei et al. (2014) to choose a subset of 200 Tweets that we annotate using the expert annotators and use to train a logistic regression model. The general form of a feature-based submodular function is

$$f(X) = \sum_{d=1}^{D} \phi\left(\sum_{i=1}^{N} X_{i,d}\right)$$

where f is an objective function that uses the concave submodular function ϕ and is operating on a data subset X that has N examples and D feature dimensions. Maximizing f encourages diversity and coverage of the features within the chosen subset.

We assign one feature for each AMT worker and use the Apricot submodular data selection framework (Schreiber et al., 2019) to solve. Tweet selection is greedy: in each iteration, we choose the Tweet with the most gain. After selecting 200 Tweets, we achieve full coverage of the entire feature space, and these 200 Tweets form the validation set, which we label with the expert annotators and use to train a logistic regression model. The features are the worker IDs of the AMT workers, and the model learns weights for each worker based on how well they agree with the experts.

- **Crowdworker-based.** We consider each AMT worker as a single labeling function that returns the label submitted by that worker for a given Tweet, or abstains if that worker did not submit a label for that Tweet.

From Table 2, we see that the Snorkel method increases the number of *hijacked* Tweets in the training set, balancing it similarly to how the expert annotations balanced the test set.

4 Methodology

To detect hashtag hijacking, we present a weakly-supervised, continuously updating approach inspired by the work of Sedhai and Sun (2018) for detecting Twitter spam. The system consists of two alternating components, a Tweet hijacking classification module and an update module. Our hijacking classification module is an ensemble of classifiers initially fit to our seed training set of 2770 Snorkel-labeled #MeToo Tweets. As new #MeToo Tweets are posted, we collect them using the Twitter streaming API, label them using the classification module, and re-fit the classifiers in the update module. We describe the two modules in detail in the rest of this section.

4.1 Hijacked Tweet Classification Module

The ensemble consists of five classifiers, each of which assigns a score between 0 (*valid*) and 1 (*hijacked*); the final predicted label is a weighted sum of these scores. We consider any Tweet with score greater than 0.8 to be *confidently* hijacked and any Tweet with score less than 0.3 to be *confidently* valid; these thresholds were tuned to maximize performance on the expert-labeled validation set.

4.1.1 Known Users Classifier

This classifier keeps two lists of users: a *blacklist* of known hijackers and a *whitelist* of trusted users. If a user has posted many hijacked Tweets, it is likely that they will do so again in the future; if a user has posted many genuine #MeToo Tweets, they are likely to continue doing so.

We use the same blacklist and whitelist definitions as Sedhai and Sun (2018): the blacklist consists of known hijackers who have posted more than 5 *hijacked* Tweets; the whitelist consists of trusted users who have never posted a hijacked Tweet and have posted at least eight *valid* Tweets. The lists are initially populated using our seed training set.

If a Tweet is posted by a user on the known hijackers blacklist, this classifier returns 1 (*hijacked*). It returns 0 (*valid*) if the user is on the trusted users whitelist and the Tweet does not contain any words from a hijacked word list; this condition prevents adversarial attacks by spammers who pretend to be legitimate users at first and post hijacked Tweets after achieving a spot on the whitelist (Yang et al., 2013). Finally, if a user is on neither blacklist nor whitelist, the classifier returns 0.5.

To generate the hijacked word list, we maintain two dictionaries: a hijacked dictionary and valid dictionary, where we store the counts of how often each word appears in hijacked and valid Tweets in our training data. We set a cutoff on the number of unique Tweets in which a word needs to appear to be included in these dictionaries: 5 and 8 for hijacked and valid, respectively. For each word w, we estimate the probability of w appearing in *hijacked* and *valid* Tweets:

$$C^b_{\text{hijack}}(w) = \text{count}^b_{\text{hijack}}(w) + \gamma C^{b-1}_{\text{hijack}}(w)$$
$$C^b_{\text{valid}}(w) = \text{count}^b_{\text{valid}}(w) + \gamma C^{b-1}_{\text{valid}}(w)$$

$$p^b_h(w) = \frac{C^b_{\text{hijack}}(w)}{C^b_{\text{hijack}}(w) + C^b_{\text{valid}}(w)}$$
$$p^b_v(w) = \frac{C^b_{\text{valid}}(w)}{C^b_{\text{hijack}}(w) + C^b_{\text{valid}}(w)}$$

$\gamma \in [0, 1]$ is a decay term that comes into effect during the batch update stage of our system (Section 4.2). When updating the hijacked word list for batch b, decay is applied to the accumulated counts C from batch $b-1$. If $p^b_h(w) > p^b_v(w)$, we add w to the hijacked word list; if $p^b_h(w) <= p^b_v(w)$, we remove w from the list, if necessary.

One concern that may arise with this classifier is that a user might be put on the blacklist and not be able to get off, even if their posting behavior changes later. While we did not find many examples of users so affected in our experiments, this issue could be addressed by adding some criteria for users to get off the blacklist. For example, if blacklisted user posts more than a certain number of Tweets that are classified as *valid* by the ensemble, they should be removed from the blacklist.

4.1.2 Tweet Text Classifier

This classifier uses TF-IDF features from the Tweet text. As a prepossessing step, we remove punctuation, URLs, emojis, and stop words, and we lowercase and lemmatize the remaining words. We also replace some of the most commonly used abbreviations with full phrases (for example, replacing "ASAP" with "as soon as possible"). After preprocessing, we convert each Tweet into a vector of TF-IDF scores and fit a logistic regression model to label them. This is the only classifier in our ensemble that focuses on the Tweet text itself.

4.1.3 Social Classifier

This classifier focuses on how a Tweet and its user interact with other Tweets and users. We train a random forest model using features based on the Twitter spam analysis of Sedhai and Sun (2017):

- Number of users who follow the posting user.
- Number of users that the posting user follows.
- Whether or not the posting user is verified.
- Number of times the Tweet is retweeted.
- Number of times the Tweet is liked.
- Number of hashtags used in the Tweet.

This classifier uses the number of retweets and likes, which can vary greatly depending on how recently a Tweet was posted; a very new Tweet will have substantially lower values than the older Tweets in the seed training dataset. To address this issue, the number of likes and retweets are fetched again each time the update module runs.

4.1.4 User Profile Classifier

Sedhai and Sun (2017) argue that legitimate users are more likely to provide Twitter profile descriptions than spammers. Further, we hypothesize that, if a user is an active member of a hashtag activism movement, his or her profile description is more likely to be related to the movement. The user profile classifier labels Tweets that are posted by users with non-empty profile descriptions using a simple bag-of-words logistic regression model; for users without a profile description, this classifier simply labels the Tweet as *hijacked*.

4.1.5 Ensemble Voting

If a Tweet is labeled by the known users classifier, we consider it to be *confidently* labeled. Otherwise, we label it with the remaining classifiers, experimenting with three voting strategies:

- **Simple Average** returns the label corresponding to the average of the classifiers' scores.
- **Majority Vote** converts each classifier score into a binary label, *hijacked* or *valid*, and returns the majority label.
- **Stacking Meta-Learner** uses a gradient boosting meta-learner to weight the classifiers. If the weighted score is greater that 0.5, the Tweet is *hijacked*, and *valid* otherwise.

4.2 Batch Update Module

Since hijackers may adapt their strategies over time to fool the hijacking classification module, our system must adapt over time to correctly detect new hijacking cases. In the batch update module, we first select *confident* labels from among the system's predictions since the last batch update and add them to the training data. We then update the known users lists and retrain the Tweet text, social, and user profile classifiers, as well as the Stacking Meta-Learner. In the experiments below, we compare different sampling strategies for adding Tweets to the training data:

- **No Update** does not perform any updates and continues to use the seed-trained model.
- **Update All** adds all *confidently* labeled Tweets from the previous batch.
- **Update Equal** preserves class balance in the training set. If there are n *hijacked* and m *valid* Tweets, this strategy adds $\min(n, m)$ of each, selecting the most confident labels (ie. closer to 1 or 0) first.

5 Seed Model Results and Analysis

We report the results of our initial seed-trained model on the Expert Test set. While there aren't existing systems (Section 2) that are directly comparable with our framework, we use the closest, Jain et al. (2015), as a baseline; Van Dam and Tan (2016) focused on predicting whether a given trending hashtag was being hijacked, rather than detecting individual hijacked Tweets, and Virnami et al. (2017) required much larger amounts of hand-labeled training data than we have available, as well as non-generalizable domain knowledge, like dictionaries of related hashtags and URLs.

Jain et al. detected hijacking for general hashtags using an unsupervised approach. They used

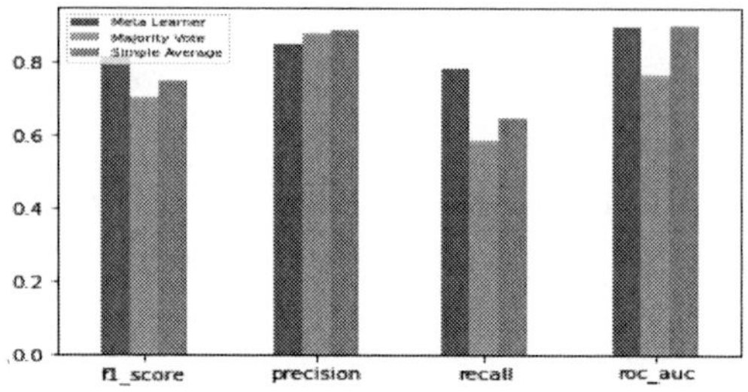

Figure 3: Comparison of ensemble voting strategies.

TF-IDF scores to create a dictionary of common words for each category of related hashtags, arguing that since hijacked Tweets are rare, they can be identified as having fewer words in common with their category. To use Jain et al.'s approach as a baseline, we use all 14,262 #MeToo Tweets that we collected, which we treat as a single category, and we collect an additional 500 Tweets for each month between October 2017 and November 2019 from each of Jain et al.'s categories (Table 3), totaling 13,000 Tweets per category.

We compare the performance of our seed-trained model with Jain et al. (2015), as well as random, majority, and minority baselines in Table 4. For the Stacking Meta-Learner, we report average scores across 100 runs. We see that our framework beats all baselines on all scores. The Stacking Meta-Learner outperforms each individual classifier on recall, while preserving relatively high precision, showing the importance of taking into account different aspects of a Tweet. Although the Tweet text classifier alone works well, the other classifiers boost the ensemble's performance on all metrics except precision, where it scores slightly lower. The Jain et al. baseline performs exactly the same as the minority baseline, labeling all Tweets as *hijacked*. This is likely due to hashtag activism Tweets using a more diverse vocabulary than general trending hashtags, resulting in Jain et al.'s TF-IDF dictionaries being less reliable for the #MeToo tweets.

5.1 Ensemble Voting Strategies

Figure 3 shows the performance of the three voting strategies using ROC-AUC score, precision, recall and F-measure as evaluation metrics. Both Simple Average and Stacking outperform Majority Vote. Simple Average and Stacking are very close, but we use Stacking in the rest of our experiments because it can adapt to changes in classifier performance over time by re-fitting the meta-learner at each batch update (Section 6).

5.2 Challenging Tweets

Figure 4 shows some Tweets that demonstrate why hijacking can be difficult to identify, even for human judges. Figure 4a could be considered spam, since they are promoting a product, but the product is related to #MeToo. Is "#MeToo merch" relevant to the social movement, or just taking advantage of it? This Tweet was labeled "hard to tell" by our expert annotators and omitted from the training set.

Figure 4b is an example of non-spam hijacking. This Tweet is about a different social movement targeting hunger in Sudan, and it hijacks several hashtags, including #MeToo. The Tweet uses language similar to that of social movement Tweets in general and was labeled *valid* by our system.

Figure 4c shows a joke Tweet from a user that exclusively posts off-color jokes and was added to the known hijackers blacklist during seed set training. However, this particular Tweet is arguably related to #MeToo, showing that even blacklisted users can occasionally post non-hijacked Tweets.

Finally, Figure 4d quotes a #MeToo-related Tweet, illustrating why we filter out Tweets that are replies to other Tweets. While this Tweet was correctly labeled as *valid* by our system, it would be impossible to tell that it is relevant without the quoted content; if it had been a reply instead of a quote, the required context would be missing.

6 Batch Update Results and Analysis

To evaluate how our framework performs over time, we collect all #MeToo Tweets posted from Februrary to May 2020, totaling 122,792 *Live* Tweets, and use the batch update module to update the system every 24 hours: we use the previous model to label all Tweets posted in the next 24-hour window, update the training set with any new *confidently* labeled Tweets, and retrain the model. For evaluation, we sample 120 Live Tweets from each month[2], evenly split between predicted *hijacked* and predicted *valid* Tweets, and we use our expert annotators to obtain gold labels (Table 2).

Table 5 shows the performance of our ensemble using two different voting strategies, Stacking Meta-Learner and Simple Average, as well as the Tweet text classifier alone. We see that while the seed-trained Stacking Meta-Learner (top section)

[2]We sample only 20 Tweets from April, as some days are missing due to an interruption in our collection script.

Category	Hashtags
Technology	#Android, #Apple, #Smartphone,#ios,#dell
Entertainment	#CSKvsMI, #Filmfare ,#MissWorld,#Maroon5,#Justin
Politics	#namo, #congress, #AAP, #BJP,# namobirthday
Brands	#puma, #adidas,#Samsung,#Lakme
Others	#happy, #Birthday, #Rain, #Sunny, #KillMe

Table 3: Hashtag categories used in the Jain et al. (2015).

Model	ROC-AUC	Precision	Recall	F-measure
Known User Classifier-BL	0.562	0.812	0.153	0.257
Known User Classifier-WL	0.519	**1.000**	0.038	0.074
Text Classifier	0.839	0.858	0.782	**0.818**
Social Classifiers	0.722	0.769	0.588	0.667
User Profile Classifier	0.666	0.760	0.447	0.563
Stacking Meta-Learner	**0.896**	0.847	0.784	0.814
Jain et al.	0.500	0.450	1.000	0.620
Random Baseline	0.514	0.463	0.518	0.489
Majority Baseline	0.500	0.000	0.000	0.000
Minority Baseline	0.500	0.450	**1.000**	0.620

Table 4: Experimental results for the seed-trained models. The top section shows the performance of individual classifiers, the middle shows the ensemble using the Stacking Meta-Learner, and the bottom shows baselines.

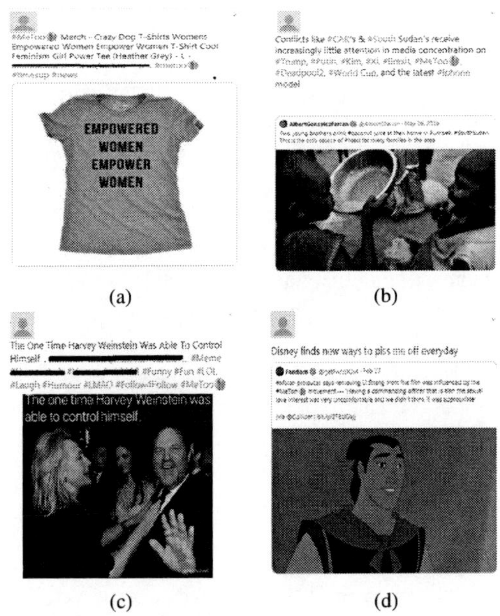

Figure 4: Examples of challenging Tweets. Coarse language used in Tweet (c) is omitted.

and Simple Average (middle section) perform similarly on the Expert Test set (Figure 3), the updated Stacking Meta-Learner significantly outperforms updated Simple Average on the Expert Live Sample set. The bootstrapping approach used by the batch update module risks adding incorrect, noisy labels to the training set; the Stacking Meta-Learner has the advantage of being able to lower the weights of classifiers badly affected by such noise.

The seed-trained Tweet text classifier performs similarly to the seed Stacking Meta-Learner ensemble (Table 4). However, with the No Update strategy, the Tweet text classifier loses about 0.16 F-measure on the Expert Live Samples set compared to on the Expert Test set, while the Stacking Meta-Learner ensemble loses less than 0.1 F-measure, suggesting that the lexical features of the Tweet text classifier are more strongly affected by changes over time, while the other classifiers in the ensemble help mitigate this effect.

The Update All strategy also affects the Tweet text classifier much worse than it does the Stacking Meta-Learner. The seed training set is constructed to be balanced between *hijacked* and *valid* Tweets. However, *hijacked* Tweets are much rarer than *valid* Tweets "in the wild," and as the batch update module adds new Tweets to the training data, the *valid* Tweets quickly outnumber the *hijacked* Tweets. With this unbalanced training set, the Update All strategy results in very high precision and abysmally low recall for the Tweet text classifier. Again, the Stacking Meta-Learner ensemble is more robust; while its performance using the Update All strategy is worse than with No Update or Update Equal, it is not affected as strongly; it is able to lower the weights of classifiers, like Tweet text, that become less reliable as the training data grows imbalanced. Overall, the Update Equal

Model	ROC-AUC	Precision	Recall	F-measure
Stacking Meta-Learner with No Update	**0.764**	0.767	0.675	0.718
Stacking Meta-Learner with Update All	0.664	0.589	0.656	0.621
Stacking Meta-Learner with Update Equal	0.751	0.658	**0.801**	**0.722**
Simple Average with No Update	0.673	0.732	0.470	0.573
Simple Average with Update All	0.621	0.750	0.318	0.447
Simple Average with Update Equal	0.723	0.629	0.775	0.694
Text Classifier with No Update	0.727	0.806	0.550	0.654
Text Classifier with Update All	0.638	**0.885**	0.305	0.453
Text Classifier with Update Equal	0.759	0.856	0.589	0.698

Table 5: Experimental results using three different update strategies. The top section shows the performance of the ensemble using the Stacking Meta-Learner, the middle shows the ensemble using Simple Average voting, and the bottom section shows the Tweet text classifier trained alone, without the other classifiers.

strategy performs the best, adding an equal number of *hijacked* and *valid* Tweets at each batch update to preserve class balance in the training set.

Figure 5 shows Tweets that are labeled correctly by our Live Update system, but incorrectly by the seed-trained system. Figure 5a is correctly labeled as *hijacked* after Live Updates, while the seed system is mislead by the political hashtags. Figure 5b is correctly labeled as *valid* by the Live Update system, while the seed system labels it as *hijacked*, likely because of hashtags referring to actor Johnny Depp, coupled with the word "media."

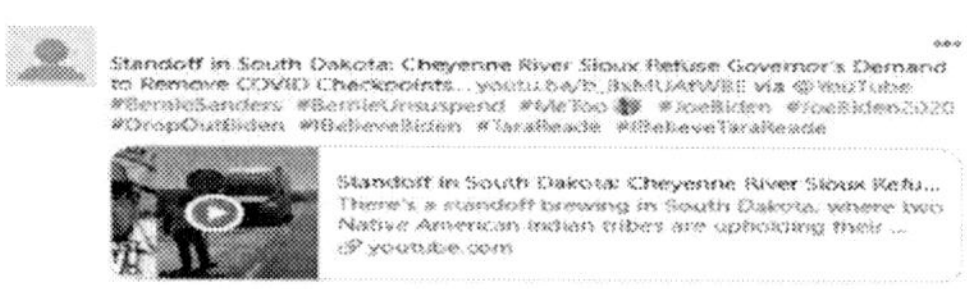

(a)

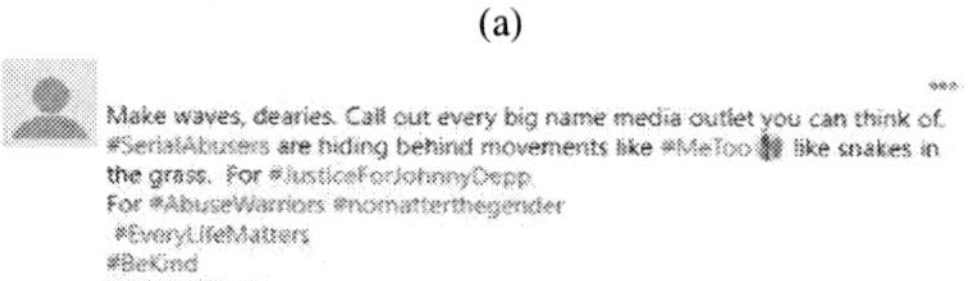

(b)

Figure 5: Examples of Tweets labeled correctly by our Live Update system but not by the seed systems.

7 Conclusion

We have presented a weakly-supervised, bootstrapping framework to detect Tweet-level hashtag hijacking targeting social movements, using a combination of features based on the Tweet text, user profile, and other Tweet properties. We focus on the #MeToo movement, but our methodology can be applied to any movement or hashtag. Our approach is not limited to specific contexts and takes into account the changing characteristics of hashtag use over time. To best of our knowledge, this is the first time that a semi-supervised method is used to detect hashtag hijacking at the Tweet level.

Avenues for future work include addressing the class imbalance and error propagation that results in lower system performance over time, as well as exploring other types of classifiers. A potential solution to the error propagation problem may be to use active learning to obtain human-labeled samples at regular intervals to regulate our system. To reduce the expense of such annotation, submodular data subset selection can again be used to choose the most informative examples to label. Additional classifiers, such as one that scrapes linked webpages, or one that handles embedded images, could boost the overall performance of the ensemble.

We hope that this work encourages others to address the task of detecting Tweet-level hashtag hijacking and to develop other weakly-supervised approaches for Twitter data.

References

Leticia Bode, Alexander Hanna, JungHwan Yang, and Dhavan Shah. 2015. Candidate networks, citizen clusters, and political expression: Strategic hashtag use in the 2010 midterms. *The ANNALS of the American Academy of Political and Social Science*, 659:149–165.

Philipp Darius and Fabian Stephany. 2019. Twitter "hashjacked": Online polarisation strategies of germany's political far-right.

Marco Deseriis. 2017. Hacktivism: On the use of botnets in cyberattacks. *Theory, Culture & Society*, 34(4):131–152.

Hongyu Gao, Yan Chen, Kathy Lee, Diana Palsetia, and Alok N Choudhary. 2012. Towards online spam filtering in social networks. In *NDSS*, volume 12, pages 1–16.

N. Hampson. 2012. Hacktivism: A new breed of protest in a networked world. *Boston College international and comparative law review*, 35:511.

Xia Hu, Jiliang Tang, and Huan Liu. 2014. Online social spammer detection. In *Proceedings of the AAAI Conference on Artificial Intelligence*, volume 28.

Xia Hu, Jiliang Tang, Yanchao Zhang, and Huan Liu. 2013. Social spammer detection in microblogging. In *Twenty-third international joint conference on artificial intelligence*. Citeseer.

Nikita Jain, Pooja Agarwal, and Juhi Pruthi. 2015. Hashjacker — detection and analysis of hashtag hijacking on twitter. *International journal of computer applications*, 114(19).

Jan Kalbitzer, Thomas Mell, Felix Bermpohl, Michael Rapp, and Andreas Heinz. 2014. Twitter psychosis a rare variation or a distinct syndrome? *The Journal of nervous and mental disease*, 202:623.

Kyumin Lee, James Caverlee, and Steve Webb. 2010. Uncovering social spammers: social honeypots+ machine learning. In *Proceedings of the 33rd international ACM SIGIR conference on Research and development in information retrieval*, pages 435–442.

Simon Lindgren. 2019. Movement mobilization in the age of hashtag activism: Examining the challenge of noise, hate, and disengagement in the #metoo campaign. *Policy & Internet*, 11(4):418–438.

Alexander Ratner, Stephen H. Bach, Henry Ehrenberg, Jason Fries, Sen Wu, and Christopher Ré. 2017. Snorkel. *Proceedings of the VLDB Endowment*, 11(3):269–282.

Jacob Schreiber, Jeffrey Bilmes, and William Stafford Noble. 2019. apricot: Submodular selection for data summarization in python.

S. Sedhai and A. Sun. 2018. Semi-supervised spam detection in twitter stream. *IEEE Transactions on Computational Social Systems*, 5(1):169–175.

Surendra Sedhai and Aixin Sun. 2017. An analysis of 14 million tweets on hashtag-oriented spamming*. *J. Assoc. Inf. Sci. Technol.*, 68(7):1638–1651.

Rukundo Solomon. 2017. Electronic protests: Hacktivism as a form of protest in uganda. *Computer Law Security Review*, 33(5):718–728.

Paul A. Taylor. 2005. From hackers to hacktivists: speed bumps on the global superhighway? *New Media & Society*, 7(5):625–646.

Courtland VanDam and Pang-Ning Tan. 2016. Detecting hashtag hijacking from twitter. In *Proceedings of the 8th ACM Conference on Web Science*, WebSci '16, pages 370–371, New York, NY, USA. ACM.

Deepali Virmani, Nikita Jain, Ketan Parikh, and Abhishek Srivastava. 2017. Hashminer: Feature characterisation and analysis of hashtag hijacking using real-time neural network. *Procedia Computer Science*, 115:786 – 793. 7th International Conference on Advances in Computing Communications, ICACC-2017, 22-24 August 2017, Cochin, India.

Alex Hai Wang. 2010. Don't follow me: Spam detection in twitter. In *2010 International Conference on Security and Cryptography (SECRYPT)*, pages 1–10.

Kai Wei, Yuzong Liu, Katrin Kirchhoff, Chris Bartels, and Jeff Bilmes. 2014. Submodular subset selection for large-scale speech training data. pages 3311–3315.

C. Yang, R. Harkreader, and G. Gu. 2013. Empirical evaluation and new design for fighting evolving twitter spammers. *IEEE Transactions on Information Forensics and Security*, 8(8):1280–1293.

Guobin Yang. 2016. Narrative agency in hashtag activism: The case of# blacklivesmatter. *Media and Communication*, 4(4):13.

Sarita Yardi, Daniel Romero, Grant Schoenebeck, and Danah Boyd. 2010. Detecting spam in a twitter network. *First Monday*, 15.

A Mechanical Turk Interface and Instructions

Figure 6 shows screenshots of the instructions and interface for the Human Intelligence Task we use to label the seed training set.

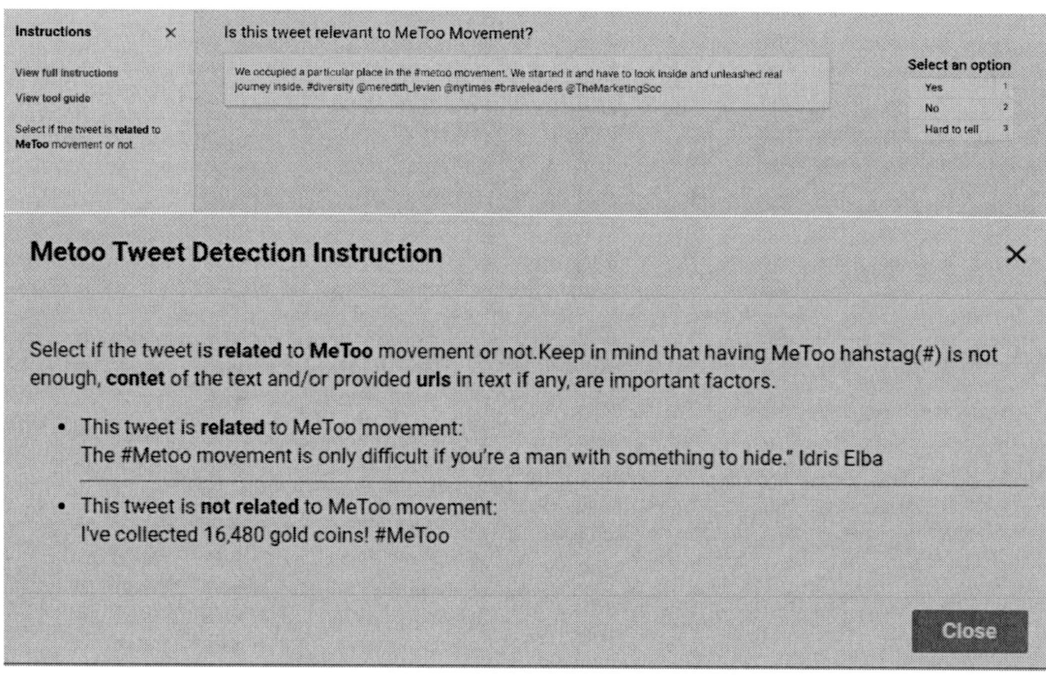

Figure 6: Our AMT task interface and instructions.

NLP for Consumer Protection: Battling Illegal Clauses in German Terms and Conditions in Online Shopping

Daniel Braun
Technical University of Munich
Department of Informatics
daniel.braun@tum.de

Florian Matthes
Technical University of Munich
Department of Informatics
matthes@tum.de

Abstract

Online shopping is an ever more important part of the global consumer economy, not just in times of a pandemic. When we place an order online as consumers, we regularly agree to the so-called "Terms and Conditions" (T&C), a contract unilaterally drafted by the seller. Often, consumers do not read these contracts and unwittingly agree to unfavourable and often void terms. Government and non-government organisations (NGOs) for consumer protection battle such terms on behalf of consumers, who often hesitate to take on legal actions themselves. However, the growing number of online shops and a lack of funding makes it increasingly difficult for such organisations to monitor the market effectively. This paper describes how Natural Language Processing (NLP) can be applied to support consumer advocates in their efforts to protect consumers. Together with two NGOs from Germany, we developed an NLP-based application that legally assesses clauses in T&C from German online shops under the European Union's (EU) jurisdiction. We report that we could achieve an accuracy of 0.9 in the detection of void clauses by fine-tuning a pre-trained German BERT model. The approach is currently used by two NGOs and has already helped to challenge void clauses in T&C.

1 Introduction

NLP, and technology more broadly, has improved the access to knowledge in many domains. It is no longer necessary to pay thousands of dollars for a lexicon like the Encyclopædia Britannica or to hire a translator to understand texts in other languages. The legal domain is arguably one of the biggest resistance to digitisation efforts. While, in some aspects, it still struggles to catch up with other industries, technology has started to change the landscape of legal service provision. So far, consumers rarely benefit from this development. On the contrary, mostly big companies and law firms benefit. Most of the existing so-called "LegalTech" tools, like Lexis Advance[1], Lexical Labs[2], and ANVI [3], to name just a few, are tailored to the needs of companies and law firms, rather than consumers and consumer protection agencies. Thereby, LegalTech tools are not only missing the opportunity to democratise access to legal advice, by making it more affordable and available, they are actively increasing the current imbalance of power between companies and consumers.

In this paper, we describe, how we apply NLP technology to automatically assess clauses in German T&C from consumer online shops, to find void clauses and help to protect consumers from them. Unlike the, relatively little, existing work (see Section 2), we focus on organisations that represent consumer interests as users. By focusing on such organisations, rather than individual consumers, we hope to be able to increase the impact of our work. While tools for individual consumers usually only benefit those who are using them, consumer protection agencies legally challenge void T&C they find, forcing their change and hence benefiting all consumers. We also believe that the task of ensuring that companies adhere to consumer contract and distance selling laws should not be left to consumers alone.

2 Related Work

As mentioned before, the existing research in the area of the legal analysis of T&C focuses on individual consumers as users.

The project "Terms of Service; Didn't Read" (ToS;DR) from Binns and Matthews (2014) uses

[1] https://www.lexisnexis.com/en-us/products/lexis-advance.page
[2] https://www.lexicallabs.com/
[3] https://anvilegal.com/

Proceedings of the 1st Workshop on NLP for Positive Impact, pages 93–99
Bangkok, Thailand (online), August 5, 2021.

crowd-sourcing to provide manually generated summarisations of the ToS from many major online platforms, like Facebook and Twitter. However, the fact that ToS;DR is crowd-sourced affects the scalability and topicality of the project.

The SaToS project (Software-aided analysis of Terms of Services) (Braun et al., 2017, 2018, 2019a,b) automatically summarise and assess T&C for consumers using dependency parsing and other rule-based approaches, however, only covering a few selected aspects of T&C.

CLAUDETTE is a project at the European University Institute (Micklitz et al., 2017; Lippi et al., 2017; Contissa et al., 2018b,a; Lippi et al., 2019b,a,c; Liepina et al., 2019) which focuses on the detection of unfair clauses in terms of the legislation of the EU. Originally focused on Terms of Services from tech giants like Netflix, Google, Microsoft, and Snapchat, CLAUDETTE now mainly focuses on the analysis of privacy policies.

Since the introduction of the General Data Protection Regulation (GDPR) in the EU, the interest in the analysis of privacy policies has increased in general (see e.g. Harkous et al. (2018) and Torre et al. (2020)).

3 The Role of NGOs in Consumer Protection

The folk wisdom that being right does not automatically lead to getting justice is specifically true for the area of consumer protection, where there is regularly a strong imbalance of power between the involved parties, a single consumer on one side and a potentially large corporation on the other side. In acknowledgement of this fact, many legislators have given NGOs in the area of consumer protection special and extensive rights to assist and represent consumers and their interests. At the same time, consumer advocates and consumer protection agencies are chronically underfunded in many countries. With their limited financial means, consumer advocates all over Europe struggle to keep up with the demand generated by the increasing importance of digital offerings. In 2018, the consumer protection agencies in Germany received in total 184,579 complaints from consumers. 65,370 of these complaints (more than 35%) were related to digital offerings. In comparison, only 36,945 complaints (20%) were received about products and services from the financial industry (Verbraucherzentrale Bundesverband e.V., 2019). In addition to providing individual counselling to consumers, consumer advocates increasingly try to monitor (digital) markets proactively and react to negative developments before consumers are harmed. Monitoring markets as big as eCommerce and proactively act against void clauses in standard form contracts is, at scale, simply not possible without automation of the underlying processes.

For the work presented in this paper, we collaborated with two consumer protection NGOs from two different German states, which are mainly funded by the government and enjoy special privileges when it comes to taking legal actions on behalf of consumers. We worked with five legal experts from these organisations over a period of three years, from 2017 to 2020.

4 Data Corpus

Building a corpus for the automated legal assessment of T&C is far from trivial. On the one hand, we want to have a realistic distribution of clauses in our corpus, with regard to their legality and topics, on the other hand, we need a sufficient number of void clauses in order to be able to train statistical classification models. If we would only use complete T&C, we would need thousands of contracts to find a sufficient number of void clauses.

4.1 Sources

We, therefore, decided to combine three approaches for gathering data:

- We took 78 clauses from a database that is maintained by the organisations we collaborated with. This database contains clauses that have been successfully challenged legally by the organisations and are therefore void.
- We randomly selected 24 complete T&C from the corpus provided by Braun and Matthes (2020), which together consist of 968 clauses.
- The experts actively searched on the internet for clauses about topics they identified as specifically relevant for their everyday work and also specifically for void clauses from these topics. Additional 140 clauses were collected in this way.

Overall, the corpus consists of 1,186 clauses. On average, a clause in our corpus consists of more than 55 words.

Since contracts, under German law, are protected by copyright, we are not allowed to publish the corpus. However, it can be shared on request for non-commercial, scientific purposes.

4.2 Annotation

The 78 clauses which were extracted from the existing database were not manually labelled, because they already have been classified as void by successful legal proceedings.

For all other clauses in the corpus, we had each clause labelled independently by two experts with (potentially) "void" or "valid". Generally speaking, a contract clause is void, if it contains a regulation that violates the law. The final decision of whether a clause is void or not, can, therefore, only be made by a court of law. However, given their expertise and experience in consumer protection law, the experts we worked with can make reasonable assumptions about whether or not a given clause could be ruled to be void, based on the law and existing court decisions.

Some German laws governing the drafting of T&C contain very specific regulations. For example, §355 No. 2 of the German civil code (Bürgerliches Gesetzbuch, BGB) states that *"The withdrawal period is 14 days."* All clauses providing less than 14 days of withdrawal period for consumers are therefore void. Other regulations, however, are more vague. §307 No. 1 BGB, for example, states that clauses are void, if *"[...] they unreasonably disadvantage the other party to the contract [...]"*. Such vague terms need to be interpreted, e.g. by court decisions or legal literature. Therefore, we asked the experts to shortly justify each of their assessment in a commentary and give references to laws or court decisions where appropriate. We then compared the annotations and provided the experts with a list of the conflicting annotations, which they then resolved together by agreeing on one common assessment.

We found the old prejudice of "two lawyers, three opinions" to carry a certain amount of truth. The inter-annotator agreement (before the resolution phase) was between 76% (for the annotation of complete T&C) and 64% (for the annotation of the hand-picked clauses).

4.3 Analysis

Table 1 shows which topics the clauses in the corpus cover and how many clauses for each topic are void. Since a clause can belong to multiple topics, the sum of the counts is larger than the number of clauses. The numbers are also not representative, since the experts actively searched for (void) clauses covering specific topics. The fact that more than 41% of all payment clauses were void, but just about 12% of all delivery clauses, hence, gives no indication about whether payment clauses are generally more likely to be void.

Therefore, we want to focus only on data from T&C that were annotated completely for a moment, because they provide a more realistic picture of the situation. The experts annotated 24 complete T&C. In these 24 T&C, they found 73 void clauses, about three clauses per contract. The contracts consist of 50 clauses per contract on average, which means that about 6% of all clauses are void. The experts were surprised that the ratio of void clauses is that high. They said they never before analysed all aspects of such a large number of T&C and would not have expected to find so many void clauses, and also decided to take actions about some of the clauses they found during the annotation process. So already at this stage, our work had a (small) impact and helped to protect consumers better.

Many void clauses differ only in relatively small aspects from their valid counterparts. A clause about default interest, for example, becomes void if the default interest is set at six percentage points above the base interest rate, instead of five percentage points. The clause *"In the event of a default in payment by the buyer, the seller is entitled to charge interest on the amount outstanding at the rate of six percentage points above the central bank rate at the time payment is due."*, would therefore be void. Such clauses are, linguistically, almost identical. However, there are also a few types of clauses, e.g. defining automatic price increases for subscriptions, that are virtually always void in the data set, independent from the individual phrasing of the clause.

It should be noted that the data in Table 1 only covers clauses that were present and void. In cases of an existing information obligation, the absence of a specific clause might also be unlawful. The fact that the corpus includes 24 T&C, but we found only 18 arbitration clauses imply that at least six companies may not have fulfilled their legal obligation to inform consumers about the EU Online Dispute Resolution (ODR) platform (European Parliament and Council of the European Union, 2013).

Topic	#clauses	#void
minimum age	12	0
applicability	22	1
applicable law	12	1
arbitration	18	1
changes	3	0
conclusion of contract	135	8
delivery	117	14
description	8	0
disposal	8	0
intellectual property	21	0
language	9	1
liability	99	43
party	26	0
payment	305	126
personal data	64	1
place of jurisdiction	11	2
prices	38	9
retention of title	26	4
severability	13	6
text storage	10	0
warranty	43	9
withdrawal	209	26

Table 1: Distribution of clause topics and void clauses in the corpus

5 Approach

The BERT language model (Devlin et al., 2019) has been shown to be effective on a wide range of tasks in the legal domain, including Named Entity Recognition (Chalkidis et al., 2020), annotation of legal concepts (Chalkidis et al., 2020), and evidence retrieval (Soleimani et al., 2020).

Additionally, there is a pre-trained German language model available "bert-base-german-cased" (Chan et al., 2020) that was trained, among other sources, on a large corpus of legal texts. It is trained on cased German texts and, like the original BERT model, has 12 hidden layers with a size of 768, 12 attention heads per attention layer, and 110 million parameters. The model was trained on the German Wikipedia and a web corpus gathered by Suárez et al. (2019), which account for more than 90% of the data the model was trained on. However, the model was also trained on the Open Legal Data set from Ostendorff et al. (2020), which consists of more than 100,000 German court decisions.

6 Evaluation

We used the HuggingFace transformers library (Wolf et al., 2019) to fine-tune the pre-trained language model with our data set on the binary classification task of deciding whether a clause is void or not. We split our corpus into a training (80%) and a test set (20%) and first perform a stratified five-fold cross-validation on the training set to identify the best performing hyper-parameters for the fine-tuning. We started our search with the values suggested in the original BERT paper: batch size 16 or 32, learning rate 5e-5, 3e-5 or 2e-5, and 2, 3 or 4 epochs (Devlin et al., 2019). However, the authors also note that the optimal hyper-parameters are task-specific and that small data sets (which they define as less than 100,000 labels) are more sensitive to the choice of parameters than larger ones, therefore we also tried a smaller batch size (8) and higher numbers of epochs (8, 12, 16, 21). In the end, we found that batch size 16, learning rate 3e-5, and three epochs performed best.

With these hyper-parameters, we evaluated the approach on our test data set, which consists of 237 clauses, of which 192 are valid and 45 are void. BERT performed very well in the classification of void clauses and achieved an accuracy of 0.9, as well as a precision and recall of 0.9.

Out of the 45 void clauses in the test data, only four clauses have falsely not been identified as void (false negatives). Since our approach is meant to be a support tool for experts, all results will be double-checked by a human expert, which makes a high recall desirable.

A deeper analysis of the results showed that, while some types of clauses, as mentioned before, are virtually always void in the data set, others are virtually never. This might have (positively) influenced the classification performance.

7 Ethical and Societal Implications

The goal of this work is to support consumer advocates in order to further consumer protection and address the imbalance of power between corporations and consumers. While these are, by most standards, worthy and ethical goals, just because something is well-intended does not mean it can not have critical or at least ambivalent consequences. In this section, we want to highlight some of the issues that can arise from the research presented in this thesis and the goals it pursues. The laws governing T&C are changing comparably fast. For small companies, without in-house legal counselling, it can therefore be expensive and challenging to keep up with the changing legislation and keep T&C always up to date. In such cases, honest mistakes might be made in drafting and maintaining T&C which do not intend to harm consumers. Nevertheless, such mistakes can make companies vulnerable to cease-and-desist orders from competitors and organisations which specialise in sending out cease-and-desist orders, not in order to protect consumer interests but for personal financial benefit. Therefore, we choose organisations to collaborate with that are dedicated to consumer protection and bound to that aim by their statute and their state given mission. However, it can not be prevented that our research can also be used by less well-intended actors. While this poses a potential threat, it can also allow companies on the other side to use our results in the same way on their own T&C and hence make sure they match the rule of law.

A second, arguably more philosophical issue that arises, not just from our research, but from the perspective of consumer-focused LegalTech in general, is whether our legal system is prepared for lowering the bar for accessing the system. The legal and moral standpoint on this issue is quite clear. The charter of fundamental rights of the EU guarantees in article 47 that "everyone whose rights and freedoms guaranteed by the law of the Union are violated has the right to an effective remedy before a tribunal". While the legal situation is clear, it is also clear that there are, in fact, barriers in place which make access to justice harder, whether they are of financial or procedural nature. And while it could be denied that they purposefully do so, it is difficult to deny that these barriers help to keep up the in many countries already stretched legal systems. If we would be able to denounce our neighbours by the click of a button every time they disturb the nighttime, this could not just have implications for the viability of our legal systems but also for the kind of society we live in and how we interact with each other. Concerning our work, we would argue that, if it has any influence on the legal system at all, it is designed to reduce its load. While the number of cease-and-desist orders sent out by consumer advocates might rise, we would hope that subsequently, this would lead to fewer cases brought on by consumers about void clauses in T&C.

Finally, if a system that automatically T&C for their lawfulness would be successful and widely adopted, one of the implications would very likely be that companies could start trying to "gamble" the system. This is a phenomenon that can be observed very well in the area of search engine optimisation (Malaga, 2008) and security (Mansfield-Devine, 2018). This could potentially lead to a situation where such a system would mostly fail to detect clauses that were purposefully drafted in a consumer-aversive way and would potentially be left detecting mostly clauses that are unintentionally void, e.g., by honest mistake, and were never intended to harm consumers. If we can learn anything from search engine optimisation and security, then that there is no easy or permanent fix to such problems. We, therefore, try to build our system in a way that it can be easily adapted, so that consumer advocates can change the system in a way that it will be able to detect such clauses, once they became aware of it, entering an "arms race" with malicious companies. And while "security through obscurity" is generally discouraged, search engine providers have shown that obfuscating the exact criteria helps to stay ahead of attempts to manipulate the ranking of websites. Therefore, our decision to focus on consumer advocates as users, rather than consumers themselves, can also help to mitigate the problem since companies will not be able to directly test different versions of their clauses.

8 Conclusion

In this paper, we have given an example of how NLP can be used to further the goal of consumer protection and address the existing imbalance of power between consumers and companies. We have argued that, in order to support consumers as broadly and effectively as possible, one should not (only) target individual consumers as potential users, but rather target organisations that represent consumers and their interests and have the power and means to pursue legal battles.

Together with experts from consumer protection agencies, we labelled a corpus of more than 1,100 German clauses from T&C from online shops with regard to their lawfulness. We showed that the labelling process already generated an impact on consumer protection, by enabling consumer advocates to send cease-and-desist orders against clauses that were identified as void and by providing new insights to consumer advocates, e.g. about the average share of void clauses in T&C.

We used this corpus to fine-tune a pre-trained BERT model that can identify void clauses in T%C with an accuracy of 0.9.

So far, the project and the developed classifier resulted in ten cease-and-desist orders that were sent to companies using void clauses in their T&C and hence protecting potentially hundreds of consumers. The approach is currently used in a test mode by two NGOs. By further integrating the technology into the existing workflows of consumer protection agencies and building a pipeline to continuously improving the model, based on manual annotations and corrections made by experts, we hope to be able to contribute to the protection of many more consumers in the future.

Acknowledgements

The project is supported by funds of the Federal Ministry of Justice and Consumer Protection (BMJV) based on a decision of the Parliament of the Federal Republic of Germany via the Federal Office for Agriculture and Food (BLE) under the innovation support programme.

References

Reuben Binns and David Matthews. 2014. Community structure for efficient information flow in'tos; dr', a social machine for parsing legalese. In *Proceedings of the 23rd International Conference on World Wide Web*, pages 881–884. ACM.

Daniel Braun and Florian Matthes. 2020. Automatic detection of terms and conditions in german and english online shops. In *Proceedings of the 16th International Conference on Web Information Systems and Technologies - WEBIST,*, pages 233–237. INSTICC, SciTePress.

Daniel Braun, Elena Scepankova, Patrick Holl, and Florian Matthes. 2017. Satos: Assessing and summarising terms of services from german webshops. In *Proceedings of the 10th International Conference on Natural Language Generation*, pages 223–227, Santiago de Compostela, Spain. Association for Computational Linguistics.

Daniel Braun, Elena Scepankova, Patrick Holl, and Florian Matthes. 2018. Customer-centered legaltech: Automated analysis of standard form contracts. In *Tagungsband Internationales Rechtsinformatik Symposium (IRIS) 2018*, pages 627–634. Editions Weblaw.

Daniel Braun, Elena Scepankova, Patrick Holl, and Florian Matthes. 2019a. Consumer protection in the digital era: The potential of customer-centered legaltech. In *INFORMATIK 2019: 50 Jahre Gesellschaft für Informatik – Informatik für Gesellschaft*, pages 407–420, Bonn. Gesellschaft für Informatik e.V.

Daniel Braun, Elena Scepankova, Patrick Holl, and Florian Matthes. 2019b. The potential of customer-centered legaltech. *Datenschutz und Datensicherheit - DuD*, 43(12):760–766.

Ilias Chalkidis, Manos Fergadiotis, Prodromos Malakasiotis, Nikolaos Aletras, and Ion Androutsopoulos. 2020. LEGAL-BERT: The muppets straight out of law school. In *Findings of the Association for Computational Linguistics: EMNLP 2020*, pages 2898–2904, Online. Association for Computational Linguistics.

Branden Chan, Stefan Schweter, and Timo Möller. 2020. German's next language model. *arXiv preprint arXiv:2010.10906*.

Giuseppe Contissa, Koen Docter, Francesca Lagioia, Marco Lippi, Hans-W Micklitz, Przemysław Pałka, Giovanni Sartor, and Paolo Torroni. 2018a. Claudette meets gdpr: Automating the evaluation of privacy policies using artificial intelligence. Technical report, European Consumer Organisation (BEUC).

Giuseppe Contissa, Francesca Lagioia, Marco Lippi, Hans-Wolfgang Micklitz, Przemyslaw Palka, Giovanni Sartor, and Paolo Torroni. 2018b. Towards consumer-empowering artificial intelligence. In *International Joint Conference on Artificial Intelligence*, pages 5150–5157.

Jacob Devlin, Ming-Wei Chang, Kenton Lee, and Kristina Toutanova. 2019. BERT: Pre-training of deep bidirectional transformers for language understanding. In *Proceedings of the 2019 Conference of the North American Chapter of the Association for Computational Linguistics: Human Language Technologies, Volume 1 (Long and Short Papers)*, pages 4171–4186, Minneapolis, Minnesota. Association for Computational Linguistics.

European Parliament and Council of the European Union. 2013. Regulation (eu) no 524/2013 of the european parliament and of the council of 21 may 2013 on online dispute resolution for consumer disputes and amending regulation (ec) no 2006/2004 and directive 2009/22/ec (regulation on consumer odr). `https://eur-lex.europa.eu/legal-content/EN/TXT/?uri=CELEX%3A32013R0524`. Accessed 2020-07-10.

Hamza Harkous, Kassem Fawaz, Rémi Lebret, Florian Schaub, Kang G Shin, and Karl Aberer. 2018. Polisis: Automated analysis and presentation of privacy policies using deep learning. In *27th {USENIX} Security Symposium ({USENIX} Security 18)*, pages 531–548.

Ruta Liepina, Giuseppe Contissa, Kasper Drazewski, Francesca Lagioia, Marco Lippi, Hans-Wolfgang

Micklitz, Przemysław Pałka, Giovanni Sartor, and Paolo Torroni. 2019. Gdpr privacy policies in claudette: Challenges of omission, context and multilingualism. In *Proceedings of the Third Workshop on Automated Semantic Analysis of Information in Legal Texts co-located with the 17th International Conference on Artificial Intelligence and Law (ICAIL 2019)*.

Marco Lippi, Giuseppe Contissa, Francesca Lagioia, Hans-Wolfgang Micklitz, Przemysław Pałka, Giovanni Sartor, and Paolo Torroni. 2019a. Consumer protection requires artificial intelligence. *Nature Machine Intelligence*, 1(4):168–169.

Marco Lippi, Przemyslaw Palka, Giuseppe Contissa, Francesca Lagioia, Hans-Wolfgang Micklitz, Yannis Panagis, Giovanni Sartor, and Paolo Torroni. 2017. Automated detection of unfair clauses in online consumer contracts. In *JURIX*, pages 145–154.

Marco Lippi, Przemysław Pałka, Giuseppe Contissa, Francesca Lagioia, Hans-Wolfgang Micklitz, Giovanni Sartor, and Paolo Torroni. 2019b. Claudette: an automated detector of potentially unfair clauses in online terms of service. *Artificial Intelligence and Law*, 27(2):117–139.

Marco Lippi, Przemysław Pałka, Giuseppe Contissa, Francesca Lagioia, Hans-Wolfgang Micklitz, Giovanni Sartor, and Paolo Torroni. 2019c. Claudette: an automated detector of potentially unfair clauses in online terms of service. *Artificial Intelligence and Law*, 27(2):117–139.

Ross A Malaga. 2008. Worst practices in search engine optimization. *Communications of the ACM*, 51(12):147–150.

Steve Mansfield-Devine. 2018. The malware arms race. *Computer Fraud & Security*, 2018(2):15–20.

Hans-W Micklitz, Przemysław Pałka, and Yannis Panagis. 2017. The empire strikes back: digital control of unfair terms of online services. *Journal of consumer policy*, 40(3):367–388.

Malte Ostendorff, Till Blume, and Saskia Ostendorff. 2020. Towards an open platform for legal information. *arXiv preprint arXiv:2005.13342*.

Amir Soleimani, Christof Monz, and Marcel Worring. 2020. Bert for evidence retrieval and claim verification. In *European Conference on Information Retrieval*, pages 359–366. Springer.

Pedro Javier Ortiz Suárez, Benoît Sagot, and Laurent Romary. 2019. Asynchronous pipeline for processing huge corpora on medium to low resource infrastructures. In *7th Workshop on the Challenges in the Management of Large Corpora (CMLC-7)*. Leibniz-Institut für Deutsche Sprache.

Damiano Torre, Sallam Abualhaija, Mehrdad Sabetzadeh, Lionel Briand, Katrien Baetens, Peter Goes, and Sylvie Forastier. 2020. An ai-assisted approach for checking the completeness of privacy policies against gdpr. In *in Proceedings of the 28th IEEE International Requirements Engineering Conference (RE'20)*.

Verbraucherzentrale Bundesverband e.V. 2019. Jahresbericht 2018. `https://www.vzbv.de/content/bericht-2018`. Accessed 2020-05-04.

Thomas Wolf, Lysandre Debut, Victor Sanh, Julien Chaumond, Clement Delangue, Anthony Moi, Pierric Cistac, Tim Rault, Rémi Louf, Morgan Funtowicz, Joe Davison, Sam Shleifer, Patrick von Platen, Clara Ma, Yacine Jernite, Julien Plu, Canwen Xu, Teven Le Scao, Sylvain Gugger, Mariama Drame, Quentin Lhoest, and Alexander M. Rush. 2019. Huggingface's transformers: State-of-the-art natural language processing. *ArXiv*, abs/1910.03771.

A Research Framework for Understanding Education-Occupation Alignment with NLP Techniques

Renzhe Yu
University of California, Irvine
Irvine, CA, USA
renzhey@uci.edu

Subhro Das
MIT-IBM Watson AI Lab, IBM Research
Cambridge, MA, USA
subhro.das@ibm.com

Sairam Gurajada
IBM Research – Almaden
San Jose, CA, USA
sairam.gurajada@ibm.com

Kush R. Varshney
IBM Research – T. J. Watson Research Center
Yorktown Heights, NY, USA
krvarshn@us.ibm.com

Hari Raghavan
IBM Corporate Social Responsibility
New York, NY, USA
hraghav@us.ibm.com

Carlos X. Lastra-Anadon
IE University
Madrid, Spain
clastra@faculty.ie.edu

Abstract

Understanding the gaps between job requirements and university curricula is crucial for improving student success and institutional effectiveness in higher education. In this context, natural language processing (NLP) can be leveraged to generate granular insights into where the gaps are and how they change. This paper proposes a three-dimensional research framework that combines NLP techniques with economic and educational research to quantify the alignment between course syllabi and job postings. We elaborate on key technical details of the framework and further discuss its potential positive impacts on practice, including unveiling the inequalities in and long-term consequences of education-occupation alignment to inform policymakers, and fostering information systems to support students, institutions and employers in the school-to-work pipeline.

1 Introduction

One important role of higher education is to prepare students for the workforce, but not all college graduates benefit equally from their degrees: more than 40% of recent college graduates are either unemployed or work in jobs not requiring a degree (Federal Reserve Bank of New York, 2020). On the other side of the equation, 45% employers worldwide report having difficulty "finding the right skills or talent" (Manpower Group, 2018). Are there significant gaps between what higher education offers and what employers look for? What are the sources of these gaps? Addressing these questions can bring substantial policy implications and positive societal impacts, such as mitigating inequalities in labor market outcomes across student groups and major areas.

Given that college education is delivered predominantly through structured coursework (Kuh et al., 2007), we assume that curricular content and its correspondence with employers' demand may be an important driver of differences in student outcomes in the labor market. Nonetheless, there has been little consensus on the definition of this correspondence and the understanding of how it contributes to the observed gaps (Cleary et al., 2017). One challenge behind this void is the lack of data that can capture the dynamics of labor market demands and the details of curricular content on a large scale. With the recent availability of digitized records of course content and job requirements as well as advances in computational methods, granular and scalable analysis of the correspondence between the two becomes possible (Börner et al., 2018).

In this paper, we present a novel research framework to measure the alignment between curricular content and labor market demands. We leverage neural network-based language models and other NLP techniques to learn representations of relevant documents. Based on these representations and theoretical insights, we incorporate three lenses through which to measure the alignment: skill overlap (economic), instructional design features (educational), and semantic text similarity (technical). This framework represents the first comprehensive and scalable approach for connecting the content of

Proceedings of the 1st Workshop on NLP for Positive Impact, pages 100–106
Bangkok, Thailand (online), August 5, 2021.

education and workforce, which was either treated as a black box or investigated on a small scale in prior research (Walker, 2020; Hora, 2019). Moreover, the computational capacity of this framework can empower system-wide policy research as well as local practices regarding curricular alignment and workforce preparation, thereby bringing positive societal impacts. For example, university stakeholders can track the downstream consequences of ill-aligned curricula especially for students from marginalized groups.

In Section 2, we briefly summarize prior research related to the technical and substantive aspects of our work. Section 3 details our three-dimensional framework that measures education-occupation alignment. Section 4 envisions the societal benefits of our framework through assisting downstream policy research and field practice of different stakeholders in the school-workforce pipeline. Finally, we conclude with a summary and next steps in Section 5.

2 Related Work

2.1 Natural Language Processing

Recent advances in language models have shown promising results in representing texts for different downstream NLP applications. Pre-trained language models such as GloVe (Pennington et al., 2014), ELMo (Peters et al., 2018), and BERT (Devlin et al., 2019) encode a sentence (or a document) into multi-dimensional vectors (a.k.a. embeddings). More recently, specialized long-text document encoders (Adhikari et al., 2019; Beltagy et al., 2020) have emerged and achieved state-of-the-art performance in benchmark tasks.

Based on these embeddings, one can learn the alignment, or similarity, between different documents with sentence-pair regression models (Reimers and Gurevych, 2019) or twin networks architectures such as Siamese networks (Bromley et al., 1993). Alternatively, document alignment can be evaluated via labels. Each document can be attached to one or multiple pre-defined labels, and two documents align well if they share a decent proportion of labels. Under this formulation, the core task becomes attaching labels which is essentially a text classification problem. In our context, for example, the "labels" that curricular and job content share are skills. Due to the sheer volume of possible skills, this becomes an extreme multi-label classification task (XMC) as recently pointed out by Bhola et al. (2020). In their closely relevant work, BERT models are employed to learn an embedding for a job description and XMC models then classify each embedding into a subset of skills over a large pool of predetermined skills set.

2.2 Content Analysis of Curricula, Jobs, and Their Relationships

Curricular content is key in teaching and learning research, but most prior research is built upon a small sample and/or requires extensive human coding (Hong and Hodge, 2009). In recent years, large-scale computational analyses of digitized curricular documents (e.g., textbooks, syllabi) have emerged to inform both instructors and policymakers (Lucy et al., 2020; Jiang and Pardos, 2020). The majority of these pioneering works employ bag-of-words representations of the documents and there remains abundant scope for deeper dives into intellectual and pedagogical features beyond the surface level.

There is a large literature documenting changes in job market demands in advanced economies. Only until the recent decade real-time data on job vacancies has enabled detailed assessment of the evolving skills required by jobs (Deming and Noray, 2020). For instance, Das et al. (2020) document the increase in the demand for jobs in the fields of big data and artificial intelligence (AI), Fleming et al. (2019) show that high- and low-wage jobs are gaining tasks and earning more.

The microscopic relationship between curricular content and job requirements is a novel topic, although it is essentially built upon the literature on labor market returns to education (Walker, 2020) with the recent availability of big data. To our knowledge, Börner et al. (2018) presented the first study on this relationship, using textual content of syllabi and job postings. Another relevant work examines the interplay between curricular content and academic research in a similar manner (Biasi and Ma, 2021). Our work expands on these attempts and incorporates more disciplinary perspectives to create a holistic research framework.

3 Measuring Education-Occupation Alignment

3.1 Problem Framing

As described in Section 2.2, the textual content of curricular offerings and job requirements have been increasingly available in machine-readable formats in the digital era. In general, different types of curricular documents include information such as subject matter content, learning objectives, instructional design, etc. Job-related documents, on the other hand, commonly describe required skills, responsibilities, qualifications, etc. Our framework is intended to be largely agnostic of specific document types and datasets as long as they include most of the aforementioned information and each document represents an individual course or professional position. In the descriptions below, we use course syllabi and job postings as examples of such documents.

The focus of our framework is measuring education-occupation alignment. Specifically, given a syllabus S_i, we want to learn an alignment metric $align\,(i;j)$ to capture how much it aligns with job posting P_j, and then use this metric to derive macroscopic alignment measures depending on the scope of analysis. Note that the metric is not symmetric and anchored to course syllabi, because educational providers (programs, institutions, etc.) in practice have more motivation and power to accommodate the labor market than the opposite. Building upon the existing literature, our framework incorporates the following three disciplinary dimensions along which to operationalize $align\,(i;j)$.

3.2 Economic Dimension: Skill Overlap

First, we treat skills as the bond between jobs and courses, because economists have highlighted skills as organizing units of the labor market (Acemoglu and Autor, 2011). In this sense, education-occupation alignment can be conceptualized as the extent to which a course syllabus covers skills required by the labor market. Intuitively, we have:

$$align\,(i;j) = \frac{|D_{ij}|}{|D_j|} \tag{1}$$

where $D_{ij} = \{s|s \in S_i, s \in P_j\}$, $D_j = \{s|s \in P_j\}$, and s is a specific skill in a finite skill pool.

Most job documents include expected skills, but curricular documents are not necessarily skill-focused. Therefore, computing Equation (1) translates into the task of predicting skills from the content of syllabi. There can be multiple NLP approaches for this task, and here we present an example inspired by Bhola et al. (2020) who frame skill identification as a multilabel classification problem. Specifically, we describe a BERT-LSTM architecture as illustrated in Figure 1. The lower part of the graph serves to learn document representations. It takes in a curricular or job document, leverages a pretrained BERT (Devlin et al., 2019) to learn a vector representation (`[CLS]` token) for each sentence, and feeds these sentence vectors through an LSTM (Hochreiter and Schmidhuber, 1997) model in sequential order to get the document-level representation (the last hidden state). This two-level stacked architecture is used because BERT is typically used to handle sentence-level tasks and both syllabi and job postings are usually longer than the recommended maximum sequence length. The top part of Figure 1 is a multilabel classifier constructed as a feed-forward neural network where the prediction targets are skill labels. Additional tweaks such as Correlation Aware Bootstrapping (Bhola et al., 2020) can be simply added for the sake of performance.

In the application scenario mentioned above, this skill prediction architecture can be trained and validated (except for the pre-trained BERT) on the job posting data and used to map course syllabi to the same skill space.

3.3 Educational Dimension: Instructional Design Features

Second, we focus on identifying the extent to which courses equip students with general social and cognitive skills, such as problem solving and communication, as research has validated their long-term economic returns (Deming, 2017). This dimension complements the last one because the focus on skill overlap is better at differentiating specialized skills that are concentrated in a smaller cluster of jobs, compared to general competencies that appear in almost every single posting (Coffey et al., 2020) and therefore are harder to predict in the multilabel classification framework (Figure 1).

In the educational literature, most of these general skills are aligned with the target competencies in a variety of teaching and learning frameworks (Fink, 2013; Krathwohl, 2002), which in most cases further connect to specific learning activities and instructional design. While not all curricular documents include detailed descriptions of course design, it is worth exploring the possibility of NLP-assisted coding of course design features. Table 1 presents an example of research-informed rubric, where each item captures a design feature which is associated with one (or more) competency. Some of the features are simply occurrences of

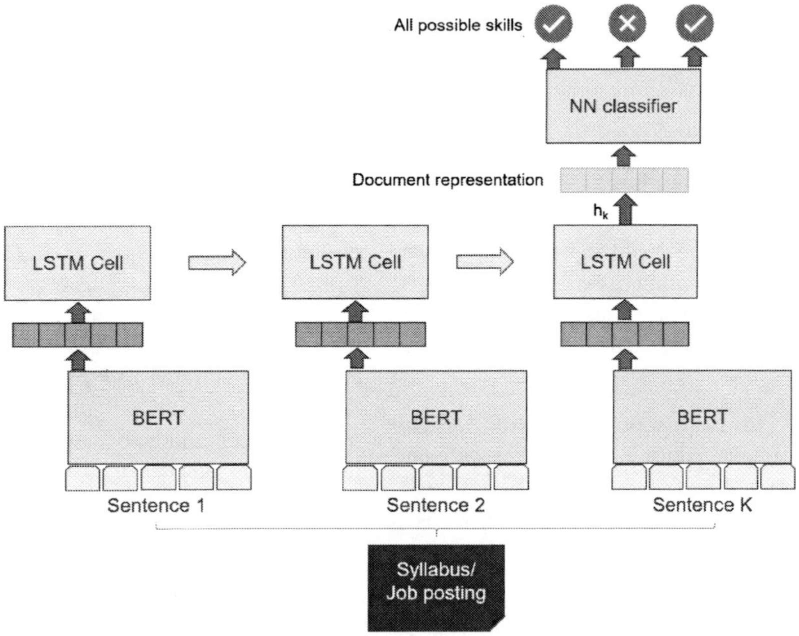

Figure 1: BERT-LSTM architecture to predict skills from course syllabi or job postings

Course design	**Competency**
Require group project	Collaboration
Require in-class presentation	Communication
Space out assignments	Time management
Encourage reflections	Critical thinking

Table 1: Example rubric of course design features mapped to general competencies

certain learning activities while others need more holistic examination of the course structure. To automatically code these items from a syllabus, a model architecture similar to that in Figure 1 might be useful, where the output skill labels are replaced by course design items. Admittedly, neither a comprehensive rubric connecting course design to higher-order competencies nor an NLP-assisted item coding pipeline is well researched, but both are promising directions.

With this setup, education-occupation alignment is not directly captured by $align\,(i;j)$ for individual pairs of documents; instead, a simple count of predicted course design items in syllabus S_i that are associated with any of predetermined general competencies will serve as the overall alignment measure for S_i.

3.4 Technical Dimension: Semantic Text Similarity

The last dimension is holistic and purely data-driven. Because scholarly understanding of the detailed language in curricular versus job documents is still limited, we assume that the overall semantic text similarity between them might reflect latent aspects of education-occupation alignment such as culture or values. As a prerequisite, we still wish to learn a vector representation for each document such that the similarity between S_i and P_j can be expressed as a simple function such as cosine similarity:

$$align\,(i;j) = \frac{\boldsymbol{v_i} \cdot \boldsymbol{v_j}}{\|\boldsymbol{v_i}\|\|\boldsymbol{v_j}\|} \tag{2}$$

where $\boldsymbol{v_i}$ and $\boldsymbol{v_j}$ are the document vectors of S_i and P_j, respectively. To learn these vectors, predictive architecture like in Figure 1 is not applicable because there is no target available to train the LSTM component for. Instead, we suggest feeding each document into pretrained Longformer (Beltagy et al., 2020) for the output representation (`[CLS]` token with global attention). To ensure that the document vectors are comparable through cosine similarity, siamese and triplet networks need to be created to update model weights following Reimers and Gurevych (2019). Alternatively, the earlier "doc2vec" model (Le and Mikolov, 2014) can also be used, as the resulting vectors are ready to use for cosine similarity.

4 Positive Impact

4.1 For Policy Research

With an established alignment metric for individual pairs of educational and job documents, we can aggregate them within different temporal, geographical or disciplinary boundaries to answer policy-relevant questions, such as the two examples below.

Inequalities in Education-Occupation Alignment. Traditional educational statistics were unable to collect information about curricular content. With the education-occupation alignment metric, we are able to systematically evaluate the differences across major areas and institutional characteristics in how well they prepare students for the workforce. From an equity perspective, if institutions with more students from underrepresented groups exhibit lower levels of labor market alignment, it suggests that the current landscape of higher education might exacerbate inequities in economic mobility. In other words, students' socio-economic gaps that originate from their family background might propagate into their professional career.

Education-Occupation Alignment and Student Outcomes. Does better education-occupation alignment contribute to better student outcomes? The established alignment metric and the nationwide standard for administrative data[1] together make it possible to provide an empirical answer to this kind of question on a large scale, where important student outcome metrics may include graduation and earnings. If this alignment is an important driving force of student outcomes, institutional effort to prepare students for workforce should be directed more towards curricular reforms. Additionally, the fine-grained alignment metric enables us to examine if it forecasts longer-term student outcomes with different levels of confidence at different types of institutions and different time points.

4.2 For Practitioners

From a practical perspective, the capacity to quantify education-occupation alignment at scale can provide actionable insights to various stakeholders. Such insights might well be incorporated into some standard information system to directly facilitate the decision-making of these people.

College students. Existing research has shown that students at different institutions have limited knowledge about the returns associated with different degree majors (Baker et al., 2018); and that simple interventions such as providing earning prospects have the potential to help individual students make optimal choices. In a similar vein, our computational framework could help a student understand the possible alignment or lack of alignment between a prospective degree program and local labor market demands, based on the summary of detailed course-level analysis within that program or a similar program at another institution, assuming a certain degree of generalizability.

Higher education administrators. Our framework could help administrators identify potential curricular "hidden gems" or "problem areas" at their institution that might align well or not well with skills demanded by the labor market. Motivated by a desire to improve institutional effectiveness and students' labor market outcomes, they could on one hand pursue curricular reforms and/or industry partnerships for the "problematic areas", while sustaining resources for student recruitment, employer engagement and other operational aspects of the "hidden gems."

Employers. Our framework could help employers refine or update their student recruitment strategies, if necessary, based on the alignment levels across major fields and institution types in their target area(s). The goal of this practice is to hire graduate talents whose skills are better suited for the employer's needs. In some scenarios, such efficiency-oriented decisions might ultimately extend opportunities to students who previously were not as likely to be considered for certain roles with the employer due to the lack of granular analysis of course content. In this case, the use of our framework might eventually contribute to the diversity, equity, and inclusion (DEI) goals of the employer and of the local community in general.

5 Summary

We propose a research framework for measuring the alignment between curricular content and job requirements by leveraging NLP techniques. Based

[1] https://nces.ed.gov/ipeds/

on neural representations of curricular and job documents, our framework includes three dimensions for quantifying education-occupation alignment: 1) amount of specialized knowledge and skills shared by the two types of documents, 2) quantity of instructional design features associated with general social and cognitive competencies, and 3) overall semantic text similarity between the two corpora. We discuss how the framework can help researchers answer education and economic policy questions, and empower stakeholders in practice to make more informed decisions around recruitment, course development, major/course choice, etc.

We focus on sketching the high-level picture of the proposed framework through examples, while leaving plenty of space for technical details and future work by ourselves and others. Given the importance of education-occupation alignment especially in the post-pandemic era, and the widely available yet underutilized corpora data of curricular and job content, we call for more cross-disciplinary collaborations on the topic to contribute to healthier education-occupation dynamics of the future.

Acknowledgments

This work was conducted under the auspices of the IBM Science for Social Good initiative.

References

Daron Acemoglu and David Autor. 2011. Skills, tasks and technologies: Implications for employment and earnings. In *Handbook of Labor Economics*, volume 4, pages 1043–1171. Elsevier.

Ashutosh Adhikari, Achyudh Ram, Raphael Tang, and Jimmy Lin. 2019. Docbert: Bert for document classification.

Rachel Baker, Eric Bettinger, Brian Jacob, and Ioana Marinescu. 2018. The effect of labor market information on community college students' major choice. *Economics of Education Review*, 65:18 – 30.

Iz Beltagy, Matthew E. Peters, and Arman Cohan. 2020. Longformer: The long-document transformer.

Akshay Bhola, Kishaloy Halder, Animesh Prasad, and Min-Yen Kan. 2020. Retrieving skills from job descriptions: A language model based extreme multi-label classification framework. In *Proceedings of the 28th International Conference on Computational Linguistics*, pages 5832–5842.

Barbara Biasi and Song Ma. 2021. The Education-Innovation Gap.

Katy Börner, Olga Scrivner, Mike Gallant, Shutian Ma, Xiaozhong Liu, Keith Chewning, Lingfei Wu, and James A. Evans. 2018. Skill discrepancies between research, education, and jobs reveal the critical need to supply soft skills for the data economy. *Proceedings of the National Academy of Sciences*, 115(50):12630–12637.

Jane Bromley, Isabelle Guyon, Yann LeCun, Eduard Säckinger, and Roopak Shah. 1993. Signature verification using a "siamese" time delay neural network. In *Proceedings of the 6th International Conference on Neural Information Processing Systems*, NIPS'93, page 737–744, San Francisco, CA, USA. Morgan Kaufmann Publishers Inc.

Jennifer Lenahan Cleary, Monica Reid Kerrigan, and Michelle Van Noy. 2017. Towards a New Understanding of Labor Market Alignment. In Michael B. Paulsen, editor, *Higher Education: Handbook of Theory and Research*, volume 32, pages 577–629.

Clare Coffey, Gwen Burrow, Rob Sentz, Kevin Kirschner, and Yustina Saleh. 2020. Resilient skills: The survivor skills that the class of covid-19 should pursue. Technical report, Emsi.

Subhro Das, Sebastian Steffen, Wyatt Clarke, Prabhat Reddy, Erik Brynjolfsson, and Martin Fleming. 2020. Learning Occupational Task-Shares Dynamics for the Future of Work. In *Proceedings of the AAAI/ACM Conference on AI, Ethics, and Society*.

David J. Deming. 2017. The Growing Importance of Social Skills in the Labor Market. *The Quarterly Journal of Economics*, 132(4):1593–1640.

David J Deming and Kadeem Noray. 2020. Earnings Dynamics, Changing Job Skills, and STEM Careers. *The Quarterly Journal of Economics*, 135(4):1965–2005.

Jacob Devlin, Ming-Wei Chang, Kenton Lee, and Kristina Toutanova. 2019. BERT: Pre-training of deep bidirectional transformers for language understanding. In *Proceedings of the 2019 Conference of the North American Chapter of the Association for Computational Linguistics: Human Language Technologies, Volume 1 (Long and Short Papers)*, pages 4171–4186, Minneapolis, Minnesota. Association for Computational Linguistics.

Federal Reserve Bank of New York. 2020. The Labor Market for Recent College Graduates.

L Dee Fink. 2013. *Creating significant learning experiences: An integrated approach to designing college courses*. John Wiley & Sons.

Martin Fleming, Wyatt Clarke, Subhro Das, Phai Phongthiengtham, and Prabhat Reddy. 2019. The future of work: How new technologies are transforming tasks. Technical report, MIT-IBM Watson AI Lab.

Sepp Hochreiter and Jürgen Schmidhuber. 1997. Long short-term memory. *Neural computation*, 9(8):1735–1780.

Philip Young P Hong and David R Hodge. 2009. Understanding social justice in social work: A content analysis of course syllabi. *Families in Society*, 90(2):212–219.

Matthew T Hora. 2019. *Beyond the skills gap: Preparing college students for life and work.* Harvard Education Press.

Weijie Jiang and Zachary A Pardos. 2020. Evaluating sources of course information and models of representation on a variety of institutional prediction tasks. In *Proceedings of the 13th International Conference on Educational Data Mining*.

David R Krathwohl. 2002. A revision of bloom's taxonomy: An overview. *Theory into practice*, 41(4):212–218.

George D. Kuh, Jillian Kinzie, Jennifer A. Buckley, Brian K. Bridges, and John C. Hayek. 2007. Piecing Together the Student success puzzle: Research, Propositions, and Recommendations. *ASHE Higher Education Report*, 32(5):1–182.

Quoc Le and Tomas Mikolov. 2014. Distributed representations of sentences and documents. In *Proceedings of the 31st International Conference on Machine Learning*, volume 32 of *Proceedings of Machine Learning Research*, pages 1188–1196, Bejing, China. PMLR.

Li Lucy, Dorottya Demszky, Patricia Bromley, and Dan Jurafsky. 2020. Content analysis of textbooks via natural language processing: Findings on gender, race, and ethnicity in texas us history textbooks. *AERA Open*, 6(3):2332858420940312.

Manpower Group. 2018. Solving the Talent Shortage: Build, Buy, Borrow and Bridge. Technical report, Manpower Group.

Jeffrey Pennington, Richard Socher, and Christopher D. Manning. 2014. Glove: Global vectors for word representation. In *Empirical Methods in Natural Language Processing (EMNLP)*, pages 1532–1543.

Matthew E. Peters, Mark Neumann, Mohit Iyyer, Matt Gardner, Christopher Clark, Kenton Lee, and Luke Zettlemoyer. 2018. Deep contextualized word representations. In *Proceedings of the 2018 Conference of the North American Chapter of the Association for Computational Linguistics: Human Language Technologies, Volume 1 (Long Papers)*, pages 2227–2237, New Orleans, Louisiana. Association for Computational Linguistics.

Nils Reimers and Iryna Gurevych. 2019. Sentence-BERT: Sentence embeddings using Siamese BERT-networks. In *Proceedings of the 2019 Conference on Empirical Methods in Natural Language Processing and the 9th International Joint Conference on Natural Language Processing (EMNLP-IJCNLP)*, pages 3982–3992, Hong Kong, China. Association for Computational Linguistics.

Ian Walker. 2020. Heterogeneity in the returns to higher education. In *The Economics of Education*, pages 75–90. Elsevier.

Dialogue Act Analysis for Alternative and Augmentative Communication

E. Margaret Perkoff
University of Colorado Boulder
margaret.perkoff@colorado.edu

Abstract

Augmentative and Alternative Communication (AAC) devices and applications are intended to make it easier for individuals with complex communication needs to participate in conversations. However, these devices have low adoption and retention rates. We review prior work with text recommendation systems that have not been successful in mitigating these problems. To address these gaps, we propose applying Dialogue Act classification to AAC conversations. We evaluated the performance of a state of the art model on a limited AAC dataset that was trained on both AAC and non-AAC datasets. The one trained on AAC (accuracy = 38.6%) achieved better performance than that trained on a non-AAC corpus (accuracy = 34.1%). These results reflect the need to incorporate representative datasets in later experiments. We discuss the need to collect more labeled AAC datasets and propose areas of future work.

1 Introduction

Dialogue Act classification takes a conversation transcript as input and identifies the appropriate intent for each turn in a conversation. For example, the sentence "How are you?" might be classified as an Open Ended Question. The exact tags that are used to label sentences depend on the context. The Switchboard DAMSL tag set (Jurafsky et al., 1997) is frequently used as a standard initial classification model which has forty-two distinct classes. Once labeled conversational data is available, it can be used to create generative statistical systems that take a sentence and a prior Dialogue Act as input and provide the next most like Dialogue Act for the conversation. Prior research has used this information to analyze both human-human conversations and better facilitate human-machine conversations (Ahmadvand et al., 2019).

However, research in Dialogue Act classification has not included conversations with individuals who do not rely solely on verbal speech to communicate. As of the 2010 United States census, approximately 15.7 million adults were listed as having a communicative disability (Brault, 2012). The communicative disability domain includes individuals who identify as having either a visual, hearing, or speech impairment or some combination of the three. Many of these individuals communicate through non-verbal methods including Augmentative and Alternative Communication (AAC) technology; we will refer to this population as AAC communicators.

AAC communicators leverage a broad set of tools to supplement their verbal speech or to replace it entirely. Speech language pathologists may recommend AAC as part of a treatment plan for an individual in order to maximize their ability to effectively communicate in their environment. In addition to providing more communication methods, research has proven that AAC technology can actually improve language development skills in children (Light et al., 2019). These systems vary in technical sophistication from picture boards corresponding to concepts to tablets or application based speech-generating devices (Elsahar et al., 2019). Figure 1 depicts two such devices, both of which include touch-based text displays. There are standalone or dedicated AAC devices available that only provide a communication interface whereas application-based solutions may run on a personal tablet or mobile device. In addition to touch access, devices can also incorporate eye-gaze, switch, or brainwave input. Some devices will allow individuals to switch between different access modes to account for fatigue levels they may experience at different times. (Elsahar et al., 2019)

The exact system used is tailored to the individual based on their cognitive, communicative, and

Proceedings of the 1st Workshop on NLP for Positive Impact, pages 107–114
Bangkok, Thailand (online), August 5, 2021.

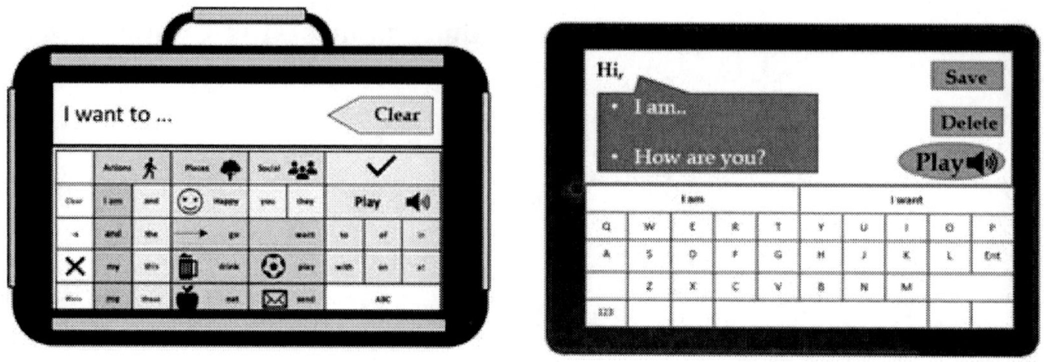

(a) (b)

Figure 1: Two examples of AAC devices, a) is a dedicated AAC device using touch-input and b) is an AAC application running on a non-dedicated device. (Elsahar et al., 2019)

physical profile. An ideal system will maximize the individual's ability to express themselves while minimizing the cognitive and physical demands of using the system. Speech pathologists will perform an initial AAC evaluation to match a patient with the appropriate device to fit their immediate needs and long term communication goals and define an AAC intervention plan to track progress on these goals. Over the course of intervention, the system may be adjusted in order to better suit the needs of the individual whether it be physical changes to accommodate improved or worsening motor functionality or word selection adjustments to introduce more complicated vocabulary.

Over the last few decades, AAC devices have improved significantly, but satisfaction and retention rates for them remain low (Waller, 2019). There has been some effort to improve on-screen word prediction, but it has yet to provide sufficiently relevant suggestions during conversations or improve communication rates for AAC communicators. As we will discuss in the Related Work section, the application of NLP to AAC technology has been primarily limited to word prediction, despite the expansion of the field to a multitude of other tasks. We hypothesize that incorporating Dialogue Act information into AAC technology will improve the ease of use of these devices and in turn positively impact the ability of AAC communicators to participate in conversations.

In this paper, we address the potential benefits of applying Dialogue Act classification to conversations that include a participant communicating via an AAC device. We will start by presenting the previous NLP applications that have been used to enhance AAC software as well as currently available representative datasets. Then, we evaluate the performance of an existing state-of-the-art model on a small dataset of transcribed conversations between an AAC communicator and one of their daily communication partners. Finally, we present the challenges that inhibit work in this context. Ultimately, we hope that future researchers will recognize the value of applying language models to conversations with AAC communicators in order to improve their ability to independently participate in educational, social, and career settings.

2 Related Work

2.1 Natural Language Processing For AAC Users

There have been numerous efforts to incorporate different aspects of language processing into AAC. In 2011, (Higginbotham et al., 2011) conducted a review of the use of Natural Language Processing for Augmentative and Alternative Communication. These proposed enhancements are often aimed at improving the ease of use of devices or the rate of communication. The rate of communication for a device indicates how quickly an AAC communicator can respond using the technology. This is a critical element for being an active conversational participant. At the time, the relevant systems used optimized keyboards to improve input, word prediction, and speech recognition. There were different variations on improvements to word prediction including incorporating key noun phrases used by communication partners to enhance the on-screen suggestions. (Wisenburn and Higginbotham, 2009). However, none of the word prediction methods used were found to improve the rate of communication for AAC users.

Nearly a decade later, language processing research in AAC has not expanded much outside of the realm of word prediction. The research has focused on incorporating additional context to the word suggestions provided to users on device with the intent of improving communication rates as well as relevance of the suggestions themselves. Fried-Oken, M., Jakobs, T., & Jakobs, E. (2018) developed SmartPredict, an application-based AAC that leverages a statistical language model, the communicator's recent vocabulary, and content suggestions from their conversational partner via a partner application. Their hypothesis was that information provided by conversational partners would enhance the overall ease of use with the application. Initial findings from their experiments show a slight improvement in the number of selections that the AAC communicators required to indicate their desired intent, but these have not been expanded to a larger group yet. Garcia et al. (2015) investigated the use of location-aware language models for word and sentence prediction and found that they did not provide statistically significant improvements for participants' conversational rate. Location information was later used for pictogram prediction in a pictogram-based AAC device (Garcia et al., 2016) where the location based models also did not result in significant improvements in AAC usage. Outside of predictive models for word or pictogram-based devices, there has also been research into how NLP can be used to improve new AAC technology. Oken et al. (2014) were the first researchers to use NLP to enhance a Brain Computer Interface (BCI) system. Their system works by presenting the individual with a single letter for 2.5 seconds at a time and using non-invasive sensors to determine if this is the individual's target character. Instead of scanning through the entire alphabet, their statistical model presents the next letter based on what is most likely to occur following the previous letter. An enhanced BCI system has the potential to improve communication methods available to individuals with extremely limited or no voluntary motor control, including those with Locked-In Syndrome.

Research in the AAC space has remained limited to a small number of language processing tasks in the last several decades. Effort has been made to improve ease of use of AAC devices and communication rates by incorporating geographic, temporal, and contextual information into word prediction systems. Yet, as mentioned above, these additions have not significantly impacted the rate of communication or device retention rates of AAC communicators. Future work in this space needs to include experimental AAC designs that leverage a greater breadth of NLP applications to better meet the needs of this population.

2.2 Data including Individuals with Complex Communication Needs

In order to pursue further NLP applications for AAC, there is a need to collect or aggregate representative training data sets for these models. The most comprehensive dataset including conversational data for AAC communicators is the AAC and non-AAC Workplace Corpus (Friginal et al., 2013). This corpus includes transcripts of over two hundred hours of data captured with eight participants using AAC devices in their workplace environment. A single corpus of conversational transcripts is not sufficient to create statistical models that will provide significant benefit.

However, despite a lack of transcribed conversations, audio datasets have been greatly expanded upon to include speech samples that represent a variety of different language disorders. There are multiple corpora available that include samples of speech from adult Parkinson's patients (Tsanas et al., 2014) (Orozco et al., 2014) (Jaeger et al., 2019). Other audio datasets have been collected to study the dysarthric speech of individuals with Cerebral Palsy and Amyotrophic Lateral Sclerosis (Rudzicz et al., 2010). Little et al. (2007)'s corpus includes speech samples from individuals with a mixed set of language disorders. In addition to covering a range of language impairment types, the audio data that has been collected is also representative of individuals from different age groups. As an example, the Child's Pathological Speech Database (Ringeval et al., 2011) includes speech data from children with either autism spectrum disorder or a different language impairment. There is also the CSLU Autism Speech Corpus which contains data from speech pathology evaluations on forty-five children conducted from 2005-2012 (Gale et al., 2019) amounting to 1.5 hours of audio data with a total of 1,022 utterances.

Of the datasets mentioned above, the AAC and non-AAC Workplace Corpus is the only one that includes individuals communicating with an AAC device. It is also the only corpus that is coded for linguistic characteristics, including part-of-speech tagging. Even if speech-to-text applications were run to convert all of the audio corpora mentioned above to transcript formats, they would still need to be coded by linguistic features in order to be usable as training data for certain language processing tasks. For these reasons, additional effort to collect and label representative conversational data of AAC communicators is needed to make meaningful progress with NLP advancements.

3 Implications of Dialogue Act Analysis for AAC

Applying Dialogue Act classification to conversations including communicators reliant on AAC has the potential to improve their ability to communicate as well as enhance the AAC intervention and evaluation processes.

3.1 Benefits for AAC Communicators

The ultimate goal of AAC intervention is to increase the communicative competence of an individual. This covers not only the ability to communicate in the workplace or classroom setting, but also the ability to engage in personal conversations with friends and family. The current set of AAC devices and applications has yet to provide an adequate solution for individuals with complex communication needs. Many individuals who have been prescribed high-tech AAC devices end up abandoning them due to bad user interface, physical access limitations, the cognitive load required to learn them, or due to a lack of access to an expert (Waller, 2019). Those that continue to use their devices face limitations with conversational agency in terms of conversational, task, and device constraints (Valencia et al., 2020).

Incorporating Dialogue Act information into an AAC interface would improve the ability of AAC communicators to participate in conversations. A generative Dialogue Act model built into an AAC application would be able to predict the most likely next Dialog Act in a conversation. This information could then be used to provide the AAC communicator with partial or full phrases that correspond to the appropriate Dialog Act. Smart phrase recommendations may enhance the rate of communication, making it easier for the AAC communicator to respond to the topic in a timely manner. For example, if their conversational partner asks, a *Wh-Question: What are you doing this weekend."* the system could provide partial phrase recommendations that conform to a *Statement-Non-Opinion* such as "I'm going to ... ". Dialog Act suggestions also have the potential to impact ease of use with the device by reducing the amount of navigation required to find desired words or phrases. These improvements would reduce the cognitive and physical load imposed on the AAC communicator and potentially make them more motivated to continue to use their device.

3.2 AAC Evaluation and Intervention Improvements

Dialogue Act classification could also be used to quickly analyze speech pathology transcripts to improve both initial AAC evaluations and ongoing AAC intervention. As part of the initial AAC assessment, the conversations between the patient and members of the AAC team are coded for communicative functions such as requests, information sharing, and wh-questions. (Beukelman and Light, 2020) Speech language pathologists record these sessions and transcribe them on their own or send them to a transcription service. Once they have a written version, they review either the audio or written files and annotate them for the appropriate communicative function.

Communicative functions could be treated as Dialogue Act classes and annotated by speech pathologists on representative samples of atypical speech. A Dialogue Act classification model could then be trained on this gold standard data in order to automate this process in the future. This type of automation would make it easier for speech pathologists to evaluate patients for an initial AAC device as well as fitting them to a new device at a later stage in their treatment. As a result, their patients could gain access to an appropriate AAC device and improve their ability to communicate more quickly.

Following the initial assessment, Dialogue Act classification could then be used to track the progress of the patient with their initial evaluation goals. Current speech pathology research stresses the importance of evidence-based intervention for individuals with complex communication needs (Light et al., 2019). By using a Dialogue Act classification model, speech pathologists and conversational partners could quickly code interactions and identify how often the individual is able to express the communicative functions that correspond to their intervention goals. This provides more frequent feedback on goals and allows the AAC team to adjust appropriately. Additionally, models could be trained to identify the method by which the individual is communicating, either through vocalization or a device. Then multi-class models could associate particular communicative functions with communication methods. This would provide deeper insight into whether the individual can vocalize a particular communicative function or if they require a device to fulfill particular conversational needs. Automated transcription would also allow for conversations to be evaluated at home instead of in a speech pathologists office, reducing potential burden on the individual and their AAC team.

4 Experiments

To explore the potential of Dialogue Act classification for conversations including individuals using AAC, we will evaluate the accuracy of a state of the art model on a small representative dataset.

4.1 Data

The data used consists of written transcripts of unscripted conversation between an individual using a speech generating device and one of their regular communication partners. The data was collected at the University of Buffalo (Higginbotham, 2021). Each of the individuals involved in the original study had amyotrophic lateral sclerosis (ALS) which has impacted their ability to communicate vocally. Participants were prompted to discuss trips that they had taken in the past. There are ten unique transcripts which each correspond to a conversation between one of the communicative partner pairs In total, there are four hundred and thirty six utterances present in the dataset.

In addition to the AAC dataset, some of the models were trained on the Switchboard training corpus (Jurafsky et al., 1997). The Switchboard corpus contains labeled data from 1,155 5-minute conversations. The training set contains a total of 197,489 utterances. Both datasets were annotated with the Switchboard DAMSL tags which are described in detail below.

Dialogue Act Tag	Count
Statement-non-opinion	155
Statement-opinion	36
Yes-No-Question	26
Repeat-phrase	24
Open-Question	20
Other	19
Yes Answers	19
Agree/Accept	16
Response Acknowledgement	15
Backchannel in question form	14

Table 1: Counts of dialogue act tags in the ALS Dataset.

Dialogue Act Annotation We annotated the sentences based on the Switchboard DAMSL Dialogue Act tags (Jurafsky et al., 1997) which are currently the standard benchmark for evaluating the accuracy Dialogue Act classification models. The DAMSL model consists of forty-two distinct classes of dialogue acts meant to represent the meaning of a particular utterance. The top ten most frequent set of dialogue act tags present in the dataset can be seen in Table 1. The standards followed are based on the examples provided in the Switchboard manual.

A sample conversation snippet with the associated dialogue act tags can be seen in the conversation below. AC refers to the AAC communicator and P is their conversational partner.

P: *20 years together you can't think of one thing?* [Rhetorical-Question]
AC: *We don't take many trips* [Statement-non-opinion]
AC: *Florida was cool when we went to Universal Studios* [Statement-opinion]
P: *Yeah* [Yes Answers]

4.2 Classification Model

To establish a baseline of model performance, we picked the top implementation currently available for Dialogue Act analysis based on existing leaderboards (Ruder, 2021). The classification model from Ravi and Kozareva (2018)'s is currently ranked as the highest performing solution with an accuracy of 83.1 on the Switchboard dataset. This approach avoids the need to use pretrained word embeddings and instead uses projection transformations to transform the input. This avoids the need for us to train word embeddings on

Training Set	Validation Set	Accuracy	Loss
AAC	AAC	0.386	2.655
SWBD	SWBD	0.341	2.787
SWBD	AAC	0.341	2.787

Table 2: We evaluated all three versions of our Dialogue Act Classification models with a subset of the AAC datset based on categorical accuracy and crossentropy loss. AAC indicates that the training or validation set was sampled from the AAC dataset whereas SWBD indicates that the sampling was from the Switchboard corpus.

our limited dataset. We used the publicly available implementation which closely follows the original algorithm, but achieves a maximum accuracy of 73.1 (Suarez, 2021). Our experiments used a neural network with 2 hidden layers with 256 units. The Dialogue Act labels were mapped to one-hot encoding vectors of size 42. All of the models are trained with stochastic gradient descent for 100 epochs.

We compared three methods of training a classification model based on different combinations of the AAC data and the Switchboard dataset. The goal of these experiments was to understand whether the AAC transcripts alone could be used to train a classification model as well as whether training a model on the Switchboard corpus would be sufficient for classifying AAC conversational data. The first model relies on only the ALS transcript data for training and validation. We randomly sampled 80% of the sentences from the transcripts to use for training data, 10% for validation, and 10% for testing. The second model was trained and validated with the Switchboard corpus and then tested with the same test set of AAC sentences. Lastly, we trained a model on the Switchboard training corpus and validated with samples from the AAC set. The same sample set of sentences was used for validation in the first and third models. For each model variation, we calculate the categorical crossentropy loss and the categorical accuracy on the test set of AAC sentences.

5 Results

The results in Table 2 show that the first model, which was trained and validated on the AAC corpus outperforms both of the others, which were trained on the Switchboard dataset. This indicates that the Switchboard dataset is an inadequate training set for AAC conversations. It also suggests that the use of representative data in model training has a positive impact on classification accuracy. However, the low 38.6% accuracy of this model reflects the fact that our current AAC dataset is not adequate for training a statistical Dialogue Act classification model. A larger representative dataset would be needed to improve results for a model trained on AAC-data only. The use of AAC data only in the validation phase of model training, during which hyperparameters are set, seems to have minimal impact on the accuracy of the model. This could be due to the small size of the validation set or further evidence that the Switchboard training data does not generalize to the AAC sentence data.

The low accuracy scores could also be reflective of the need to use better annotation tags. The AAC conversational data used for future experiments could benefit from AAC context specific Dialogue Act tags. Although the DAMSL tags work well for comparison to results on existing datasets, it would be more beneficial to use a refined tag set that is specific to the AAC data that is being analyzed. Ideally, the tags should be modified depending on the context in which they are being used. A speech pathologist may choose to use a specific set of classes for coding sentences that are closely related to the goals of the individual's intervention. These tags are different from a set that would be used to provide real-time suggestions on a device during a typical conversation. Once a set of context appropriate tags has been established, the AAC data should be annotated by a group of annotators who are familiar with interpreting AAC output, such as speech pathologists in order to establish more accurate standard tags and inter-annotator agreement.

6 Conclusion

In this paper, we introduced the possibility of applying Dialogue Act classification to conversations that include one or more individuals communicating via AAC devices. We have discussed the potential benefits for applying this NLP technique to AAC applications as well as speech pathology transcriptions. In the experiments, we trained a Dialogue Act classification model on a small subset of AAC data and determined that a model trained on the Switchboard corpus does not perform as well on AAC conversational data as one that has been trained on a representative corpus. However, with the current AAC corpus available, the accuracy for the Dialogue Act classification model is far from the current benchmarks for these models on the Switchboard corpus. This indicates the need for more experiments to improve Dialogue Act classification accuracy in this context.

Future experiments will require labeled AAC conversational data for model training. The data collection task is a daunting proposition due to the fact that AAC devices are inherently personalized. Each AAC intervention session is tailored to the patient, the devices chosen, and goals set are meant to be the best choice for that individual. A representative dataset would need to be sufficiently large to incorporate individuals with different communication impairments, different degrees of impairment, and those from different age groups. The data must also be collected in a manner to preserve the privacy of the individuals' included. Furthermore, the current limitations of AAC devices may bias the data that could be collected. If a person is currently limited in their communicative ability due to poor user design with the device, the speech that they output will not be reflective of their full communicative desires. To mitigate this risk, further research needs to be done with this population to better incorporate their conversational goals into a representative dataset. Additionally, any model proposed should have a personalizable component. This component would allow for supplemental training data that is based on the individual's recent conversation history or a bootstrapping period. The inclusion of a personalization training period would provide enhanced conversational agency as well as incorporating an individual's communication style into their AAC device.

Once a sufficiently accurate Dialogue Act classification model is available, it can be embedded into a standalone AAC device or AAC application. This prototype should be designed alongside individuals who currently communicate via AAC as well as their AAC team. Through a collaborative research and design process, we hope to see improvements in usage rates for AAC devices and higher satisfaction rates by AAC communicators. More importantly, we anticipate that as AAC devices improve, AAC communicators will find themselves able to participate in more professional, educational, and social conversational opportunities.

References

Ali Ahmadvand, Jason Ingyu Choi, and Eugene Agichtein. 2019. Contextual dialogue act classification for Open-Domain conversational agents. In *Proceedings of the 42nd International ACM SIGIR Conference on Research and Development in Information Retrieval*, SIGIR'19, pages 1273–1276, New York, NY, USA. Association for Computing Machinery.

David R Beukelman and Janice C Light. 2020. *Augmentative et alternative communication : supporting children and adults with complex communication needs*. Paul H. Brookes Publishing Co.

Matthew W Brault. 2012. Americans with disabilities: 2010. Technical Report P70-131, U.S. Census Bureau, Washington, D.C.

Yasmin Elsahar, Sijung Hu, Kaddour Bouazza-Marouf, David Kerr, and Annysa Mansor. 2019. Augmentative and alternative communication (AAC) advances: A review of configurations for individuals with a speech disability. *Sensors*, 19(8).

Fried-Oken, M., Jakobs, T., & Jakobs, E. 2018. Smart-Predict: AAC app that integrates partner knowledge into word prediction. Annual Conference of the Assistive Technology Industry Association (ATIA).

Eric Friginal, Pamela Pearson, Laura Di Ferrante, Lucy Pickering, and Carrie Bruce. 2013. Linguistic characteristics of AAC discourse in the workplace. *Discourse Studies*, 15(3):279–298.

Robert Gale, Liu Chen, Jill Dolata, Jan van Santen, and Meysam Asgari. 2019. Improving ASR systems for children with autism and language impairment using Domain-Focused DNN transfer techniques. *Interspeech*, 2019:11–15.

Luís Filipe Garcia, Luís Caldas de Oliveira, and David Martins de Matos. 2016. Evaluating pictogram prediction in a location-aware augmentative and alternative communication system. *Assist. Technol.*, 28(2):83–92.

Luís Filipe Garcia, Luís Caldas De Oliveira, and David Martins De Matos. 2015. Measuring the performance of a Location-Aware text prediction system. *ACM Trans. Access. Comput.*, 7(1):1–29.

D Jeffery Higginbotham, Gregory W Lesher, Bryan J Moulton, and Brian Roark. 2011. The application of natural language processing to augmentative and alternative communication. *Assist. Technol.*, 24(1):14–24.

J Higginbotham. 2021. Communication and assistive device laboratory - AAC shared narrative corpora:ALS.

Hagen Jaeger, Dhaval Trivedi, and Michael Stadtschnitzer. 2019. Mobile device voice recordings at king's college london (MDVR-KCL) from both early and advanced parkinson's disease patients and healthy controls.

Dan Jurafsky, Liz Shriberg, and Debra Biasca. 1997. *WS-97 Switchboard DAMSL Coders Manual.*

Janice Light, David McNaughton, David Beukelman, Susan Koch Fager, Melanie Fried-Oken, Thomas Jakobs, and Erik Jakobs. 2019. Challenges and opportunities in augmentative and alternative communication: Research and technology development to enhance communication and participation for individuals with complex communication needs. *Augment. Altern. Commun.*, 35(1):1–12.

Max A Little, Patrick E McSharry, Stephen J Roberts, Declan A E Costello, and Irene M Moroz. 2007. Exploiting nonlinear recurrence and fractal scaling properties for voice disorder detection. *Biomed. Eng. Online*, 6:23.

Barry S Oken, Umut Orhan, Brian Roark, Deniz Erdogmus, Andrew Fowler, Aimee Mooney, Betts Peters, Meghan Miller, and Melanie B Fried-Oken. 2014. Brain-computer interface with language model-electroencephalography fusion for locked-in syndrome. *Neurorehabil. Neural Repair*, 28(4):387–394.

Juan Rafael Orozco, Julian D Arias-Londoño, J Francisco Vargas-Bonilla, and Elmar Noeth. 2014. New spanish speech corpus database for the analysis of people suffering from parkinson's disease. In *International Conference on Language Resources and Evaluation*. unknown.

Sujith Ravi and Zornitsa Kozareva. 2018. Self-Governing neural networks for On-Device short text classification. In *Proceedings of the 2018 Conference on Empirical Methods in Natural Language Processing*, pages 887–893, Brussels, Belgium. Association for Computational Linguistics.

Fabien Ringeval, Julie Demouy, György Szaszak, Mohamed Chetouani, Laurence Robel, Jean Xavier, David Cohen, and Monique Plaza. 2011. Automatic intonation recognition for the prosodic assessment of Language-Impaired children. *IEEE Trans. Audio Speech Lang. Processing*, 19(5):1328–1342.

Sebastian Ruder. 2021. NLP-progress.

Frank Rudzicz, Aravind Kumar Namasivayam, and Talya Wolff. 2010. The TORGO database of acoustic and articulatory speech from speakers with dysarthria. *Language Resources and Evaluation*, 46(4):1–19.

Andres Suarez. 2021. SGNN.

Athanasios Tsanas, Max A Little, Cynthia Fox, and Lorraine O Ramig. 2014. Objective automatic assessment of rehabilitative speech treatment in parkinson's disease. *IEEE Trans. Neural Syst. Rehabil. Eng.*, 22(1):181–190.

Stephanie Valencia, Amy Pavel, Jared Santa Maria, Seunga (gloria) Yu, Jeffrey P Bigham, and Henny Admoni. 2020. Conversational agency in augmentative and alternative communication. In *Proceedings of the 2020 CHI Conference on Human Factors in Computing Systems*, CHI '20, pages 1–12, New York, NY, USA. Association for Computing Machinery.

Annalu Waller. 2019. Telling tales: unlocking the potential of AAC technologies. *Int. J. Lang. Commun. Disord.*, 54(2):159–169.

Bruce Wisenburn and D Jeffery Higginbotham. 2009. Participant evaluations of rate and communication efficacy of an AAC application using natural language processing. *Augment. Altern. Commun.*, 25(2):78–89.

Improving Policing with Natural Language Processing

Anthony Dixon
School of law
University of Leeds
mml8acd@leeds.ac.uk

Daniel Birks
School of Law
University of Leeds
D.Birks@leeds.ac.uk

Abstract

This article explores the potential for Natural Language Processing (NLP) to enable a more effective, prevention focused and less confrontational policing model that has hitherto been too resource consuming to implement at scale. Problem-Oriented Policing (POP) is a potential replacement, at least in part, for traditional policing which adopts a reactive approach, relying heavily on the criminal justice system. By contrast, POP seeks to prevent crime by manipulating the underlying conditions that allow crimes to be committed. Identifying these underlying conditions requires a detailed understanding of crime events - tacit knowledge that is often held by police officers but which can be challenging to derive from structured police data. One potential source of insight exists in unstructured free text data commonly collected by police for the purposes of investigation or administration. Yet police agencies do not typically have the skills or resources to analyse these data at scale. In this article we argue that NLP offers the potential to unlock these unstructured data and by doing so allow police to implement more POP initiatives. However we caution that using NLP models without adequate knowledge runs the risk of perpetuating existing, or introducing new, biases that have the potential to produce unfavourable outcomes.

1 Introduction

This article will first provide a brief overview of Problem-oriented Policing (POP) and demonstrate that it is an efficient crime prevention strategy. It will show that by implementing POP processes and reducing criminal opportunities less people are likely to commit crime and end up within the criminal justice system. It will then demonstrate that while POP has previously been successful the analytical burden it places on crime analysts is substantial and is an impediment for wider adoption. Subsequently, we will argue that NLP methods have the potential to support efforts to overcome these challenges - enabling at-scale systematic extraction of insights from police free text data sets that can support the POP process. We will conclude by discussing several ethical challenges that must be overcome if NLP is to help deliver positive societal outcomes by supporting those who seek to reduce crime.

2 Problem-Oriented Policing

POP is a model of policing proposed in 1979 by Herman Goldstein (Goldstein, 1979) as an accompaniment to the traditional policing model. Traditional policing focuses resources on reactive response, investigations and arrests. Arrests lead to prosecution, court, prison and probation costs and the criminalisation of, mostly, young males. By contrast, POP seeks to re-balance this traditional reactive approach (Goldstein, 1990) to include preventative efforts which act before the crime or problem arises (Tilley, 2008).

To this end, POP seeks to prevent problems from reoccurring by analysing how previous similar events occurred then intervening in that generation process to prevent recurrence - see Fig 1 for a pictorial representation. In this regard, an essential element for conducting POP is understanding the conditions that allowed crime to occur in the first instance. POP is based upon understanding crime as a socio-physical process that occurs when three separate elements coincide. Much like a fire relies on a fuel, a spark and oxygen to occur, crime relies on the convergence of a motivated offender, a suitable target in a setting without a capable guardian (Cohen and Felson, 1979). POP seeks to understand how these elements, known as the crime triangle, coalesce and therefore how the triangle can be disrupted to prevent crime opportunities.

Proceedings of the 1st Workshop on NLP for Positive Impact, pages 115–124
Bangkok, Thailand (online), August 5, 2021.

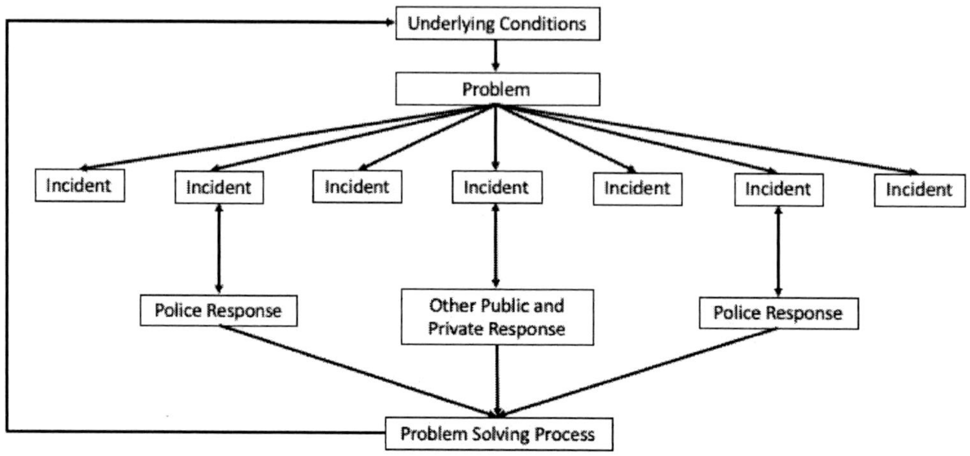

Figure 1: A schematic for POP. Reproduced from (Eck and Spelman, 1987)

POP is generally regarded as a successful police model when implemented correctly. There are systematic reviews that provide evidence for POP's increased effectiveness in crime prevention over the traditional model. A recent systematic review (Hinkle et al., 2020) found that POP was much more effective at preventing crime than traditional policing. A second review (Braga et al., 2014), also found that when targeted alongside another police tactic, hot-spot policing, POP was also more successful than traditional policing. Moreover, a number of randomized controlled trials have shown that POP is more effective at preventing crime than traditional policing approaches (Taylor et al., 2011; Braga et al., 1999).

From a social justice perspective POP has the effect of reducing opportunities for crime across communities, and thereby reducing the attractiveness of crime in areas where it is traditionally higher. With reference to the crime triangle, high crime areas may contain similar quantities of potential offenders to low crime areas, but lack capable guardians or security measures, thus creating more viable opportunities for crime. A decreased reliance on the criminal justice system also means less people are criminalised. In what follows we outline the POP process, provide some illustrative examples, identify some key criticisms and challenges associated with its application, and describe how NLP might be used to overcome these and facilitate positive impact.

2.1 POP Framework - SARA

The POP analytical framework is typically based upon a four stage process - Scanning, Analysis, Response and Assessment (SARA):

1. **Scan.** Firstly the problem space is scanned for collections of incidents that represent a potential problem to be addressed. Typically this scanning is completed by the police in conjunction with the community, either directly or indirectly through received complaints. The *scan* is wide but analytically shallow. The output is a reduced collection of incidents that share the same characteristics indicating common underlying causes.

2. **Analysis.** After the problem space is defined, it is then analysed with the aim of identifying underlying conditions that might be manipulated to prevent the crime - these are often known as pinch points. This stage is typically the most arduous from an analytical perspective, as the details of each crime need to be thoroughly understood to allow common pinch points to be identified and understood. In comparison to the *scan* stage, *analysis* is much more focused delving deeper into the crimes selected.

3. **Response.** The third stage - *response* - the is aimed at the pinch points identified in the previous stage. By manipulating these pinch points the conditions for crime are altered, with the aim of making criminal opportunities less attractive, more risky, more difficult or removing them altogether.

4. **Assessment.** The final *assessment* stage seeks to assess the effectiveness of the intervention, capturing information that can enhance the response and inform future POP users.

We now illustrate this this framework by means of an example from an op rational policing environment in the UK.

2.2 POP Example

An example of POP implementation is included to demonstrate how the process operates and how success is achieved. The example is centred on residential burglary reduction in Durham UK.[1] Durham Constabulary, situated in Northern England, had experienced consistently high rates of residential burglary. Reliance on traditional policing methods had not addressed the problem with burglary rates remaining high even after offenders had been caught and convicted. In response a different approach was sought through POP.

1. **Scan.** Durham's burglary data from a number of years was anyalysed to identify the type of dwelling, items stolen and modus operandi (how burglary was committed) associated with residential burglaries. These factors were used to highlight areas where the same types of burglary occurred - that is the *scan* of the whole force area identified smaller areas where the same types of crime were being committed, thus allowing an investigation into the underlying causes. At this stage large volumes of crimes are analysed (typically there are around 4000 burglaries in Durham a year) in order to select a coherent manageable group of crimes for further analysis in the following stage.

2. **Analysis.** Once the areas for enhanced analysis had been determined, crimes were further explored to understand how and (where possible) by whom they had been committed. Combined analyses of police records and intelligence data led to the identification of opportunistic as well as organised gang burglaries, and identified poor residential security as an underlying issue along with insufficient informal guardianship in selected areas.

3. **Response.** After *analysis* of the problems and a shift away from relying on the criminal justice system, the police garnered public support to change community behaviours. This made the areas less attractive to burglars by enhancing informal guardianship. In addition, the police provided home security packs to the most vulnerable residents. The result was a reduction in burglaries in the majority of the POP response areas, against a backdrop of rising burglaries across the region. Not only was this intervention cost effective relative to a traditionally criminal justice response, it also, more importantly, meant that significantly fewer residents had their homes violated.

4. **Assessment.** The *assessment* phase was conducted by comparing levels of crime in the intervention and control areas pre- and post-response. This was carried out using simple count data and tracked whether the POP initiatives had reduced crime in the target areas relative to control areas. While this approach was able to estimate the impact of the *response* in the target area, it still exhibited a key weakness, in that without further detailed analyses it could not provide insights into how offences had been prevented or how their nature may have changed as a result of the response. Consequently this assessment was of limited value for considering how such tactics might be improved or adapted for use in other areas.

2.3 Impediments to POP

Significant information that is required for POP is contained in textual data. Some of this will be in police generated crime notes - such as the modus operandi described above, witness statements, forensic reports or other sources such as complaints from the community. Analyses of these data is largely completed manually (Goldstein, 1990), and as such it is often a long and laborious task, and given resource pressures, the work often has to be completed selectively. Unlocking access to this information would enable analysts

[1] https://popcenter.asu.edu/sites/default/files/17-04.pdf

and officers access to a much wider source of information with which to implement POP responses. In a guide to POP, Scott and Kirby (2012) cite the need to both get and train the right staff (Chapter 9) and the requirement for enhanced analytical support is highlighted at great length (Chapter 17). POP requires appropriate knowledge, skills and experience to be delivered effectively, but because these skills are not required for the traditional response policing model, they are often lacking in within police agencies.

To chronologically bookend this point, a lack of analytical skills was identified by Goldstein in 1990, (Goldstein, 1990), and was still seen as an issue in 2016 (Scott et al., 2016). A recent review of POP in England and Wales (Sidebottom et al., 2020) concluded that "recurrent weaknesses in the application of SARA...concerned the depth and quality of problem analysis.", additionally they also found that "43% of survey respondents said they did not have access to information necessary to perform effective problem-solving". Given that the crux of POP lies in the understanding of the problem at hand, yet the police agencies that want to implement POP do not have the necessary skills available in sufficient quantities, it is hardly surprising that POP usage is not widespread. However, it is encouraging to note that it would largely appear to be a resourcing issue, rather than a systemic POP problem as where analytical resourcing have been sufficient, often as a result of collaborations with academia, POP implementations have been more successful.

With these constraints in mind, it seems clear that if some components of the POP process could be supported through automation, then at least one obstacle to expanding POP implementations would be overcome. It is here that we believe modern NLP techniques have the potential to facilitate rapid exploitation of police free text information, in turn contributing to a significant lowering of the analytical burdens associated with successful POP implementation. Yet, to simply burden police analytical staff with yet another complex tool will likely not produce a desirable outcome. Instead, tools need to be simplified and packaged so that time-poor analysts without extensive training can leverage the technology even if that means not harnessing the full potential of NLP technologies.

3 Police Free-Text

In many countries, including the United Kingdom, the police have a legal requirement to record and document crimes. This documentation can vary depending on the severity of the crime and procedures within individual agencies. As can be seen from example texts in (Birks et al., 2020) and (Kuang et al., 2017) police free text includes misspellings and specialised vocabulary like acronyms and contractions. Police free text is also generally unedited, capital case rules are liberally applied and often there is little formal grammar. All this sets police free-text apart from the data sets that are generally used to train existing NLP models, suggesting that the nature of the text will require model adaptations to reach similar results to those achieved using the types of data sets existing models are trained on. Despite these differences, some preliminary experimental work carried out by the author has shown that existing models give sufficient coverage to the language without adaption. Work to understand the utility of part-of-speech taggers showed that using a universal dependency parser based on the English Web Tree Bank[2] (Silveira et al., 2014) an overall token accuracy of 90% was achieved when tested on Burglary Modus Operandi text, although that did mean that around 67% of sentences contained at least one error.

A further challenge is the sensitivity of police data. Police free-text data can contain personal information and so are often subject to local laws and regulatory frameworks (such as GDPR in the UK and EU). These protections present challenges. Police agencies, as we have previously discussed, typically do not have the expertise to conduct the detailed analyses in house and almost certainly do not have access to GPUs or other accelerators to build some of the more powerful models from scratch. At the same time, timely sharing of sensitive data in ways that facilitate academic research can present significant logistical challenges. This means that the NLP analytical engines will most likely have to travel to the data located in the police IT systems, unless systems can be developed to securely move and store the data. Any NLP implementation would, ideally, have low hardware requirements and be packaged so that it can be used by practitioners who may be quantitatively competent, but not be experts in NLP or machine learning tech-

[2]Work was completed in R using udpipe package with model english-ewt-ud-2.4-190531

niques. In order to overcome these data sharing obstacles we have initially adopted a very low risk approach with a partner agencies to release data for experimental research. This approach is characterised by the following methods:

1. Low risk data. Requests for data are designed from the outset to be low risk, we request modus operandi data which is designed to be shared with other parts of the criminal justice system and as such is not supposed to contain personal data.

2. In-house pre-processing. To add an additional level of security we have also developed a simple approach to further pre-process data in police systems prior to sharing. Our white-listing approach simply redacts all tokens that are not found within a list of commonly used words(circa 10,000). Crucially this list does not contain common names, again minimising the risk of disclosure of personal data. While this approach may be sub optimal relative to other methods it is deterministic and easily explainable.

3. Safe place. All data are held in modern secure environments. We have utilised a secure area (ISO27001 compliant) that can only be accessed by members of the project team.

4. Safe people. Members of the research team are vetted by the police force in question to ensure they meet necessary standards for data handling.

5. Shared insights. We agree to share all insights with our police partners. All publications detailing research are vetted by multiple parties from both police and academia prior to submission.

Clearly these approaches will have an impact on the data received and therefore the generalisation of NLP applicability to different types of data (e.g. witness statements). However this approach does offer a promising beginning to understand how and if NLP can be useful for POP processes.

4 Related Work

Machine learning, text mining and data science have, unsurprisingly already been seen as useful tools by crime scientists (Marshall and Townsley, 2006). However, as a recent review into the intersection of crime and AI has shown (Campedelli, 2020), although some methods of AI and machine learning exist in the criminological literature, there is a general paucity of NLP related research compared to other areas. In this section we concentrate on analyses of free-text police data only.

Much of the existing crime free-text analysis is dominated either by unsupervised learning and revolves around the problem of crime linkage rather than crime reduction (Hassani et al., 2016). Crime-linkage seeks to identify crimes that are committed by the same individual(s), whereas POP typically requires crimes grouped according to enabling characteristics. Notable examples of unsupervised learning with Police Free-text data are Birks et al. (2020) and Kuang et al. (2017) who use unsupervised natural language processing to understand how crimes may be grouped relative to how they were committed rather than traditional crime classifications. Birks et al. (2020) completes this within a single crime classification and Kuang et al. (2017) conducted this across multiple crime classifications. This is referred to as crime topic modelling and seeks to understand crime from an ecological perspective.

In addition to the previous studies a pair of recent studies conducted with police data from Brazil, (Basilio et al., 2020, 2019) utilise unsupervised NLP techniques to cluster crimes with the hope of understanding what policing strategies will be suited to different areas of the city. The authors cluster crimes, then show police officers a representative sample of the clusters and ask them to nominate a suitable policing style (traditional, POP or hot-spot). They do not report if the styles were subsequently adopted or if they were successful.

Recently the complexities of models used with crime data has increased and there has been work to extract specific information directly from police free text data, see for example the work by Karystianis et al. (2018, 2019) who seek to explore relationships between mental health and types of domestic violence through rule-based information extraction. However, information extraction requires significant efforts to build rules and dictionaries, and whilst this approach is undoubtedly more effective than manually trawling through thousands of records it still likely represents an implementation hurdle that is too great for routine adoption.

For NLP to aid POP, algorithms need to be developed that can assist with the characterisation of crime events. Whether this is with known characteristics, such as presence of alcohol or type of victim-offender relationship, or perhaps unknown characteristics that are discovered through unsupervised learning. The extant research discussed above provides a foundation for further explorations into the utility of NLP, but to the authors' knowledge no current research focuses on characterising crime events for the purposes of aiding crime prevention, more so if one also considers the desire for such solutions to operate without the need of high performance computing. Thus, the focus of future research to enable POP should be on examining how existing NLP models can be utilised against police generated free text data, in a low resource environment, with the aim of enhancing the characterisation of crime events.

5 NLP Applications

Policing encompasses a diverse set of tasks and responsibilities. It is conceivable that NLP methods could be used to support a broad array of processes associated with these functions. This section will focus on those NLP applications that we believe may offer direct benefit to POP processes, in turn reducing the aforementioned analytical burden associated with their application in real world police settings.

5.1 Classification

Police agencies often flag crimes with keywords to help understand contextual factors associated with a particular offence. For instance, a common flag is to record if an offender is under the influence of alcohol or illegal drugs. Often these flags are not completed thoroughly (there may be hundreds of flags to select from) because police officers are under time-pressure to deal with the situation at hand. Classification algorithms can be used to check these flags and broaden the coverage where officers have described the presence of a flag but not separately recorded it, thereby giving police analysts a more complete picture of known factors. In reference to the Durham example highlighted above classification may have been used to understand if force had been used to enter a given residence or if the residence had been deliberately targeted for example to steal a high performance motor vehicle. This kind of classification can be very useful for the *scan* stage of POP, as enhancing the structured data with additional and more complete crime characteristics from text data can assist in grouping crimes with a similar context or process to form the nucleus of a POP intervention.

5.2 Named Entity Recognition

Named Entity Recognition (NER) may be used by POP analysts to extract specific elements of a crime from crime reports, modus operandi or related intelligence data. For instance, it may be used in assault cases to extract a weapon type, or in domestic abuse cases to understand the relationship between the victim and the offender. Matching on key characteristics like this will facilitate better problem grouping, and will be an improvement on current information availability as quite often this level of detail is not included in a structured manner. In the case of the Durham example NER might have been used to further understand the method of entry - for instance distinguishing between entry methods such as smashing a window or the breaking of a particular type of lock. Crime prevention strategies work best when they are specific, for examples denying entry through snapping patio door locks requires a different strategy to that of combating burglars who exploit insecure properties. NER has the ability to extract this level of detail from crime reports and thereby vastly reducing the time spent in the *analysis* phase of the POP cycle where currently police analysts have to trawl manually through the detail to retrieve this information in order to form an appropriate POP response.

5.3 Clustering

The two previous techniques rely on searching for known characteristics. Unsupervised clustering may improve on this by allowing similar crimes to be grouped so that POP Responses (the R in SARA) can be targeted more efficiently. This would build on the work mentioned above (Kuang et al., 2017; Birks et al., 2020) enabling analysts to be free from the strictures of pre-existing administrative categories and pre-conceived notions of the main causal factors. This clustering can also be extended to encompass other variables, such as time and location information, enabling a richer scan for problems than would otherwise be the case. In the example of burglary, clustering may provide insights into the emergence of new modus operandi. In the past techniques such as hooking keys through letterboxes or snapping certain door locks have emerged and have only been tackled once in widespread use.

Unsupervised techniques could also be useful in the *assessment* phase of the POP framework, as understanding how criminals are adapting to POP responses is an important part of ensuring lasting impacts from POP interventions. The emergence or shift of crime clusters after a POP evaluation can indicate that perhaps new techniques are being used in order to overcome the POP intervention.

6 Ethical Implications

While NLP may offer a range of opportunities to police agencies, utilisation of free-text information from police activities will be subject to similar ethical considerations and biases as other usages of NLP. However, in the case of police usage the a key consideration must be the potential societal impact of biases.

There is a real risk that improper or careless uses of NLP may introduce or perpetuate biases that serve to undermine relationships with the communities that the police are there to serve, thus adding to problems rather than solving them. For this reason it is imperative that ethical considerations, particularly around potential biases are considered before implementation and at all stages of the utilisation, by those devising analytical solutions, analysts who apply them, and those officers that formulate the POP responses. Here we envisage three main areas where use of NLP may be effected by bias. Typically these areas are likely to produce resource allocation biases (Blodgett et al., 2020).

6.1 Data Coverage

Police do not know about all crime, in the UK it is estimated that only around 40% of crime is reported to the police (Tarling and Morris, 2010). The single biggest factor for reporting crime is the seriousness of the offence and in other research (Baumer, 2002) the level of disadvantage in a neighbourhood has correlated with lower reporting rates. This lack of coverage could lead to biases in areas where reporting of crime to the police is lower than in other areas (similar problems already exist when analysing structured police data). That is, NLP could bias resource allocation to areas where recording is more complete and POP implementations are therefor easier to implement, thus leading to an unfair distribution of resources.

6.2 Data Richness

When utilising free-text information the quality of the information extracted is wholly dependent on the information recorded in the first instance. If there are systematic imbalances in the detail of recorded crime across areas, communities or particular groups then these biases will be resident within the free-text data and are likely to be replicated into the available information for POP responses. These biases will need to be guarded against, and as part of the development of NLP for POP there will need to be research into the richness and overall quality of information that is recorded across victim characteristics and crime types. Failure to guard against these biases could see an uneven application of POP activities favouring areas where the police-community information flows are more efficient.

6.3 Algorithmic Bias

Crime is highly concentrated both in space and in relation to particular victims (Farrell, 2015). That is, we would expect different crime types to disproportionately affect different parts of society. Similar crimes are also likely to have similar written descriptions as they describe similar processes. The danger is that if the description of certain crimes are not well understood by certain models, (e.g. certain crime descriptions might use unusual language in the context of the original training data for pre-trained language models) then this will mean poorer information retrieval for certain crimes and therefore potentially for certain victim profiles. This is an example of algorithmic bias (Hooker, 2021) where model selection can effect the distribution and quality of model outputs. Consequently, it will be important to review all models in the context of the specific crimes for which they are to be utilised. This suggests that model applicability will need to be judged at a crime-specific level. This approach should allow metrics to be reviewed for each crime type to make sure that no crimes, and, in turn, victim types are misrepresented. Relatedly, biases in errors from models, perhaps reflecting some of the existing recording practices, will also likely need to be monitored to ensure that particular crimes and/or victims are not disadvantaged by particular models.

7 Pre-Trained Language Models

With the recent proliferation and success of large pre-trained natural language models (e.g. BERT (Devlin et al., 2018)), it is natural to ask whether any of these models can be utilised in the contexts described above. Not only have these models proven powerful across a range of NLP tasks and domains (Lee et al., 2020; Chalkidis et al., 2020; Beltagy et al., 2019), but they also reduce some of the pre-processing burden such as feature engineering and embedding generation. For example, Hugging Face have recently introduced an autoNLP[3] service that allows access to high powered NLP models with very little training. While pre-trained language models are good candidates for facilitating POP through NLP, the ethical challenges discussed above remain pertinent. Commercial offerings of pre-packaged auto-NLP have the potential to be successful within police agencies, and are likely to offer good general results with a relatively low training burden. However, as suggested above, the richness and completeness of the data and the selection and usage of particular models are all potential sources of bias. To combat against these biases, users of the system must be able to understand the models, or be partnered with an agency that can, so that the models can be leveraged in an appropriate fashion. Police will need to delve beneath the surface of potential headline metrics to ensure that the models are not creating new, or perpetuating existing biases. If the police are ill-equipped to do this then it is, in our view, the responsibility of the academic community to investigate these potential problems before systems are used in an operational settings.

8 Societal Implications

Authors submitting to the NLP for Positive Impact workshop were challenged to define what they felt positive impact meant to them in the context of their work. Positive impact for us would be, firstly, the more wide spread adoption of problem oriented policing. This would see more police agencies devoting more of their time to proactive activities and thus to crime prevention rather than focusing on reactive detection and arrest of offenders. The positive societal impact of this would be less people embroiled in the criminal justice system, as the conditions for crime would not manifest themselves as often, and so the opportunities to commit crime would be reduced (Felson and Clarke, 1998). These may seem lofty aims for an analytical technique, and perhaps they are, but in this instance NLP would serve as one part of a new approach to understanding crime. NLP can be the key enabler to unlock the latent potential in a policing technique that will allow a shift away from the contentious response-arrest based policing style to a more balanced system. A balanced system that promotes preventing people, often young and disadvantaged, from becoming criminalised. A system that values a problem prevented over an arrest made or a person incarcerated. In this context, a positive impact would see police agencies more aligned with their communities needs and more focused on preventing crime harms before they occur.

9 Conclusion

Problem-oriented Policing (POP) can be an effective method for reducing crime. Empirical evidence suggests it is more effective than the traditional response model in many situations. However, the key requirement of effective POP is an understanding of the crime event, information that is often stored but is too resource intensive to extract from police administrative free text data. Here we have argued that NLP has the potential to be applied in a range of ways that could lower the analytical burden of police who seek to take a POP approach, thus enabling it to be adopted more extensively. Widespread adoption of POP has the potential to have a positive impact on society. By reducing opportunities for crime, POP is capable of reducing the societal harms that stem from both victimisation and offending. Moreover, the preventative approach advocated by POP relies less heavily on traditional arrest-based response method of policing which can create tensions between the police and local communities that they serve alongside producing a range of social and economic costs downstream.

NLP is not, however, without its drawbacks, and chief among these are the technical knowledge required to utilise the models and a need to account for potential biases. This all means that the introduction of NLP to police agencies will have to be carefully considered, with biases understood, quantified and addressed in ways that minimise undue harm. Generally speaking, police agencies do not have the expertise to do this themselves, and pri-

[3]https://huggingface.co/autonlp

vate providers who might offer such expertise often have a vested interests in protecting their technologies which in turn reduces transparency. As such, it is incumbent on the academic community to investigate how NLP might support such policing efforts and better understand how the aforementioned challenges might be met prior to them manifesting in negative outcomes. If applied correctly and with appropriate safeguards, NLP has the potential to unlock the power of prevention-focused policing techniques, thereby reducing crime and the diverse societal harms associated with its occurrence.

Acknowledgements

We thank the anonymous reviewers for their insightful and helpful comments which have undoubtedly served to enhance the paper. This research was supported by the Economic and Social Research Council.

References

M.P. Basilio, G.S. Brum, and V. Pereira. 2020. A model of policing strategy choice: The integration of the latent dirichlet allocation (lda) method with electre i. *Journal of Modelling in Management*, 15(3):849–891. Cited By 1.

M.P. Basilio, V. Pereira, and G. Brum. 2019. Identification of operational demand in law enforcement agencies: An application based on a probabilistic model of topics. *Data Technologies and Applications*, 53(3):333–372. Cited By 2.

Eric P Baumer. 2002. Neighborhood disadvantage and police notification by victims of violence. *Criminology*, 40(3):579–616.

Iz Beltagy, Kyle Lo, and Arman Cohan. 2019. Scibert: A pretrained language model for scientific text. *arXiv preprint arXiv:1903.10676*.

Daniel Birks, Alex Coleman, and David Jackson. 2020. Unsupervised identification of crime problems from police free-text data. *Crime Science*, 9(1):18.

Su Lin Blodgett, Solon Barocas, Hal Daumé III, and Hanna Wallach. 2020. Language (technology) is power: A critical survey of" bias" in nlp. *arXiv preprint arXiv:2005.14050*.

Anthony A Braga, Andrew V Papachristos, and David M Hureau. 2014. The effects of hot spots policing on crime: An updated systematic review and meta-analysis. *Justice quarterly*, 31(4):633–663.

Anthony A Braga, David L Weisburd, Elin J Waring, Lorraine Green Mazerolle, William Spelman, and Francis Gajewski. 1999. Problem-oriented policing in violent crime places: A randomized controlled experiment. *Criminology*, 37(3):541–580.

Gian Maria Campedelli. 2020. Where are we? Using Scopus to map the literature at the intersection between artificial intelligence and research on crime. *Journal of Computational Social Science*.

Ilias Chalkidis, Manos Fergadiotis, Prodromos Malakasiotis, Nikolaos Aletras, and Ion Androutsopoulos. 2020. Legal-bert: The muppets straight out of law school. *arXiv preprint arXiv:2010.02559*.

Lawrence E Cohen and Marcus Felson. 1979. Social change and crime rate trends: A routine activity approach. *American sociological review*, pages 588–608.

Jacob Devlin, Ming-Wei Chang, Kenton Lee, and Kristina Toutanova. 2018. Bert: Pre-training of deep bidirectional transformers for language understanding. *arXiv preprint arXiv:1810.04805*.

John E Eck and William Spelman. 1987. Problem-solving: Problem-oriented policing in newport news.

Graham Farrell. 2015. Crime concentration theory. *Crime prevention and community Safety*, 17(4):233–248.

Marcus Felson and Ronald V Clarke. 1998. Opportunity makes the thief. *Police research series, paper*, 98:1–36.

H. Goldstein. 1990. *Problem-oriented Policing*. Temple University Press.

Herman Goldstein. 1979. Improving policing: A problem-oriented approach. *Crime and Delinquency*, 25(2):236–258.

Hossein Hassani, Xu Huang, Emmanuel S Silva, and Mansi Ghodsi. 2016. A review of data mining applications in crime. *Statistical Analysis and Data Mining: The ASA Data Science Journal*, 9(3):139–154.

Joshua C Hinkle, David Weisburd, Cody W Telep, and Kevin Petersen. 2020. Problem-oriented policing for reducing crime and disorder: An updated systematic review and meta-analysis. *Campbell Systematic Reviews*, 16(2):e1089.

Sara Hooker. 2021. Moving beyond "algorithmic bias is a data problem". *Patterns*, 2(4):100241.

George Karystianis, Armita Adily, Peter Schofield, Lee Knight, Clara Galdon, David Greenberg, Louisa Jorm, Goran Nenadic, and Tony Butler. 2018. Automatic extraction of mental health disorders from domestic violence police narratives: text mining study. *Journal of medical internet research*, 20(9):e11548.

George Karystianis, Armita Adily, Peter W Schofield, David Greenberg, Louisa Jorm, Goran Nenadic, and Tony Butler. 2019. Automated analysis of domestic violence police reports to explore abuse types and victim injuries: text mining study. *Journal of medical Internet research*, 21(3):e13067.

Da Kuang, P Jeffrey Brantingham, and Andrea L Bertozzi. 2017. Crime topic modeling. *Crime Science*, 6(1):12.

Jinhyuk Lee, Wonjin Yoon, Sungdong Kim, Donghyeon Kim, Sunkyu Kim, Chan Ho So, and Jaewoo Kang. 2020. Biobert: a pre-trained biomedical language representation model for biomedical text mining. *Bioinformatics*, 36(4):1234–1240.

Ben Marshall and Michael Townsley. 2006. Needles or needless? Technical report, Jill Dando Institute, UCL.

Michael Scott, John Eck, Knutsson Johannes, and Herman Goldstein. 2016. Problem-oriented policing. In Richard Wortley and Michael Townsley, editors, *Environmental criminology and crime analysis*, 2 edition, chapter 11, pages 227–258. Taylor & Francis.

Michael Scott and Stuart Kirby. 2012. Implementing pop: leading, structuring and managing a problem-oriented police agency.

A Sidebottom, K Bullock, R Armitage, M Ashby, C Clemmow, S Kirby, Gloria Laycock, and Nick Tilley. 2020. Problem-oriented policing in england and wales 2019.

Natalia Silveira, Timothy Dozat, Marie-Catherine de Marneffe, Samuel Bowman, Miriam Connor, John Bauer, and Christopher D. Manning. 2014. A gold standard dependency corpus for English. In *Proceedings of the Ninth International Conference on Language Resources and Evaluation (LREC-2014)*.

Roger Tarling and Katie Morris. 2010. Reporting crime to the police. *The British Journal of Criminology*, 50(3):474–490.

Bruce Taylor, Christopher S Koper, and Daniel J Woods. 2011. A randomized controlled trial of different policing strategies at hot spots of violent crime. *Journal of experimental criminology*, 7(2):149–181.

Nick Tilley. 2008. Modern approaches to policing: community, problem-oriented and intelligence-led. *Handbook of policing*, 2.

Empathy and Hope: Resource Transfer to Model Inter-country Social Media Dynamics

Clay H. Yoo[♣] **Shriphani Palakodety**[♡] **Rupak Sarkar**[◇] **Ashiqur R. KhudaBukhsh**[♣*]
[♣]Carnegie Mellon University
[♡]Onai
[◇]Maulana Abul Kalam Azad University of Technology
hyungony@andrew.cmu.edu, spalakod@onai.com,
rupaksarkar.cs@gmail.com, akhudabu@cs.cmu.edu

Abstract

The ongoing COVID-19 pandemic resulted in significant ramifications for international relations ranging from travel restrictions, global ceasefires, and international vaccine production and sharing agreements. Amidst a wave of infections in India that resulted in a systemic breakdown of healthcare infrastructure, a social welfare organization based in Pakistan offered to procure medical-grade oxygen to assist India - a nation which was involved in four wars with Pakistan in the past few decades. In this paper, we focus on Pakistani Twitter users' response to the ongoing healthcare crisis in India. While #IndiaNeedsOxygen and #PakistanStandsWithIndia featured among the top-trending hashtags in Pakistan, divisive hashtags such as #EndiaSaySorryToKashmir simultaneously started trending. Against the backdrop of a contentious history including four wars, divisive content of this nature, especially when a country is facing an unprecedented healthcare crisis, fuels further deterioration of relations. In this paper, we define a new task of detecting *supportive* content and demonstrate that existing *NLP for social impact* tools can be effectively harnessed for such tasks within a quick turnaround time. We also release the first publicly available data set[1] at the intersection of geopolitical relations and a raging pandemic in the context of India and Pakistan.

1 Introduction

The COVID-19 pandemic started in late 2019 (Carvalho et al., 2021) and as of this writing is still ongoing. Several factors - geopolitical, economic, social among others - dramatically influenced health outcomes around the world. In this paper, we focus on the ongoing (as of May 2021) infection wave in India (CNN, 2021). After aggressive initial steps to successfully curb the spread of the virus, case counts exploded in India towards the end of April 2021. The rapidity of the spread overwhelmed the healthcare infrastructure in the country. A widespread shortage of medical-grade oxygen (BBC, 2021), overworked medical staff, and full capacity emergency rooms became the norm in major population centers.

The crisis was heavily discussed on social media and the associated hashtags were among the most discussed Twitter trends globally. In Pakistan, a neighboring country that fought four wars with India over the past seven decades (Paul and Paul, 2005), a significant volume of tweets expressed solidarity with the Indian populace primarily through two hashtags - #IndiaNeedsOxygen and #PakistanStandsWithIndia. In addition, the hashtag #EndiaSaySorryToKashmir started trending in Pakistan. The tweets using this hashtag were primarily divisive and often referenced a long-running territorial dispute at the heart of India-Pakistan relations. Amidst a far-reaching and rapidly progressing pandemic, divisive content of this nature negatively impacts the mental well-being of the affected population and can contribute to strained relations.

Hashtag based filtering, while extremely effective, cannot solely identify *supportive* content. For instance, users can hijack trending hashtags and post content that violates the spirit of the hashtag (see Table 1). Also, replies or responses to a controversial tweet with a divisive hashtag may still retain the same hashtag but the content may reflect a unifying message. Rapidly evolving crises also require a fast turnaround time which can preclude

* Ashiqur R. KhudaBukhsh is the corresponding author.
[1]Data is publicly available at https://github.com/anton-sturluson/empathy-and-hope.

Proceedings of the 1st Workshop on NLP for Positive Impact, pages 125–134
Bangkok, Thailand (online), August 5, 2021.

#PakistanStandsWithIndia	we're rivals not enemies. we breath same air speak same languages. our prayers , wishes and thoughts are with our brothers from other side of the border. We need to fight this bettle together
#PakistanstandswithIndia	karma is bitch, india deserves what's happening right now because that's what they did with people of kashmir. kashmir's can't take revenge but god has his plans for redemption.
#IndiaNeedsOxygen	Despite the fact that we have our political conflicts, but I really pray for their good health. Get well soon india. Pakistani nation is with you.
#IndiaNeedsOxygen	India deserves this . You are facing what you did to kashmir and fool pakistani supporting india on this you are just slaves to british thats all ..
#EndiaSaySorryToKashmir	Kashmir is our and it is all of it. Until the independence of Kashmir, there will be war till the destruction of India.
#EndiaSaySorryToKashmir	Political differences have their place but the prayers of us Pakistanis are with our Indian brothers and sisters. May Allah give health to all.

Table 1: Example tweets where the hashtag and the tweet content agree (highlighted in blue) and disagree (highlighted in red).

sophisticated, time-consuming solutions.

In this paper, we present a method to automatically detect *supportive* content from the tweet text (excluding hashtags, mentions, emojis, and urls). Our minimally supervised approach combines multiple soft signals - a *hope speech* classifier that detects peace-seeking content (Palakodety et al., 2020a), and an *empathy-distress* classifier trained on a well-known empathy-distress data set (Buechel et al., 2018). We further demonstrate superior performance in presence of supervision and release an annotated data set in this important humanitarian domain.

Model reusability is a major challenge in NLP applications (Arango et al., 2019; Beltagy et al., 2019). We see our paper as preliminary evidence that NLP methods for positive impact research are not isolated efforts, and solutions arising from adjacent tasks can be re-purposed to tackle newer challenges.

NLP for positive impact: Our work can be described by the following two broad themes specific to this workshop - *online well-being & positive information sharing* and *case studies for NLP for social good.* In order to create a positive impact, we believe a research contribution needs to satisfy a subset of the following conditions: (1) a problem domain with a high societal impact; (2) resource-sharing to facilitate scientific progress; and (3) a research theme that spawns a rich line of follow-up work.

Our paper has the following contributions:

Social: We analyze the bilateral relationship between countries with a contentious history amidst a raging pandemic. Our work is at the intersection of two important themes - geopolitical relations and healthcare crises. We show a significant outpouring of support and solidarity between the two nations' online communities in the context of the pandemic. Barring a few recent efforts (Palakodety et al., 2020a; Tyagi et al., 2020), there is little literature on web manifestation of the India-Pakistan relationship co-occurring with other crises. To the best of our knowledge, this is the first analysis of social media text interactions between India and Pakistan amidst a pandemic.

Resource: We present a data set of tweets exploring geopolitical relations between historic adversaries amidst a health crisis. Publicly available data sets expressing empathy and distress are scarce (Buechel et al., 2018). Beyond our immediate objective of detecting *supportive* tweets, this data set may be useful in answering several other research questions.

The reusability argument: We present a compelling case study that *NLP for positive impact applications* are not isolated tasks. Rather, multiple existing resources can be combined to tackle a new challenge in a fast turnaround time setting.

2 Task

In this paper, we consider the task of detecting *supportive* content. Supportive behavior in language has been previously studied. For example, a AAAI-2020 shared task focused on detecting *disclosure* and *supportiveness* from written accounts of casual and confessional conversations (Chhaya et al., 2020). Our task is slightly different in the sense that we are interested in detecting content where speakers are supporting a country/people severely affected by a healthcare crisis.

We define *supportive* content to be either expressing empathy, distress, or solidarity. Our def-

Empathy	Our hearts go out to our neighbours who are facing unprecedented misery. Pakistani People are praying for you ...
Distress	I am a Pakistani but seriously this is heartbreaking what i am seeing from few days about India.We are enemies but this is about humanity,If we unite in this pandemic we both countries can fight together and can win this battle together,Peace ...
Solidarity	As a human we all are together Pray for India and for all people all over the world who are suffering from COVID May Allah pak save us from this dangerous COVID-19 Stop hating start praying

Table 2: Example tweets exhibiting empathy, distress, and solidarity.

initions for empathy and distress follow (Buechel et al., 2018) that considers extensive psychology literature (Batson et al., 1987; Batson and Shaw, 1991; Sober and Wilson, 1999; Goetz et al., 2010; Mikulincer and Shaver, 2010). (Buechel et al., 2018) defines empathy as a warm, tender, and compassionate feeling for a suffering entity, and distress as a self-focused, negative affective state that occurs when one feels upset due to witnessing an entity's suffering or need. Among the several existing definitions of solidarity, we borrow the following (Wildt, 1999): a mutual attachment between individuals (groups) that encompasses two levels: (1) a *factual level* of actual common ground between the individuals (groups); and (2) a *normative level* of mutual obligations to aid each other, as and when should be necessary. In Table 2 we present three example tweets exhibiting empathy, distress, and solidarity.

Our definition for *not-supportive* content does not have a similar psychological grounding. Our annotators observed that the *not-supportive* content in this specific context, primarily (1) expressed politically motivated hate; (2) demonstrated a warmongering attitude; (3) expressed schadenfreude; (4) mentioned politically contentious issues; and (5) expressed unrelated content such as product promotion etc.

3 Resource

We use two existing resources for our work. Next, we present a short description of these resources.

3.1 *Hope speech* classifier

The *hope speech* detection task introduced in (Palakodety et al., 2020a) involves identifying social media text content with a unifying message encouraging peace, discouraging war, and highlighting the economic, social, and human costs of conflict against the backdrop of the 2019 India-Pakistan conflict. A detailed definition of *hope speech* with illustrative examples is provided in (Palakodety et al., 2020a).

3.2 Empathy and Distress Classifier

We train a classifier on the empathy-distress data set introduced in (Buechel et al., 2018). The data set is grounded in prior psychology literature on empathy and distress (Batson et al., 1987; Batson and Shaw, 1991; Sober and Wilson, 1999; Goetz et al., 2010; Mikulincer and Shaver, 2010). The data set consists of 418 news article excerpts from popular news platforms and responses to them from 403 annotators, resulting in a total of 2,015 responses (5 articles per annotator). Upon filtering responses that deviated from the task description, the pruned final data set consists of 1,860 responses (empathy: 916, distress: 905). We split this data into train and test sets in 90/10 ratio and train a binary classifier using `BERT` (Devlin et al., 2019) (`bert-base-uncased`) using transformers library (Wolf et al., 2020).

4 Data

Our data set, $\mathcal{T}$, consists of 309,394 tweets posted by 150,289 unique users collected between 21 April 2021 and 04 May 2021. The top trending hashtags in Pakistan for April 22 and April 23 were retrieved from `https://getdaytrends.com/` and all associated tweets were obtained using the Twitter API[2]. Other closely related trending hashtags were also included (e.g., #IndiaNeedsOxygen and #IndiaNeedOxygen, or #PakistanStandsWithIndia and #PakistanStandWithIndia). Additional details are in Table 4. In this paper, any mention of a hashtag includes closely spelled variants (e.g. #IndiaNeed(s)Oxygen, #PakistanStand(s)WithIndia, or #I(E)ndiaSaySorryToKashmir). We define the following two hashtag sets: $\mathcal{H}_{supportive}$ = {#IndiaNeed(s)Oxygen, #PakistanStand(s)WithIndia} ; and $\mathcal{H}_{not\text{-}supportive}$ = {#I(E)ndiaSaySorryToKashmir}.

Subsets of interest: Two mutually disjoint subsets of $\mathcal{T}$: $\mathcal{T}_{supportive}$ and $\mathcal{T}_{not\text{-}supportive}$ are de-

[2]https://developer.twitter.com/en/docs/twitter-api

fined as follows. $\mathcal{T}_{supportive}$ includes tweets containing one or more of the $\mathcal{H}_{supportive}$ hashtags and $\mathcal{T}_{not\text{-}supportive}$ includes tweets containing one or more of the $\mathcal{H}_{not\text{-}supportive}$ hashtags. Tweets containing any intersection of the $\mathcal{H}_{supportive}$ and $\mathcal{H}_{not\text{-}supportive}$ hashtags are discarded from either subset and thus there is no intersection between $\mathcal{T}_{supportive}$ and $\mathcal{T}_{not\text{-}supportive}$. Since classification of extremely short texts is a well-established challenge (Sindhwani et al., 2009; Attenberg et al., 2010; KhudaBukhsh et al., 2015), in all of our sampling experiments involving a text classifier, we impose a length restriction of 10 or more tokens after preprocessing. Furthermore, our classifiers are only presented with the tweet text, i.e., the body of the tweet with hashtags, emojis, urls, and mentions removed.

Generating country labels for tweets: The Twitter API bundles geographic location (coordinates) with tweets. In addition, we utilized a weak signal - if a user's Twitter handle contains an India or Pakistan flag emoji, then we assume their tweets originated in India or Pakistan respectively. In the cases where the location information and our signal are both present, we notice no inconsistency, indicating our weak country signal is robust.

5 Characterization of the Tweets

5.1 Likes and Retweets

We now characterize the retweets and likes of each of these hashtags. Let $\#ht_{Ind}$, $\#ht_{Pak}$, and $\#ht_{Other}$ denote the subsets of tweets that contain the hashtag *ht* and originate in India, Pakistan, and other (or unknown), respectively. Table 5 shows that overall, the tweets containing *supportive* hashtags received fewer likes and retweets than those containing *not-supportive* hashtags. We further notice that tweets containing *supportive* hashtags that originated in Pakistan received substantially more likes than those from India. Our results though come with the following caveats. Multiple factors can influence our data collection process such as the inner workings of Twitter algorithms or the Twitter API. Also, our focus is on English tweets; previous studies have reported that Hindi is more commonly used to express negative sentiment in social media content generated in the Indian subcontinent (Rudra et al., 2016; KhudaBukhsh et al., 2020).

5.2 Hashtag Co-occurrence

We next measure in-group and out-group co-occurrence of *supportive* and *not-supportive* hashtags within a single tweet. Pair-wise Jaccard index between the tweet sets using various hashtags is computed[3] and shown in Table 3. We observe that among all hashtag pairs, ⟨#IndiaNeed(s)Oxygen and #PakistanStand(s)WithIndia⟩ occurs the most. We observe that qualitatively, there is a stark contrast between tweets containing $\mathcal{H}_{supportive}$ hashtags and tweets containing $\mathcal{H}_{not\text{-}supportive}$ hashtags with the dominant theme in the former being empathy, distress, and solidarity. Figure 1 presents a word-cloud visualization of the tweets employing the three hashtags.

6 Related Work

Social media response to the ongoing pandemic has received significant research attention: (1) health misinformation (Memon and Carley, 2020; Hossain et al., 2020; Cinelli et al., 2020), (2) polarization (Cruickshank and Carley, 2020; KhudaBukhsh et al., 2021), (3) disease modeling (Li et al., 2020), etc. Counterhate measures along the line of counterspeech research (Benesch et al., 2016; Benesch, 2014; Mathew et al., 2018; Palakodety et al., 2020b) to combat Anti-Asian hate (Ziems et al., 2020), and community blame (Saha et al., 2021) has been studied. Our work contrasts with existing literature in three ways: (1) we analyze bilateral relations of nuclear adversaries amidst a raging pandemic; (2) we release a novel data set for wider use exploring related research questions; and (3) we present a new method that combines recent *NLP for positive impact* advances in a new, timely, and important task.

While the political volatility between India and Pakistan has been extensively studied by social scientists (Malik and Wirsing, 2002; Schofield, 2010; Bose, 2009), barring few recent lines of work (Palakodety et al., 2020a; KhudaBukhsh et al., 2020; Tyagi et al., 2020), social media interactions between the civilians of India and Pakistan has received little or no attention. All recent work on Indian and Pakistani social media (Palakodety et al., 2020a; KhudaBukhsh et al., 2020; Tyagi et al., 2020) focused on a solitary incident - the 2019 India-Pakistan conflict triggered by the Pulwama terror attack across different social media platforms.

[3]Jaccard index is a statistic to gauge similarity between two sets, $\mathcal{A}$, $\mathcal{B}$, expressed as $\frac{|\mathcal{A} \cap \mathcal{B}|}{|\mathcal{A} \cup \mathcal{B}|}$.

hashtags	#IndiaNeed(s)Oxygen	#PakistanStand(s)WithIndia	#I(E)ndiaSaySorryToKashmir
#IndiaNeed(s)Oxygen	-	0.0887	0.0247
#PakistanStand(s)WithIndia	0.0887	-	0.0405
#I(E)ndiaSaySorryToKashmir	0.0247	0.0405	-

Table 3: Jaccard index of tweet subsets employing various hashtags.

(a) #IndiaNeed(s)Oxygen (b) #PakistanStand(s)WithIndia (c) #I(E)ndiaSaySorryToKashmir

Figure 1: A word cloud visualization of the tweet contents and the associated hashtag used. Hashtags and punctuations are removed as a preprocessing step.

Hashtag	Total	India	Pakistan
#IndiaNeedsOxygen	145,975	26,383	19,748
#IndiaNeedOxygen	24,488	5,049	2,400
#PakistanStandsWithIndia	96,226	12,331	21,583
#PakistanStandWithIndia	17,406	2,772	3,790
#EndiaSaySorryToKashmir	25,081	87	8,022
#IndiaSaySorryToKashmir	557	15	169
All	309,733	46,651	55,712

Table 4: Statistics of dataset crawled between 21 April 2021 and 04 May 2021.

While (Palakodety et al., 2020a) introduced a novel task of detecting hostility-diffusing, peace seeking *hope speech* and considered comments on relevant YouTube videos as the data set, (Tyagi et al., 2020) is the first work on analyzing web-manifestation (Twitter) of political polarization between the two countries and how political parties factor in these discussions.

Our work leverages two existing resources: (1) a *hope speech* classifier introduced in (Palakodety et al., 2020a); and (2) a well-known *empathy-distress* data set (Buechel et al., 2018). As already mentioned, our work differs in a key way that we re-purpose these resources for a new *NLP for positive impact* task: detecting *supportive* tweets in the context of social media discussions during a national healthcare crisis. Our work also draws inspiration from recent findings about mining stance from hashtags (Kumar, 2018).

7 Methods, Results, and Discussion

Research question: *Does sampling tweets containing $\mathcal{H}_{supportive}$ hashtags alone suffice?*

We first investigate if hashtag-based filtering alone guarantees *supportive* tweets with a high probability. We randomly sample 1,000 tweet texts from $\mathcal{T}_{supportive}$ and manually annotate them. Our annotators are provided only the tweet texts, i.e., the body of the tweet excluding hashtags, urls, mentions, and emojis. Three annotators fluent in English, Hindi, and Urdu, and well-versed with the geopolitical events between India and Pakistan first independently annotated these tweets and achieved a Fleiss' κ score of 0.76 indicating moderate agreement. Next, disagreements are resolved through a follow-up adjudication process and a higher Fleiss' κ score of 0.86 is reached. Of the randomly chosen 1,000 tweets 444 tweets, i.e., 44.4% were marked positive. This result indicates that solely relying on *supportive* hashtag will not do better than chance and underscores the importance of sophisticated methods.

In addition, we randomly sampled 1,000 tweet texts from $\mathcal{T}_{supportive} \cup \mathcal{T}_{not\text{-}supportive}$ as our test set (denoted as $\mathcal{D}_{eval}$). Throughout our annotation process, whenever consensus label is absent, following standard literature (Bowman et al., 2015), we consider the majority label as the gold-standard label. Annotator subjectivity is a well-studied research

Hashtag$_{Location}$	Like	Retweet
#IndiaNeed(s)Oxygen$_{Ind}$	2.32 ± 63.80	1631.07 ± 3393.86
#IndiaNeed(s)Oxygen$_{Pak}$	4.39 ± 96.50	322.98 ± 1107.28
#IndiaNeed(s)Oxygen$_{Other}$	2.72 ± 215.81	1306.71 ± 2934.60
#PakistanStand(s)WithIndia$_{Ind}$	2.46 ± 78.14	2313.45 ± 2898.67
#PakistanStand(s)WithIndia$_{Pak}$	8.58 ± 358.16	665.03 ± 1559.59
#PakistanStand(s)WithIndia$_{Other}$	2.65 ± 117.25	1246.58 ± 2195.85
#I(E)ndiaSaySorryToKashmir$_{Ind}$	1.49 ± 4.97	191.45 ± 266.38
#I(E)ndiaSaySorryToKashmir$_{Pak}$	1.26 ± 24.80	276.28 ± 300.87
#I(E)ndiaSaySorryToKashmir$_{Other}$	1.51 ± 37.61	248.33 ± 293.02

Table 5: Location-specific like and retweet behavior.

Label	Percentage	Like	Retweet
supportive$_{Pak}$	85.30%	6.64 ± 270.6	505.61 ± 1378.1
not-supportive$_{Pak}$	14.70%	1.26 ± 24.8	276.28 ± 300.9

Table 6: Like and retweet behavior and count of *supportive* and *not-supportive* tweets from Pakistan.

Model	Precision	Recall	F1
$\mathcal{M}^{\text{BERT}}_{supervised}$	83.28 ± 0.8	80.98 ± 1.6	81.14 ± 1.6
$\mathcal{M}^{\text{BERT}}_{informed}$	80.78 ± 0.5	80.60 ± 0.7	80.62 ± 0.6
$\mathcal{M}^{\text{BERT}}_{hashtag}$	72.93 ± 1.2	53.78 ± 1.6	48.58 ± 2.5
$\mathcal{M}^{\text{SVM}}_{supervised}$	66.38 ± 0.5	91.65 ± 0.8	76.99 ± 0.4
$\mathcal{M}^{\text{SVM}}_{informed}$	56.98 ± 0.6	94.03 ± 0.3	70.95 ± 0.5
$\mathcal{M}^{\text{SVM}}_{hashtag}$	42.69 ± 0.03	100.00 ± 0	59.83 ± 0.03

Table 7: Test performance comparison. Five runs per experiment were conducted and mean and standard deviation are presented.

area (Pavlick and Kwiatkowski, 2019), and in order to facilitate further research, we also provide individual annotator's labels.

Research question: *Do the hope speech and the empathy-distress classifiers present any discernible signal to differentiate between supportive and not-supportive tweets?*

As already described, the *hope speech* classifier is designed for a different scenario of detecting peace-seeking, hostility diffusing content from social media discussions generated during a conflict. Our current task of detecting *supportive* tweets, although related, is not identical. Furthermore, the classifier is trained on a different social media platform, YouTube, that allows unstructured text without any length restriction, whereas Twitter allows unstructured text but imposes a length restriction. Similarly, the *empathy-distress* classifier is trained on a different data set of user responses to news events. Hence, a pertinent research question is if the *hope speech* classifier or the *empathy-distress* classifier is any good in differentiating between *supportive* and *not-supportive* tweets.

We first start with a simple experiment to illustrate that the resources provide useful signal. Let $S = \{\langle x, y \rangle\}$ such that $x \sim \mathcal{T}_{supportive}$ and $y \sim \mathcal{T}_{not\text{-}supportive}$, i.e., S consists of tweet pairs $\langle x, y \rangle$ where x and y are randomly drawn from the pool of tweets with *supportive* and *not-supportive* hashtags, respectively. Let $\mathcal{P}_h(z)$ and $\mathcal{P}_e(z)$ denote the predicted *hope speech* and *empathy-distress* probabilities of tweet z. We compute: $r_h = \frac{\Sigma_{\langle x,y \rangle \in \mathcal{S}_s} \mathbb{I}(\mathcal{P}_h(x) > \mathcal{P}_h(y))}{|\mathcal{S}|}$ and $r_e = \frac{\Sigma_{\langle x,y \rangle \in \mathcal{S}_s} \mathbb{I}(\mathcal{P}_e(x) > \mathcal{P}_e(y))}{|\mathcal{S}|}$ where $\mathbb{I}$ denotes an indicator function and $|\mathcal{S}|$, i.e., the number of randomly drawn pairs, is set to 100,000. We ran this experiment five times and found r_h to be equal to $69.3 \pm 0.13\%$ and r_e to be equal to $47.8 \pm 0.12\%$, indicating that a randomly drawn sample from $\mathcal{T}_{supportive}$ is more likely to receive a higher *hope speech* score ($\mathcal{P}_h(.)$) than a randomly drawn sample from $\mathcal{T}_{not\text{-}supportive}$. However, we do not notice similar trends with our *empathy-distress* classifier.

It is unsurprising that r_h has a much higher value than r_e. The *hope speech* classifier is trained on a data set relevant to a recent India-Pakistan conflict and thus has a substantial overlap in domain. Hence, a general nature of positive dialogue may indicate a desire to put things behind and help each other. In contrast, the *empathy-distress* classifier is trained on a broad, diverse, data set of user responses to news events and has no overlap with the current domain. However, when we rank tweets from $\mathcal{T}_{supportive}$ by the classifier's probability, we notice that top predictions are of extremely high quality in both cases. We annotate top 1,000 unique tweets from $\mathcal{T}_{supportive}$ ranked by $\mathcal{P}_h(.)$ and obtain 950 positives. Similarly, top 1,000 unique tweets from $\mathcal{T}_{supportive}$ ranked by $\mathcal{P}_e(.)$ yield 899 positives upon manual annotation. Moreover, the two classifiers complement each other as among the top 1,000 unique tweets from the *hope speech* classifier and the top 1,000 unique tweets from the *empathy-*

distress classifier had minimal overlap (62 samples). This annotation task also yielded a substantially higher Fleiss' κ score (0.8068) without any follow-up adjudication process indicating that the chosen samples have less ambiguity than our earlier experiment that involved annotating randomly selected tweets from $\mathcal{T}_{supportive}$. Our results thus indicate existing resources can be harnessed for informed sampling yielding high-quality positives.

Research question: *How to leverage existing resources to design an effective classifier to detect supportive tweets?*

We utilize two existing resources, a *hope speech* classifier from (Palakodety et al., 2020a), and an *empathy-distress* data set from (Buechel et al., 2018). We first train an *empathy-distress* classifier on the *empathy-distress* data set that can classify tweets as exhibiting empathy or distress, or not.

Our pipeline utilizes the *hope speech* and *empathy-distress* classifiers and constructs a weakly labeled data set where the positive examples exhibit themes like empathy, distress, support, and solidarity - the *supportive speech*, and the negative examples exhibit themes like controversy, whataboutism, and hostility - the *not-supportive speech*. The two classifiers are used to label tweets and the positive class probability is used to rank all the tweets in the set $\mathcal{T}_{supportive} \cup \mathcal{T}_{not\text{-}supportive}$ yielding two ranked lists. $\mathcal{D}^{+}{}_{informed}$ contains all tweets using any of the top 1,000 tweets in both ranked lists (2,000 in total, 1,938 unique) are considered positive samples, and a set of negative samples, $\mathcal{D}^{-}{}_{informed}$, is constructed by randomly sampling 500 tweets each from the bottom 80% of both ranked lists (1,000 in total, 1,000 unique). The full data set construction pipeline is presented in Algorithm 1. The trained model is denoted as $\mathcal{M}_{informed}$.

Earlier research has reported hashtags as an effective way to obtain weak labels (Kumar, 2018). We contrast $\mathcal{M}_{informed}$ against a baseline that uses hashtags alone as a source of weak labels and contains the identical number of (weakly labeled) positives and negatives as $\mathcal{D}_{informed}$. Essentially, any tweet belonging to $\mathcal{T}_{supportive}$ is considered a positive and any tweet belonging to $\mathcal{T}_{not\text{-}supportive}$ is considered a negative. Positives and negative examples are randomly sampled from these sets and a data set with the same proportions as $\mathcal{D}_{informed}$ is constructed. The trained model is denoted as $\mathcal{M}_{hashtag}$.

We train our classifiers using BERT (Devlin et al., 2019) (bert-base-uncased) using the transformers library (Wolf et al., 2020) and a 90/10 train/validation split. In addition, since English social media content from the Indian subcontinent exhibits a variety of disfluencies (Sarkar et al., 2020), and since the SVM baseline has been successfully applied to the original *hope speech* detection task (Palakodety et al., 2020a), we include an SVM baseline as well that uses TF-IDF vectors as document feature representations. The trained models are evaluated on $\mathcal{D}_{eval}$, 1000 randomly sampled tweets from $\mathcal{T}_{supportive} \cup \mathcal{T}_{not\text{-}supportive}$. Note that hashtags, urls, emojis, mentions, and punctuation are removed from the tweets prior to training.

7.1 Performance Comparison

Table 7 shows that $\mathcal{M}_{informed}$ substantially outperforms $\mathcal{M}_{hashtag}$ on the test set and thus underscores why hashtag-based-filtering may not solely suffice. Also, this result indicates that the joint concept of empathy, distress, and solidarity is learnable, and in this context, the resources exhibit synergy. Understandably, a supervised solution will improve the performance since weak labels obtained using the *hope speech* and *empathy-distress* classifier, while high-quality, still had some amount of noise. Compared to the informed sampling, we observe a slight performance boost in our supervised solutions. We also notice the BERT-based classifiers outperformed SVM baselines.

While our primary focus is on Twitter, several social media platforms exist where hashtags are not as prevalent. YouTube, a highly popular social media platform, is one such example. We performed an in-the-wild test where we obtained the top 100 *supportive* predictions from a new data set consisting of 31,232 comments on 185 YouTube COVID-19-related videos from the official YouTube channel of Geo TV, a highly popular Pakistani news channel. We used the best $\mathcal{M}^{\text{BERT}}_{informed}$ model to test our minimally supervised method's in-the-wild performance. Out of 100 such comments, a manual evaluation revealed that 70 were positive. Table 8 lists a few such randomly sampled comments. A reasonably high precision of our model indicates its cross-platform viability and applicability in downstream tasks like moderation.

7.2 Discussion

Research question: *How Pakistan Responded to this crisis?* In our earlier analysis in Section 5.1, we

Algorithm 1: *Construct*($\mathcal{D}_{informed}$, $\mathcal{M}_{informed}$)

Input: $\mathcal{T}$ is the full set of tweets, $\mathcal{T}_{supportive}$, $\mathcal{T}_{not\text{-}supportive} \subset \mathcal{T}$; $\mathcal{M}_{hopeSpeech}$ is the hope speech classifier; $\mathcal{M}_{empathyDistress}$ is the empathy-distress classifier
Output: $\mathcal{D}_{informed} \subset \mathcal{T}$; and $\mathcal{M}_{informed}$ - a model trained on $\mathcal{D}_{informed}$
Procedure:
foreach tweet $t \in \mathcal{T}_{supportive} \cup \mathcal{T}_{not\text{-}supportive}$ **do**
  classify t using $\mathcal{M}_{hopeSpeech}$ and $\mathcal{M}_{empathyDistress}$ yielding positive probabilities $\mathcal{P}_h$ and $\mathcal{P}_e$.
end
Sort $\mathcal{T}_{supportive}$ using $\mathcal{P}_h$ and $\mathcal{P}_e$ yielding two ranked lists $\mathcal{R}_{supportive_h}$ and $\mathcal{R}_{supportive_e}$.
Take the top 1,000 tweets from $\mathcal{R}_{supportive_h}$ and $\mathcal{R}_{supportive_e}$ yielding 2,000 tweets - these are the positive samples - $\mathcal{D}^{+}{}_{informed}$.
Sort $\mathcal{T}_{not\text{-}supportive}$ using $\mathcal{P}_h$ and $\mathcal{P}_e$ yielding two ranked lists $\mathcal{R}_{not\text{-}supportive_h}$ and $\mathcal{R}_{not\text{-}supportive_e}$.
Sample 500 tweets from the bottom 80% of $\mathcal{R}_h$ and $\mathcal{R}_e$ yielding 1,000 tweets - these are the negative samples - $\mathcal{D}^{-}{}_{informed}$.
$\mathcal{D}_{informed} \leftarrow \mathcal{D}^{+}{}_{informed} \cup \mathcal{D}^{-}{}_{informed}$
Duplicates are discarded from $\mathcal{D}_{informed}$
$\mathcal{M}_{informed} \leftarrow$ a classifier trained on $\mathcal{D}_{informed}$
Output: $\mathcal{D}_{informed}$ and $\mathcal{M}_{informed}$

Life is dying in our neighboring country. We have differences. We have fought wars, but we are neighbors. Sighing lives in India. My lord, who will do good except you There is no religion of humanity. May Allah save the whole world including India from this epidemic. Amen
From Pakistan I request my all Muslims Humanity has no religion and no boundaries ....Pray for all world and for India
Be safe everone, wear mask everytime, may your country doesn't goes through what our country is going. Greetings from india

Table 8: Randomly sampled YouTube comments predicted as *supportive* by $\mathcal{M}^{\mathrm{BERT}}_{informed}$ in the wild.

found that tweets containing $\mathcal{H}_{supportive}$ hashtags originating in Pakistan (1) heavily outnumbered those containing $\mathcal{H}_{not\text{-}supportive}$ hashtags; and (2) received a larger share of the likes and retweets. We investigate the like and retweet behavior conditioned on the tweet text less the hashtags. Table 6 indicates an overwhelming majority of the tweets from Pakistan is classified as *supportive* by $\mathcal{M}_{supervised}$ and such tweets received substantially more likes and retweets than the *not-supportive* tweets.

8 Ethical and Societal Implications

While the setting discussed in the paper involves humanitarian tasks, the techniques can be trivially adapted with the explicit objective to censor empathetic content. In many recent conflicts in the Indian subcontinent, such systems can have adverse social effects, and thus particular care is needed before these systems are deployed. Also, language-specific features can sometimes cause syntactically similar but semantically opposite content to be surfaced underscoring the need for a human-in-the-loop setting before such systems are deployed for social media content moderation tasks. Finally, our classifier relies on a black box *hope speech* classifier and thus runs the risk of propagating possible biases from the black box model. Further case studies need to be considered before deployment and we welcome a thorough investigation of our released data set from the scientific community.

9 Conclusions

In this paper, we present a task and associated resources for a vital domain - geopolitical relations against the backdrop of a raging pandemic. We release a data set of tweets discussing the oxygen crisis and healthcare system collapse in India due to a COVID-19 wave. Our data set is geographically diverse and connects several diverse themes - a long acrimonious history between two neighboring countries that involves four wars and a recent bilateral relations breakdown, a raging pandemic that has claimed several hundred thousand lives within a few weeks and is still ongoing. Our analysis reveals a strong humanitarian streak that prioritizes health and well-being over past geographical or ethnic disputes. We then re-purpose existing resources designed for adjacent tasks like *hope speech* and *empathy distress* detection and utilize these to identify *supportive* tweets. Our experiments reveal that *NLP for positive impact* tasks can utilize existing adjacent resources to rapidly bootstrap solutions.

References

2021. Covid: India sees world's highest daily cases amid oxygen shortage. https://www.bbc.com/news/world-asia-india-56826645. Online; accessed 7-June-2021.

2021. India is spiraling deeper into covid-19 crisis. here's what you need to know. https://www.cnn.com/2021/04/26/india/india-covid-second-wave-explainer-intl-hnk-dst/index.html. Online; accessed 7-June-2021.

Aymé Arango, Jorge Pérez, and Barbara Poblete. 2019. Hate speech detection is not as easy as you may think: A closer look at model validation. In *Proceedings of the 42nd international acm sigir conference on research and development in information retrieval*, pages 45–54.

Josh Attenberg, Prem Melville, and Foster Provost. 2010. A unified approach to active dual supervision for labeling features and examples. In *Joint European Conference on Machine Learning and Knowledge Discovery in Databases*, pages 40–55. Springer.

C Daniel Batson, Jim Fultz, and Patricia A Schoenrade. 1987. Distress and empathy: Two qualitatively distinct vicarious emotions with different motivational consequences. *Journal of personality*, 55(1):19–39.

C Daniel Batson and Laura L Shaw. 1991. Evidence for altruism: Toward a pluralism of prosocial motives. *Psychological inquiry*, 2(2):107–122.

Iz Beltagy, Kyle Lo, and Arman Cohan. 2019. Scibert: Pretrained language model for scientific text. In *EMNLP*.

Susan Benesch. 2014. Defining and diminishing hate speech. *State of the World's Minorities and Indigenous Peoples*, 2014:18–25.

Susan Benesch, Derek Ruths, Kelly P Dillon, Haji Mohammad Saleem, and Lucas Wright. 2016. Counterspeech on twitter: A field study. *A report for Public Safety Canada under the Kanishka Project*.

Sumantra Bose. 2009. *Kashmir: Roots of conflict, paths to peace*. Harvard University Press.

Samuel R. Bowman, Gabor Angeli, Christopher Potts, and Christopher D. Manning. 2015. A large annotated corpus for learning natural language inference. In *Proceedings of the 2015 Conference on Empirical Methods in Natural Language Processing, EMNLP 2015, Lisbon, Portugal, September 17-21, 2015*, pages 632–642. The Association for Computational Linguistics.

Sven Buechel, Anneke Buffone, Barry Slaff, Lyle Ungar, and João Sedoc. 2018. Modeling empathy and distress in reaction to news stories. In *Proceedings of the 2018 Conference on Empirical Methods in Natural Language Processing*, pages 4758–4765, Brussels, Belgium. Association for Computational Linguistics.

Thiago Carvalho, Florian Krammer, and Akiko Iwasaki. 2021. The first 12 months of covid-19: a timeline of immunological insights. *Nature Reviews Immunology*, 21(4):245–256.

Niyati Chhaya, Kokil Jaidka, Lyle Ungar, Jennifer Healey, and Atanu Sinha. 2020. Editorial for the 3rd aaai-20 workshop on affective content analysis.

Matteo Cinelli, Walter Quattrociocchi, Alessandro Galeazzi, Carlo Michele Valensise, Emanuele Brugnoli, Ana Lucia Schmidt, Paola Zola, Fabiana Zollo, and Antonio Scala. 2020. The covid-19 social media infodemic. *Scientific Reports*, 10(1):1–10.

Iain J. Cruickshank and Kathleen M. Carley. 2020. Characterizing communities of hashtag usage on twitter during the 2020 COVID-19 pandemic by multi-view clustering. *Appl. Netw. Sci.*, 5(1):66.

J. Devlin, Ming-Wei Chang, Kenton Lee, and Kristina Toutanova. 2019. Bert: Pre-training of deep bidirectional transformers for language understanding. In *NAACL-HLT*.

Jennifer L Goetz, Dacher Keltner, and Emiliana Simon-Thomas. 2010. Compassion: an evolutionary analysis and empirical review. *Psychological bulletin*, 136(3):351.

Tamanna Hossain, Robert L Logan IV, Arjuna Ugarte, Yoshitomo Matsubara, Sean Young, and Sameer Singh. 2020. Covidlies: Detecting covid-19 misinformation on social media. In *Proceedings of the 1st Workshop on NLP for COVID-19 (Part 2) at EMNLP 2020*.

Ashiqur R KhudaBukhsh, Paul N Bennett, and Ryen W White. 2015. Building effective query classifiers: a case study in self-harm intent detection. In *Proceedings of the 24th ACM International on Conference on Information and Knowledge Management*, pages 1735–1738.

Ashiqur R. KhudaBukhsh, Shriphani Palakodety, and Jaime G. Carbonell. 2020. Harnessing code switching to transcend the linguistic barrier. In *Proceedings of the Twenty-Ninth International Joint Conference on Artificial Intelligence, IJCAI 2020*, pages 4366–4374. ijcai.org.

Ashiqur R. KhudaBukhsh, Rupak Sarkar, Mark S. Kamlet, and Tom M. Mitchell. 2021. We don't speak the same language: Interpreting polarization through machine translation. In *The Thirty-Fifth AAAI Conference on Artificial Intelligence, AAAI 2021*, page To Appear. AAAI Press.

Sumeet Kumar. 2018. Weakly supervised stance learning using social-media hashtags.

Cuilian Li, Li Jia Chen, Xueyu Chen, Mingzhi Zhang, Chi Pui Pang, and Haoyu Chen. 2020. Retrospective analysis of the possibility of predicting the covid-19 outbreak from internet searches and social media data, china, 2020. *Eurosurveillance*, 25(10):2000199.

Iffat Malik and Robert G Wirsing. 2002. *Kashmir: Ethnic conflict international dispute*. Oxford University Press Oxford.

Binny Mathew, Navish Kumar, Pawan Goyal, Animesh Mukherjee, et al. 2018. Analyzing the hate and counter speech accounts on twitter. *arXiv preprint arXiv:1812.02712*.

Shahan Ali Memon and Kathleen M. Carley. 2020. Characterizing COVID-19 misinformation communities using a novel twitter dataset. In *Proceedings of the CIKM 2020 Workshops co-located with 29th ACM International Conference on Information and Knowledge Management (CIKM 2020), Galway, Ireland, October 19-23, 2020*, volume 2699 of *CEUR Workshop Proceedings*. CEUR-WS.org.

Mario Ed Mikulincer and Phillip R Shaver. 2010. *Prosocial motives, emotions, and behavior: The better angels of our nature*. American Psychological Association.

Shriphani Palakodety, Ashiqur R. KhudaBukhsh, and Jaime G. Carbonell. 2020a. Hope speech detection: A computational analysis of the voice of peace. In *ECAI 2020 - 24th European Conference on Artificial Intelligence*, volume 325 of *Frontiers in Artificial Intelligence and Applications*, pages 1881–1889. IOS Press.

Shriphani Palakodety, Ashiqur R. KhudaBukhsh, and Jaime G. Carbonell. 2020b. Voice for the voiceless: Active sampling to detect comments supporting the rohingyas. In *The Thirty-Fourth AAAI Conference on Artificial Intelligence*, pages 454–462. AAAI Press.

Thazha Varkey Paul and Thazha Varkey Paul. 2005. *The India-Pakistan conflict: an enduring rivalry*. Cambridge University Press.

Ellie Pavlick and Tom Kwiatkowski. 2019. Inherent disagreements in human textual inferences. *Transactions of the Association for Computational Linguistics*, 7:677–694.

Koustav Rudra, Shruti Rijhwani, Rafiya Begum, Kalika Bali, Monojit Choudhury, and Niloy Ganguly. 2016. Understanding language preference for expression of opinion and sentiment: What do Hindi-English speakers do on Twitter? In *Proceedings of the 2016 Conference on Empirical Methods in Natural Language Processing*, pages 1131–1141, Austin, Texas. Association for Computational Linguistics.

Punyajoy Saha, Binny Mathew, Kiran Garimella, and Animesh Mukherjee. 2021. "short is the road that leads from fear to hate": Fear speech in indian whatsapp groups. *CoRR*, abs/2102.03870.

Rupak Sarkar, Sayantan Mahinder, and Ashiqur KhudaBukhsh. 2020. The non-native speaker aspect: Indian English in social media. In *Proceedings of the Sixth Workshop on Noisy User-generated Text (W-NUT 2020)*, pages 61–70, Online. Association for Computational Linguistics.

Victoria Schofield. 2010. *Kashmir in conflict: India, Pakistan and the unending war*. Bloomsbury Publishing.

Vikas Sindhwani, Prem Melville, and Richard D Lawrence. 2009. Uncertainty sampling and transductive experimental design for active dual supervision. In *Proceedings of the 26th Annual International Conference on Machine Learning*, pages 953–960.

Elliot Sober and David Sloan Wilson. 1999. *Unto others: The evolution and psychology of unselfish behavior*. 218. Harvard University Press.

Aman Tyagi, Anjalie Field, Priyank Lathwal, Yulia Tsvetkov, and Kathleen M. Carley. 2020. A computational analysis of polarization on indian and pakistani social media. In *Social Informatics - 12th International Conference, SocInfo 2020, Pisa, Italy, October 6-9, 2020, Proceedings*, volume 12467 of *Lecture Notes in Computer Science*, pages 364–379. Springer.

Andreas Wildt. 1999. Solidarity: its history and contemporary definition. In *Solidarity*, pages 209–220. Springer.

Thomas Wolf, Lysandre Debut, Victor Sanh, Julien Chaumond, Clement Delangue, Anthony Moi, Pierric Cistac, Tim Rault, Rémi Louf, Morgan Funtowicz, Joe Davison, Sam Shleifer, Patrick von Platen, Clara Ma, Yacine Jernite, Julien Plu, Canwen Xu, Teven Le Scao, Sylvain Gugger, Mariama Drame, Quentin Lhoest, and Alexander M. Rush. 2020. Transformers: State-of-the-art natural language processing. In *Proceedings of the 2020 Conference on Empirical Methods in Natural Language Processing: System Demonstrations*, pages 38–45, Online. Association for Computational Linguistics.

Caleb Ziems, Bing He, Sandeep Soni, and Srijan Kumar. 2020. Racism is a virus: Anti-asian hate and counterhate in social media during the COVID-19 crisis. *CoRR*, abs/2005.12423.

A Speech-enabled Fixed-phrase Translator for Healthcare Accessibility

Pierrette Bouillon[1], **Johanna Gerlach**[1], **Jonathan Mutal**[1], **Nikos Tsourakis**[1], and **Hervé Spechbach**[2]

[1]FTI/TIM, University of Geneva, Switzerland
[2]Hôpitaux Universitaires de Genève (HUG), Switzerland
{Pierrette.Bouillon, Johanna.Gerlach, Jonathan.Mutal, Nikolaos.Tsourakis}@unige.ch
Herve.Spechbach@hcuge.ch

Abstract

In this overview article we describe an application designed to enable communication between health practitioners and patients who do not share a common language, in situations where professional interpreters are not available. Built on the principle of a fixed phrase translator, the application implements different natural language processing (NLP) technologies, such as speech recognition, neural machine translation and text-to-speech to improve usability. Its design allows easy portability to new domains and integration of different types of output for multiple target audiences. Even though BabelDr is far from solving the problem of miscommunication between patients and doctors, it is a clear example of NLP in a real world application designed to help minority groups to communicate in a medical context. It also gives some insights into the relevant criteria for the development of such an application.

1 Motivation

Access to healthcare is an important component of quality of life, but it is often compromised by the language barrier which prevents effective communication. In hospitals, medical staff are increasingly confronted with patients with whom they do not share a common language. Lack of clear communication can lead to increased risk for patients (Flores et al., 2003) but also discourages vulnerable groups from seeking medical assistance. When professional interpreters are not easily available, for example in emergency situations, there is a crucial need for tools to overcome the language barrier in order to provide medical care. While many generic translation solutions are available on the web, they present numerous disadvantages, including the unreliability of machine translation (Bouillon et al., 2017), the insufficient data confidentiality of cloud services or the absence of resources for minority languages. To overcome these issues, specifically designed tools based on a limited set of pre-translated sentences have been developed. These phraselators (Seligman and Dillinger, 2013) have the advantage of portability, accuracy and reliability. Although these tools have limited coverage, and do not solve all communication issues, recent studies have shown that they are generally preferred to machine translation as they are perceived as more reliable and trustworthy in these safety critical contexts (Panayiotou et al., 2019; Turner et al., 2019).

This paper aims to provide an overview of the NLP components included in the speech-enabled phraselator called BabelDr. In Section 2 we will give an overview of BabelDr usage. We then explain the artificial training data derived from the grammar to specialise the different components in Section 3. In sections 4, 5, 6, 7 and 8 we explain BabelDr's components in detail, as well as the possible outputs available to users. We then present several usage studies with target groups in Section 9.1, report on the performance of the whole system in Section 9.2 and conclude in Section 10.

2 BabelDr

BabelDr[1] is a joint project between the Faculty of Translation and Interpreting of the University of Geneva and Geneva University Hospitals (HUG). (Bouillon et al., 2017). The aim of the project is to develop a speech to speech translation system for emergency settings which meets three criteria: reliability, data security and portability to low-resource target languages relevant for HUG. It is designed to allow French-speaking medical practitioners to carry out triage and diagnostic interviews with patients speaking Albanian, Arabic, Dari, Farsi, Spanish, Swiss French sign language and Tigrinya.

[1]More information available at https://babeldr.unige.ch/

Proceedings of the 1st Workshop on NLP for Positive Impact, pages 135–142
Bangkok, Thailand (online), August 5, 2021. ©2021 Association for Computational Linguistics

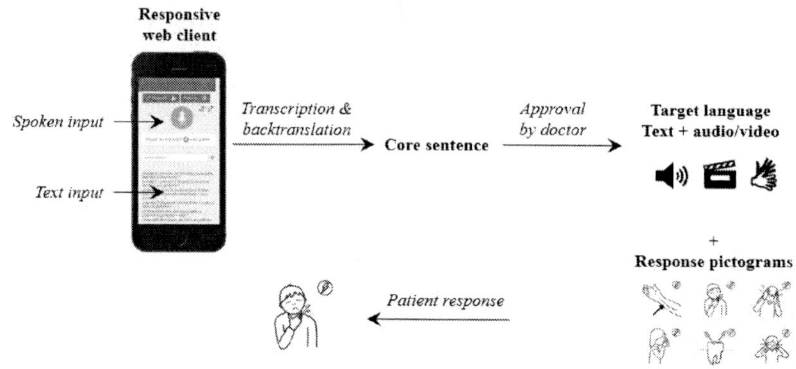

Figure 1: Overview of BabelDr usage

BabelDr is a web application designed to function on desktops and mobiles. Built on the principle of a phraselator, it relies on a limited set of pre-translated sentences, hereafter called core-sentences, collected with doctors. For improved usability and more natural interaction with the patient, it includes a speech recognition component: instead of searching for utterances in menus, medical staff can speak freely and the system will map the spoken utterances to the closest pre-translated core-sentence. This sentence is then presented for validation, in a backtranslation step, ensuring that the doctor knows exactly what is being translated for the patient. The patient can then respond by means of a pictogram-based interface. All components can be deployed on a local server with no dependency on cloud services, thus ensuring the data confidentiality that is essential for medical applications. Figure 1 illustrates the usage of BabelDr.

3 Training data and grammars

Due to confidentiality issues, training data for spoken French medical dialogues is scarce. For this reason, the first version of the system was built around a manually defined Synchronous Context Free Grammar (SCFG, Aho and Ullman, 1969), used for grammar-based speech recognition and parsing (Rayner et al., 2017). This grammar is now leveraged to generate artificial data used both for backtranslation (Section 5) and for specialising speech recognition (Section 4).

The grammar maps source variation patterns, described in a formalism similar to regular expressions, to core-sentences. Due to the repetitive nature of the content, the grammars make use of compositional sentences to make resources more compact. These sentences contain one or more variables, which are replaced by different values at system compile time. Figure 2 gives an example of a compositional utterance rule.

The current version of the grammar includes 2629 utterance rules, organised by medical domain, which expand to 10'991 core-sentences once variables are replaced by values. These core-sentences are mapped to hundreds of millions of surface sentences. Figure 3 shows an example of the aligned core-sentence - variation corpus that can be generated from the grammar.

4 Speech-to-Text

To ensure both accuracy and usability, the system uses a hybrid approach for speech recognition, combining two recognisers. The first is a grammar based speech recogniser using GRXMLs generated from the original SCFG (see Section 3). While this is fast and accurate, since it directly yields a core-sentence, it is unable to handle utterances that are out of grammar coverage. It is therefore complemented by a large-vocabulary recogniser specialised with the monolingual artificial corpus described in Section 3. The results of the two approaches are combined based on the confidence score provided by the grammar based recogniser: if the score is over a pre-defined threshold, this result is kept, else the system falls back on the large-vocabulary result. Their performance is evaluated in terms of WER, which is 38.9% for the GRXML grammar and 14.4% (see Table 2) for the large vocabulary model. In this case we have used the dataset of the user study described in (Bouillon et al., 2017).

```
Utterance
Source $$à_organe
Source ($avez_vous| $ça_fait | $ressentez_vous) ?(aussi) (mal | une douleur | des douleurs) $$à_organe
Source ?($votre_douleur) $est_elle $$à_organe
Target/french avez-vous mal $$à_organe ?       <-- core sentence (with variable)
EndUtterance

TrLex $$à_organe source="(dans le|au ?(niveau du)) genou" french="au genou"
TrLex $$à_organe source="(dans |au niveau de |à ) l'épaule" french="à l'épaule"
```

(Utterance … Source lines: *source variations*; TrLex lines: *variable values*)

Figure 2: Example of a grammar rule

avez-vous de la fièvre ?:les douleurs étaient-elles accompagnées par de la fièvre
avez-vous de la fièvre ?:vous sentez-vous fiévreux maintenant
avez-vous de la fièvre ?:vous avez une sensation d'être fiévreuse
avez-vous de la fièvre ?;êtes-vous fiévreuse en ce moment
avez-vous de la fièvre ?:sont-elles accompagnées de température
avez-vous de la fièvre ?; est-ce que vous sauriez si vous avez de la fièvre maintenant
avez-vous de la fièvre ?;fébrile
avez-vous de la fièvre ?:avez-vous de la température
avez-vous de la fièvre ?; chaud
avez-vous de la fièvre ?; ....

Figure 3: Example of the aligned corpus generated from the grammar: core-sentences with corresponding source variations

For the GRXML recogniser we use the Nuance ASR v10 and the Nuance Transcription Engine 4 for the large-vocabulary one. Both can be accessed over the network through our custom API using HTTP POST requests. The recognition is file-based and it proves to work well for any real-time interaction. The distributed nature of our back-end platform permits easy scaling and load balancing so that multiple users can interact simultaneously with the recognisers. Especially, for the GRXML case, we can load and compile grammars on the fly or change the parameters of the recogniser dynamically. We can also parse any text against a specific grammar using an HTTP request.

5 Backtranslation

The backtranslation (introduced in Section 2) is an essential step in BabelDr since it maps the speech recognition result to a core-sentence that is presented to the doctor for validation. For the GRXML recogniser, backtranslation is performed directly by the grammar. For the large vocabulary recogniser, as the set of core-sentences is limited (see Section 3), the backtranslation task can be seen as a sentence classification task where the core-sentences are the categories, or as translation task into a controlled language. As a resource, we use the bilingual corpus generated from the grammar as training data. Rayner et al. (2017) introduced an approach based on tf-idf indexing and dynamic programming (DP) achieving 91.8% on accuracy (assuming perfect speech recognition and 1-best). Mutal et al. (2019) then applied different approaches using deep learning methods, neural machine translation (NMT) and sentence classification achieving 93.2% (see Table 2) accuracy on core-sentence matching for transcriptions (assuming perfect speech recognition), improving on the previous approach. This approach is currently used in BabelDr.

6 Elliptical Sentences

In dialogues, elliptical utterances are very common, since they ensure the principle of economy and usually avoid duplication (Hamza, 2019). In BabelDr, they allow doctors to question patients in a more efficient way (Tanguy et al., 2011). However, literal translation of these utterances could affect communication as illustrated in Table 1. In BabelDr, elliptical utterances are not translated literally, but are instead mapped to the closest non-elliptical core-sentence, based on the context.

To avoid a wrong backtranslation in elliptical sentences, a context-level information (the previous accepted utterance) is added to the model. Therefore, when an utterance is identified as an ellipsis,

Utterance	Translation
do you have pain in your stomach?	¿le duele el estómago?
in your head?	*¿en tu cabeza?
Good Translation: ¿Le duele la cabeza?	

Table 1: Example of a bad translation of ellipsis. The * means a bad translation.

it is concatenated with the previous translated utterance before backtranslating. In the context of BabelDr, elliptical utterances are detected using a binary classifier. The model was trained using handcrafted features, such as sentence length, absence of verbs or nouns, part of speech of the first word, and identification of pronouns that refer to entities in the context (using morphological features). On an artificial ellipsis data set, the model achieves 98% accuracy on detecting elliptical sentences and 88% on backtranslating them to a core-sentence (see more, Mutal et al., 2020).

7 Output

After validation of the backtranslation, BabelDr presents the target language output to the patient in written and spoken form, which are both based on the same human translations of the core-sentences. In the following sections we first outline the translation approach and then describe how the translations are rendered for the patient, in audio (for spoken languages) or video format (for sign language).

7.1 Translation

High translation quality is essential for a medical phraselator, therefore the translations are produced by professional translators. Translating for BabelDr presents technical challenges, since language resources must be in a specific structured data format not easily accessible to translators. An online translation platform which includes a translation memory and allows translators to efficiently handle the compositional items was developed to facilitate the translators' task and ensure the quality and coherence of the translations (Gerlach et al., 2018).

The translations are aimed at patients with no medical knowledge and designed to be understandable by patients with a low level of literacy. Sentences were also adapted to account for cultural aspects, such as sensitive or intimate topics that are not commonly discussed, related for example to sexual habits (Halimi et al., 2020). Since the system provides translations both in written and spoken form, the translators had to choose phrasings that would function in both. A recent evaluation of the translations for two of the system's target languages (Albanian and Arabic) has shown that these translations are easy to understand, and thereby make the system more trustworthy in comparison to MT (in publication, Gerlach et al., 2021).

Ongoing developments include the extension of the system to new target languages and modalities to make the system accessible to further population groups. One addition involves translation to pictographs targeted at people with intellectual disabilities, another is translation into easy language, beginning with Simple English.

7.2 Text-to-Speech

Audio has been an important output modality for the BabelDr system, as it presents various competitive advantages for the patients. It alleviates the burden of looking on the screen, which proves to be challenging in a medical setting, e.g. positioning of the physician and patient. Especially, for illiterate users, it is an essential component, and having a system talking in their own language can improve user experience. While it would be possible to have a human record all the pre-translated sentences, due to the number and repetitive nature of the sentences, the time and cost involved in recording were considered too high. The option of a Text-to-Speech (TTS) system was therefore adopted from the beginning of the project in order to announce the translated questions of the physician. State-of-the-art systems like Nuance Vocalizer are now part of our content creation pipeline for crafting the prompts.

Systems of this kind, however, lack support for low-resource languages that the BabelDr system also targets. For this reason, we have investigated the option of building our own TTS for those languages from scratch. In a previous study, positive feedback in terms of comprehensibility was

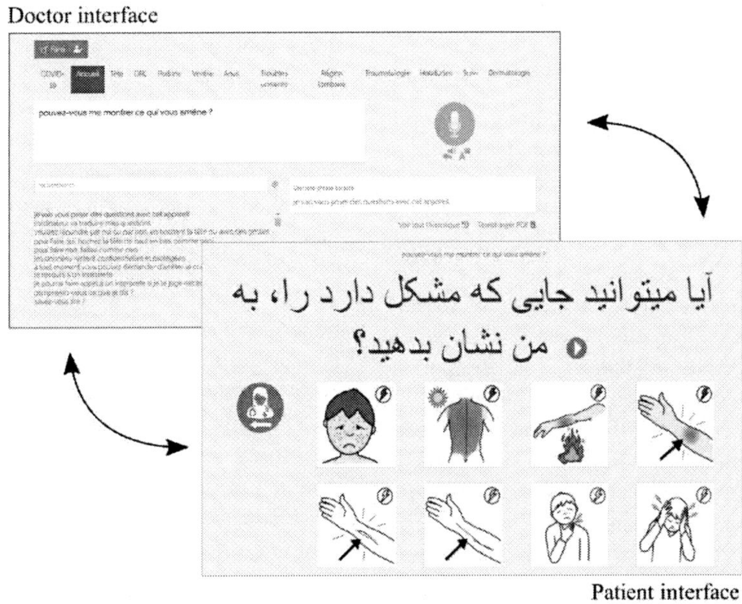

Figure 4: Doctor and patient interfaces

Task	Model	Metric	Result
Speech to Text	GRXML	WER	38.9%
	Large Vocabulary		14.4%
Back Translation	NMT	Accuracy	93.2%
Overall (3-best)		SER	5%

Table 2: Performance by component and overall

received (Tsourakis et al., 2020), after building a synthetic female voice for the Albanian language based on Tacotron 2, a neural network architecture for speech synthesis directly from text (Shen et al., 2017). Among the target languages supported by BabelDr, Tigrinya is one for which no public TTS is available.

For this reason, a female voice talent was recruited to record all the prompts that were subsequently used in the online system. This allowed us to create a corpus with 18 hours of speech that we exploit in order to create the Tigrinya synthesized voice. The training process is similar to the one found in (Tsourakis et al., 2020). As new content is constantly added to the system, new recordings of the translations are requested. This time we first generate the output with the TTS and ask the voice talent to listen to the prompts. If the result is acceptable the TTS version is kept, otherwise, a human recording is necessary. In a set of 2150 prompts the human had to record 573 files (26.7%).

7.3 French Sign Language

Establishing effective and reliable communication between a doctor and a deaf patient is a complicated task. The scarcity of professional interpreters and the lack of awareness of medical staff for deaf culture severely impedes communication. To create sign language output for our fixed-phrase translator, we have investigated two different approaches: recorded human signers and an avatar (using JASigning, Glauert and Elliott, 2011). An evaluation carried out with the deaf community showed that the recorded human signers are superior in terms of understandability and acceptability, but it was found that the avatar could be useful in this context (in print, Bouillon et al., 2021). The recorded videos were recorded by a sign language interpreter in collaboration with a deaf nurse, and are freely accessible in the online system, providing a human translation reference in sign language for medical questions. These resources present opportunities to evaluate what affects the communication task with deaf people in this specialised context.

8 Patient response interface

The original BabelDr system was limited to yes-no questions or questions where the patient could respond non-verbally, for example by pointing at a body part. This restrictive approach was problematic both for doctors, who are used to asking open questions, and for patients who had little means to actively contribute to the direction of the dialogue. To build a bidirectional version that would allow more complex responses from the patient, we considered different options. Building a system that would allow patients to respond with speech presents numerous difficulties. No speech recognisers exist for many of the minority languages targeted by our system, and few or no resources such as speech corpora are available to build such systems. A text interface, as found in traditional phraselators, while easier to implement, would not be accessible to patients with low literacy. Additionally, in the context of a fixed phrase translator, some user training is necessary to familiarise with system coverage, which is not possible for patients who arrive at an emergency service. For these reasons, we chose to add a simple pictograph based response interface, shown in Figure 4. Each core-sentence is linked to a set of corresponding response pictographs among which the patient can select their response. Evaluation of these pictographs in terms of understandability and acceptability by patients of different educational and cultural backgrounds is ongoing (Norré et al., 2020). A task-based evaluation showed that all patients prefered the bidirectional version since they could explain their symptoms more efficiently.

9 Evaluation

9.1 Task based

A translation system for the healthcare domain should be evaluated on the task it is designed to assist, which in the case of BabelDr is the diagnostic interview. To this end, we carried out several usage studies. In a preliminary study, we asked four medical students and five doctors to diagnose two standardised Arabic speaking patients, using BabelDr and Google Translate (GT). Results showed that in comparison to the generic machine translation tool, BabelDr provides higher-quality translations and led to a higher number of correct diagnoses (8/9 for BabelDr against 5/9 for GT), in particular with medical students (Bouillon et al., 2017). A subsequent crossover study where 12 French speaking doctors where asked to diagnose two Arabic speaking standardised patients using BabelDr confirmed that the application allows doctors to reach accurate and reliable diagnoses (24/24 correct). It was agreed among participating medical professionals that BabelDr could be used in their everyday medical practice (Spechbach et al., 2019).

The system is currently in use at the HUG outpatient emergency unit and a user satisfaction study is ongoing to collect patients' and doctors' feedback on system usage in real emergency settings by means of questionnaires (Janakiram et al., 2020). The study includes only patients with no understanding of French and no common language with the doctor. Overall, 90% of the 30 patients included so far reported a positive level of satisfaction. The doctors reported 87%.

9.2 System performance

To evaluate the performance of the current version of the complete system, we have used the spoken data set collected during the usage study described above (Spechbach et al., 2019). Since the system relies on human pre-translation, it is sufficient to evaluate the output in terms of backtranslation, as a correct core-sentence will result in a correct translation for the patient. We measured the performance using sentence error rate (SER), which is defined as the percentage of core-sentences that are not identical to the annotated correct core-sentences. Since the system interface presents a selection of core-sentences to the doctor, for this evaluation we considered 3-best backtranslation results, including the GRXML result when it was above the confidence threshold and two or three backtranslations of large vocabulary recogniser results. With this configuration, the system achieved 5% SER on this data set.

10 Conclusion

Healthcare translation is required to facilitate the engagement with people with diverse language, cultural, and literacy backgrounds. The development of culturally effective and patient-oriented translation tools has become increasingly urgent. Although BabelDr is far from solving the problem of miscommunication, it is an example of a concrete application of natural language processing to help minority groups communicate in a medical context.

The developed tool, resources and evaluations are a first step toward accessible healthcare apps. This research is essential to define criteria which can be used in the development and evaluation of new medical interpreting technologies with a view to enhancing the usability among patients from refugee, migrant, or other socioeconomically disadvantaged populations.

Acknowledgements

This project was supported by the "Fondation Privée des Hôpitaux Universitaires de Genève". We would also like to thank Nuance Inc for generously making their software available to us for research purposes.

References

A.V. Aho and J.D. Ullman. 1969. Syntax directed translations and the pushdown assembler. *Journal of Computer and System Sciences*, 3(1):37–56.

Pierrette Bouillon, Bastien David, Irene Strasly, and Hervé Spechbach. 2021. A speech translation system for medical dialogue in sign language - questionnaire on user perspective of videos and the use of avatar technology. In *Proceedings of the 3rd Swiss Conference on Barrier-free Communication (BfC 2020)*, Winterthur, Switzerland.

Pierrette Bouillon, Johanna Gerlach, Hervé Spechbach, Nikos Tsourakis, and Ismahene S. Halimi Mallem. 2017. *BabelDr vs Google Translate: a user study at Geneva University Hospitals (HUG)*, 20th Annual Conference of the European Association for Machine Translation (EAMT). Prague, Czech Republic. ID: unige:94511.

Glenn Flores, M. Barton Laws, Sandra J. Mayo, Barry Zuckerman, Milagros Abreu, Leonardo Medina, and Eric J. Hardt. 2003. Errors in medical interpretation and their potential clinical consequences in pediatric encounters. *Pediatrics*, 111(1):6–14.

Johanna Gerlach, Pierrette Bouillon, Rovena Troqe, Sonia Halimi, and Hervé Spechbach. 2021. *Patient acceptance of translation technology for medical dialogues in emergency situations*, Translation in Times of Cascading Crisis. Bloomsbury Academic.

Johanna Gerlach, Hervé Spechbach, and Pierrette Bouillon. 2018. *Creating an Online Translation Platform to Build Target Language Resources for a Medical Phraselator*, Proceedings of the 40th edition of Translating and the Computer Conference (TC40), pages 60–65. AsLing, The International Association for Advancement in Language Technology, Geneva. ID: unige:111776.

John Glauert and Ralph Elliott. 2011. Extending the sigml notation: A progress report. In *Second International Workshop on Sign Language Translation and Avatar Technology (SLTAT)*, Dundee, Scotland.

Sonia Halimi, Razieh Azari, Pierrette Bouillon, and Hervé Spechbach. 2020. Pee or urinate? a corpus-based analysis of medical communication for context-specific responses. Corpus exploration of lexis and genres in translation. Routledge, Taylor & Francis Group.

Anissa Hamza. 2019. *La détection et la traduction automatiques de l'ellipse : enjeux théoriques et pratiques*. Ph.D. thesis, Université de Strasbourg STRASBOURG.

Antony A. Janakiram, Johanna Gerlach, Alyssa Vuadens-Lehmann, Pierrette Bouillon, and Hervé Spechbach. 2020. *User Satisfaction with a Speech-Enabled Translator in Emergency Settings*, Digital Personalized Health and Medicine, pages 1421–1422. IOS. ID: unige:139233.

Jonathan Mutal, Pierrette Bouillon, Johanna Gerlach, Paula Estrella, and Hervé Spechbach. 2019. Monolingual backtranslation in a medical speech translation system for diagnostic interviews - a NMT approach. In *Proceedings of Machine Translation Summit XVII Volume 2: Translator, Project and User Tracks*, pages 196–203, Dublin, Ireland. European Association for Machine Translation.

Jonathan Mutal, Johanna Gerlach, Pierrette Bouillon, and Hervé Spechbach. 2020. Ellipsis translation for a medical speech to speech translation system. In *Proceedings of the 22nd Annual Conference of the European Association for Machine Translation*, pages 281–290, Lisboa, Portugal. European Association for Machine Translation.

Magali Norré, Pierrette Bouillon, Johanna Gerlach, and Hervé Spechbach. 2020. *Évaluation de la compréhension de pictogrammes Arasaac et Sclera pour améliorer l'accessibilité du système de traduction médicale BabelDr*, Handicap 2020 : technologies pour l'autonomie et l'inclusion, pages 179–182. ID: unige:144565; 11e conférence de l'IFRATH sur les technologies d'assistance.

Anita Panayiotou, Anastasia Gardner, Sue Williams, Emiliano Zucchi, Monita Mascitti-Meuter, Anita MY Goh, Emily You, Terence WH Chong, Dina Logiudice, Xiaoping Lin, Betty Haralambous, and Frances Batchelor. 2019. Language translation apps in health care settings: Expert opinion. *JMIR Mhealth Uhealth*, 7(4):e11316.

Manny Rayner, Nikos Tsourakis, and Johanna Gerlach. 2017. Lightweight spoken utterance classification with cfg, tf-idf and dynamic programming. *In: Camelin N., Estève Y., Martín-Vide C. (eds) Statistical Language and Speech Processing. SLSP 2017.*

Mark Seligman and Mike Dillinger. 2013. Automatic speech translation for healthcare: Some internet and interface aspects. In *Proceedings of 10th International Conference on Terminology and Artificial Intelligence (TIA-13)*, Paris, France.

Jonathan Shen, Ruoming Pang, Ron J. Weiss, Mike Schuster, Navdeep Jaitly, Zongheng Yang, Zhifeng Chen, Yu Zhang, Yuxuan Wang, R. J. Skerry-Ryan, Rif A. Saurous, Yannis Agiomyrgiannakis, and Yonghui Wu. 2017. Natural TTS synthesis by conditioning wavenet on mel spectrogram predictions. *CoRR*, abs/1712.05884.

Hervé Spechbach, Johanna Gerlach, Sanae Mazouri Karker, Nikos Tsourakis, Christophe Combescure, and Pierrette Bouillon. 2019. A speech-enabled fixed-phrase translator for emergency settings: Crossover study. *JMIR Med Inform*, 7(2):e13167.

Ludovic Tanguy, Cécile Fabre, Lydia-Mai Ho-Dac, and Josette Rebeyrolle. 2011. Caractérisation des échanges entre patients et médecins : approche outillée d'un corpus de consultations médicales. *Corpus, 10 |2011*, pages 137–154.

Nikos Tsourakis, Rovena Troqe, Johanna Gerlach, Pierrette Bouillon, and Hervé Spechbach. 2020. An albanian text-to-speech system for the babeldr medical speech translator. In *Digital Personalized Health and Medicine - Proceedings of MIE 2020, Medical Informatics Europe, Geneva, Switzerland, April 28 - May 1, 2020*, volume 270 of *Studies in Health Technology and Informatics*, pages 527–531. IOS Press.

Anne M Turner, Yong K Choi, Kristin Dew, Ming-Tse Tsai, Alyssa L Bosold, Shuyang Wu, Donahue Smith, and Hendrika Meischke. 2019. Evaluating the usefulness of translation technologies for emergency response communication: A scenario-based study. *JMIR Public Health Surveill*, 5(1):e11171.

A Grounded Well-being Conversational Agent with Multiple Interaction Modes: Preliminary Results

Xinxin Yan, and **Ndapa Nakashole**
Computer Science and Engineering
University of California, San Diego
La Jolla, CA 92093
x3yan@ucsd.edu, nnakashole@eng.ucsd.edu

Abstract

Technologies for enhancing well-being, healthcare vigilance and monitoring are on the rise. However, despite patient interest, such technologies suffer from low adoption. One hypothesis for this limited adoption is loss of human interaction that is central to doctor-patient encounters. In this paper we seek to address this limitation via a conversational agent that adopts one aspect of in-person doctor-patient interactions: A human avatar to facilitate medical grounded question answering. This is akin to the in-person scenario where the doctor may point to the human body or the patient may point to their own body to express their conditions. Additionally, our agent has multiple interaction modes, that may give more options for the patient to use the agent, not just for medical question answering, but also to engage in conversations about general topics and current events. Both the avatar, and the multiple interaction modes could help improve adherence.

We present a high level overview of the design of our agent, Marie Bot Wellbeing. We also report implementation details of our early prototype , and present preliminary results.

1 Introduction

NLP is in a position to bring-forth scalable, cost-effective solutions for promoting well-being. Such solutions can serve many segments of the population such as people living in medically underserved communities with limited access to clinicians, and people with limited mobility. These solutions can also serve those interested in self-monitoring (Torous et al., 2014) their own health. There is evidence that these technologies can be effective (Mayo-Wilson, 2007; Fitzpatrick et al., 2017). However, dcspite interest, such technologies suffer from low adoption(Donkin et al., 2013). One hypothesis for this limited adoption is the loss of human interaction which is central to doctor-patient encounters(Fitzpatrick et al., 2017). In this paper we seek to address this limitation via a conversational agent that emulates one aspect of in-person doctor-patient interactions: a human avatar to facilitate grounded question answering. This is akin to the in-person scenario where the doctor may point to the human body or the patient may point to their own body to express their conditions. Additionally, our agent has multiple interaction modes, that may give more options for the patient to use the agent, not just for medical question answering, but also to engage in conversations about general topics and current events. Both the avatar, and the multiple interaction modes could help improve adherence.

The human body is complex and information about how it functions fill entire books. Yet it is important for individuals to know about conditions that can affect the human body, in order to practice continued monitoring and prevention to keep severe medical situations at bay. To this end, our well-being agent includes a medical question answering interaction mode (**MedicalQABot**). For mental health, social isolation and loneliness can have adverse health consequences such as anxiety, depression, and suicide. Our well-being agent includes a social interaction mode (**SocialBot**), wherein the agent can be an approximation of human a companion. The MedicalQABot is less conversational but accomplishes the task of answering questions. The SocialBot seeks to be conversational while providing some information. And, there is a third interaction mode, the **Chatbot**, which in our work is used as a last-resort mode, it is conversational but does not provide much information of substance.

To test the ideas of our proposed agent, we are developing a grounded well-being conversational agent, called "Marie Bot Wellbeing". This paper presents a sketch of the high level design of our Marie system, and some preliminary results.

An important consideration when developing technology for healthcare is that there is *low toler-*

Proceedings of the 1st Workshop on NLP for Positive Impact, pages 143–151
Bangkok, Thailand (online), August 5, 2021.

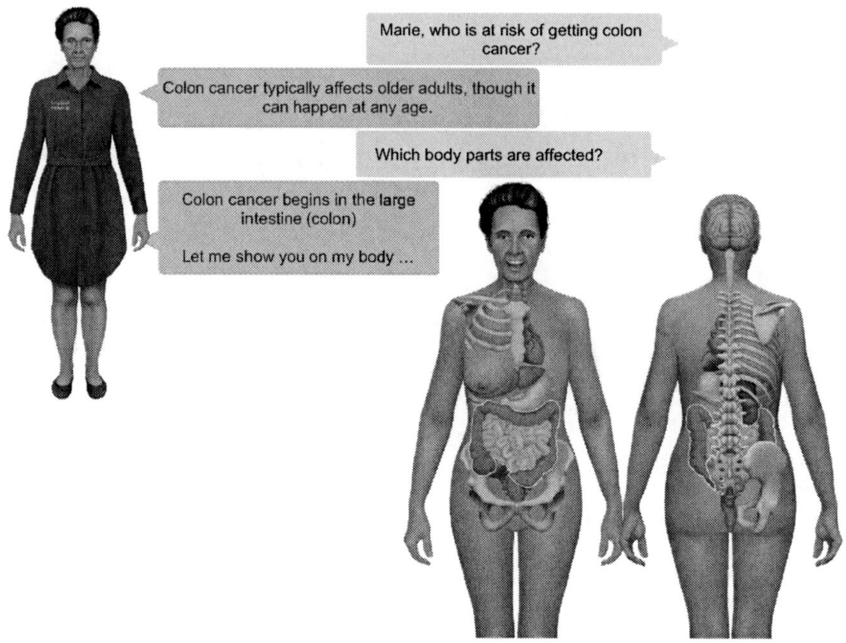

Figure 1: An illustration of the MedicalQA interaction mode. Here the agent's answer is grounded on our human avatar. The affected body part, the large intestine, is highlighted on the avatar.

ance for errors. Erroneous information can have severe negative consequences. We design the medicalQABot, and the SocialBot with this consideration in mind. Our design philosophy consists of the following tenets:

1. **Reputable answers:** Only provide answers to questions for which we have answers from reputable sources, instead of considering information from every corner of the Web.

2. **Calibrated confidence scores:** Even though the answers come from reputable sources, there are various decisions that are involved that the model must make including which specific answer to retrieve for a given question. For these predictions by our models, we must know what we do not know, and provide only information about which the model is fairly certain.

3. **Visualize**: Whenever an answer can be visualized to some degree, we should provide a visualization to accompany the text answer to help clarify, and reduce misunderstanding.

4. **Graceful failure**: when one of the interaction modes fails, another interaction mode can take over.

Organization In what follows, we discuss how the above tenets are manifested in our agent.

The rest of the paper is organized as follows: We begin with a high-level overview of the design of the different parts of the agent (Sections 2 to 4); We next discuss the current prototype implementation and preliminary results (Section 5); We next present related work (Section 6); and close with a discussion (Section 7) and concluding remarks (Section 8).

2 Interaction Modes and Dialog Management

In navigating between the different interaction modes, we design our system as follows. Based on the user utterance, we automatically predict using a binary classifier to switch between different interaction modes (MedicalQABot vs SocialBot). Suppose that the classifier predicts that the utterance is a question asking for medical information on a topic, and suppose our medicalQA determines that we have no information on that topic, our goal is to then let the SocialBot take over if it has information on that topic and can meaningfully hold a conversation about it. For the SocialBot, when missing the necessary information, our goal is to have it fall back to Chatbot mode.

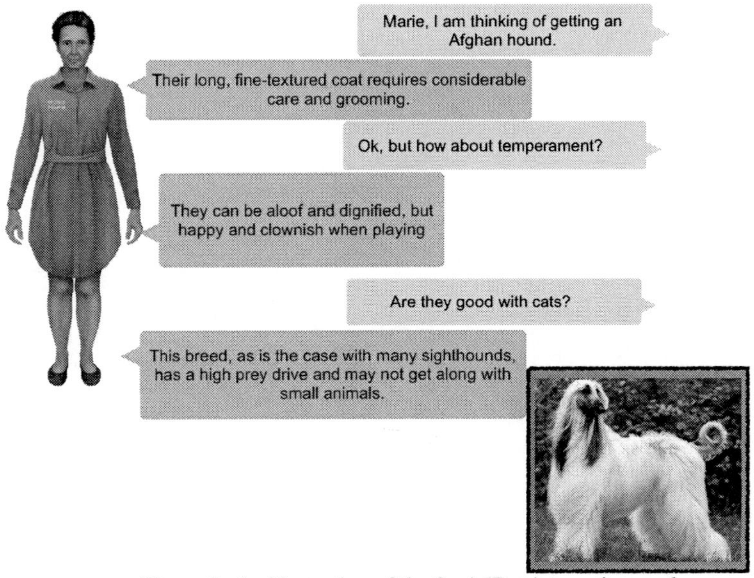

Figure 2: An illustration of the SocialBot interaction mode

3 MedicalQABot Mode

3.1 Knowledge vault of QA pairs

Some aspects of the human body are well-understood, many diseases and medical conditions have been studied for many years. Thus a lot of medical questions have already been asked, and their answers are known. Thus one approach to medicalQA is a retrieval-based one which consists of two steps: First, we collect and create a knowledge vault of frequently asked questions and their curated answers from reputable sources.

Second, given a user question, we must match it to one of the questions in the QA knowledge vault. However, when people pose their questions, they are not aware of the exact words used in the questions of the knowledge vault. We must therefore match user questions to the correct question in the knowledge vault. A simple approach is keyword search. However, this misses a lot of compositional effects. One other way is to treat this as a problem of entailment. Where given a user question, we can find, in the knowledge vault, the questions that entail the user question.

3.2 Grounding to Human Anatomy Avatar

We develop a human avatar to help users better understand medical information. And also to help them to more precisely specify their questions. The avatar is meant to be used in two ways. The human avatar was illustrated by a medical illustrator we hired from Upwork.com.

Bot → Patient: When an answer contains body parts, relevant body parts are highlighted on the avatar. "this medical condition affects the following body parts ". An illustration of this direction is shown in Figure 1.

Patient → Bot: When the user describes their condition, they can point by clicking. "I am not feeling well here".

4 SocialBot Mode

For the SocialBot, we propose to create a knowledge vault of topics that will enable the bot to have engaging conversations with humans on topics of interest including current events. For example, the bot can say “Sure, we can talk about German beer" or. "I see you want to talk about Afghan hounds"". The topics will be mined from Wikipedia, news sources, and social media including Reddit. For the SocialBot, we wish to model the principles of a good conversation: having something interesting to say, and showing interest in what the conversation partner says (Ostendorf, 2018)

5 Prototype Implementation & Preliminary Experiments

Having discussed the high-level design goals, in the following sections we present specifics of our initial prototype. Our prototype's language understanding capabilities are limited. They can be thought of as placeholders that allowed us to quickly develop a prototype. These simple capabilities will be replaced as we develop more advanced language processing methods for our system.

5.1 Data

We describe the data used in our current prototype.

Medline Data We collected Medline data [1], containing 1031 high level medical topics. We extracted the summaries and split the text into questions and answers. We generated several data files from this dataset: question-topic pair data, answer-topic pair data and question-answer pair data. The data size and split information is presented in Table 3. We will describe their usage in detail in the following sections

Medical Dialogue Data We use the MedDialog dataset(Zeng et al., 2020) which has 0.26 million dialogues between patients and doctors. The raw dialogues were obtained from healthcaremagic.com and icliniq.com.

We also use the MedQuAD (Medical Question Answering Dataset) dataset (Ben Abacha and Demner-Fushman, 2019) which contains 47457 medical question-answer pairs created from 12 NIH[2] websites.

News Category Dataset We also use the News category dataset from Kaggle[3]. It contains 41 topics. We use the data in 39 topics, without "Healthy Living" and "Wellness", which might be related to the medical domain. We extract the short description from the dataset.

Reddit Data We collected questions and comments from 30 subreddits. We treat each subreddit as one topic. The number of questions for each topic is shown in Table 7. This Reddit data is to be used for our SocialBot.

5.2 System Overview

As shown in Figure 3, our system makes a number of decisions upon receiving a user utterance. First, the system predicts if the utterance should be handled by the MedicalQABot or by the SocialBot.

If the MedicalQABot is predicted to handle the utterance, then an additional decision is made. This decision predicts which Medical topic the utterance is about. If we are not certain, the system puts the user in the loop, by asking them to confirm the topic. If the user says the top predicted topic is not the correct one, we present them with the next topic in the order, and ask them again, up to 4 times.

[1]https://medlineplus.gov/xml.html

[2]https://www.nih.gov/

[3]https://www.kaggle.com/rmisra/news-category-dataset

Train	286370
Valid	35796
Test	35797

Table 1: Interaction Mode Prediction Data

Valid accuracy	0.9970
Test accuracy	0.9972

Table 2: Interaction Mode Prediction Evaluation Results

If the SocialBot is predicted to handle the utterance, the goal is to have the system decide between various general topics and current events for which the system has collected information. If the topic is outside of the scope of what the SocialBot knows, the system resorts to a ChatBot, that may just give generic responses, and engage in chitchat dialogue.

5.3 Mode Prediction Classifier

We train this classifier to determine whether the user's input is related to the medical domain. We use the output from BERT encoder as the input to a linear classification layer trained with a cross-entropy loss function.

We choose the positive examples from MedQuAD Dataset, and negative examples from News Category Dataset. The training data information is shown in Table 1. And the evaluation results are shown in Table 2. This performance is potentially better than in real-life settings, because the medical (medline) vs non-medical (Kaggle news) data is cleanly separated. In reality, a user utterance might be "I am not happy, I have a headache" they may not want to get medical advise, but simply to just chat a bit to distract them from the headache.

5.4 MedicalQA Implementation

Medical Topic Classifier If the user utterance is routed to the MedicalQABot, the MedicalQABot first predicts the medical category of the user's input. We use Medline Data, which contains 1031 topics, to train this classifier. The dataset information is shown in Table 3. The evaluation results of our medical topic classifier is shown in Table 4.

Topic Posterior Calibration As shown in Figure 3, we ask a topic confirmation question after the topic classifier, which is used to let the user confirm the correctness of the output from Topic

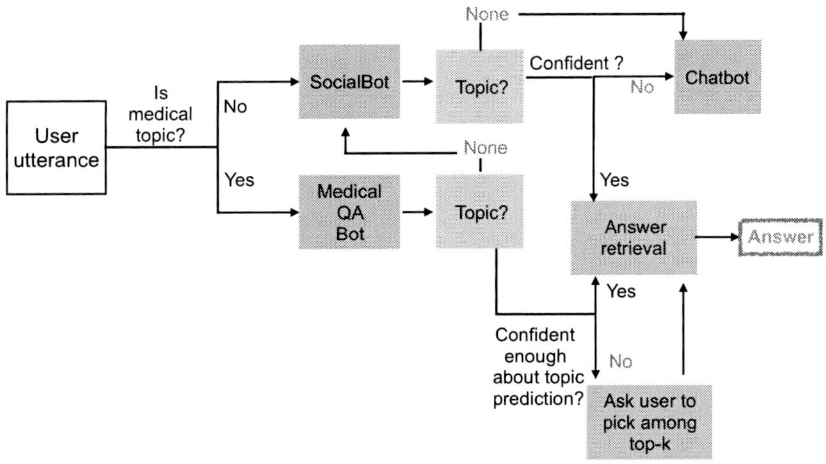

Figure 3: Our proposed pipeline. Section 5 has more details on the implementation of our current prototype.

Train	12082
Valid	3021
Test	615

Table 3: Medical Topic Classifier Training Data Information

Train accuracy	0.8812
Test accuracy	0.8358

Table 4: Medical Topic Classifier Evaluation Results

classifier. But we do not always need the confirmation. We set a threshold for the confidence score of the classifier. If the confidence score is higher than the threshold, meaning that our classifier is confident enough in the output, we will skip the confirmation question and retrieve the answer directly.

To make the classifier confidence scores more reliable, we use posterior calibration to encourage the confidence level to correspond to the probability that the classifier is correct (Chuan Guo, 2017; Schwartz et al., 2020). The method learns a parameter, called temperature or T. Temperature is introduced to the output logits of the model as follows:

$$pred = arg_i max \frac{exp(z_i/T)}{\Sigma_j exp(z_j/T)} \quad (1)$$

$\{z_i\}$ is the logits of the model and T is the temperature that needs to be optimized. T is optimized on a validation set to maximize the log-likelihood.

Precision	0.7585
Recall	0.7621
F-1 score	0.7603
Accuracy	0.7597

Table 5: MedicalQA Retriever Evaluation Results

MedicalQA Retriever After we determine the topic of the user's input, we can retrieve the answer from the Medline Dataset. We split the paragraphs in Medline data into single sentences and label them with the topics they belong to. We train the retriever using the augmented Medline data. We split the dataset into train, validation and test set using the ratio 8:1:1. The current retriever is based on BERT NextSentencePrediction model. We use the score from the model to determine the rank of each answer, and concatenate top 3 as the response of the agent. The evaluation result is shown in Table 5.

5.5 MedicalQA Grounding with Human Avatar

Our initial version for the human avatar contains 49 key body parts for front and 33 key body parts for the back. The front and back body part keywords are shown in Table 8 and 9. As future work, our goal is a more complete avatar with a comprehensive list of body parts.

Example grounded answers in our prototype system are shown in Figures 4 and 5 .

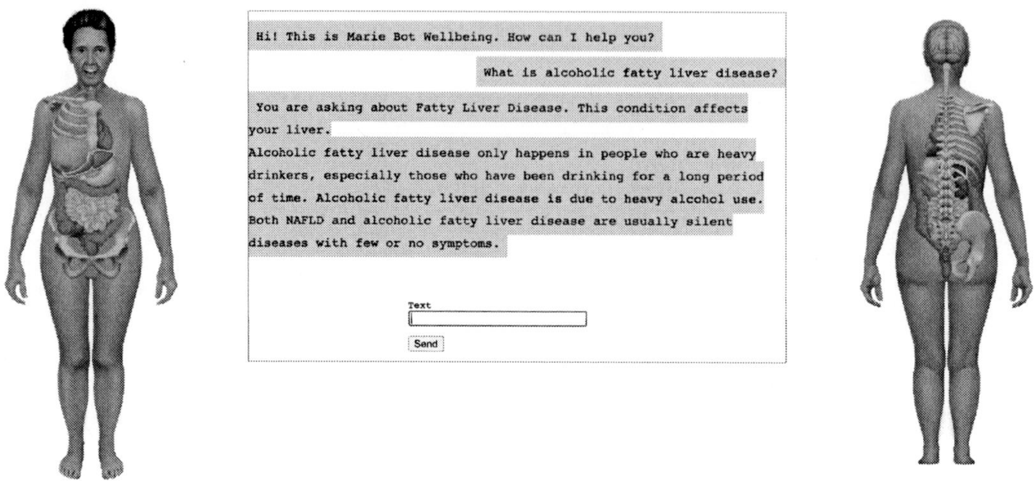

Figure 4: Human avatar visual answer example from our prototype: The affected body part, the liver, is highlighted on the avatar.

5.6 SocialBot Implementation

For our SocialBot, we currently have collected data from Reddit where each subreddits corresponds to a topic as shown in Table7. The topic classifier, posterior calibrator, and answer retriever are the same as in the MedicalQABot.

5.7 ChatBot Implementation

What is implemented is the last resort ChatBot, for which we have two versions: one is derived from a base language model, and another derived from a fine-tuned language model.

Language Models We use a large scale pre-trained language model, OpenAI GPT, as our base language model. We use the idea of transfer learning, which starts from a language model pre-trained on a large corpus, and then fine-tuned on end task. This idea was inspired by the huggingface convai project (Wolf, 2019).

Fine-tuning on Medical Dialogue Dataset: We use the Medical Dialogue Data(Zeng et al., 2020) to fine-tune the pre-trained language model. We use the questions as chat history and answers as current reply. The training set contains the portion from healthcaremagic and the test set the portion from icliniq

The evaluation results of our language model ChatBot are shown in Table 6.

	NLL	PPL
pre-trained model	5.4277	227.6291
fine-tuned model	3.2750	26.4423

Table 6: Language Model Evaluation. Negative log likelihood (NLL) and Perplexity (PPL)

6 Related Work

Medical Conversational Agents Academic and industry NLP research continues to push the frontiers of conversational agents, for example Meena from Google trained on a large collection of raw text (Daniel Adiwardana, 2020). In that work, it was found that end-to-end neural network with sufficiently low perplexity can surpass the sensibleness and specificity of existing chatbots that rely on complex, handcrafted frameworks. Medical dialogue has also been pursued from various angles for automatic diagnosis (Wei et al., 2018; Xu et al., 2019).

Grounding to Human Avatar IBM Research developed a human avatar for patient-doctor interactions (Elisseeff, 2007) with a focus on visualizing electronic medical records. By clicking on a particular body part on the avatar, the doctor can trigger the search of medical records and retrieve relevant information. Their focus on electronic medical records is different from our grounded medical question answering focus.

Another work (Charette, 2013) analyzed whether

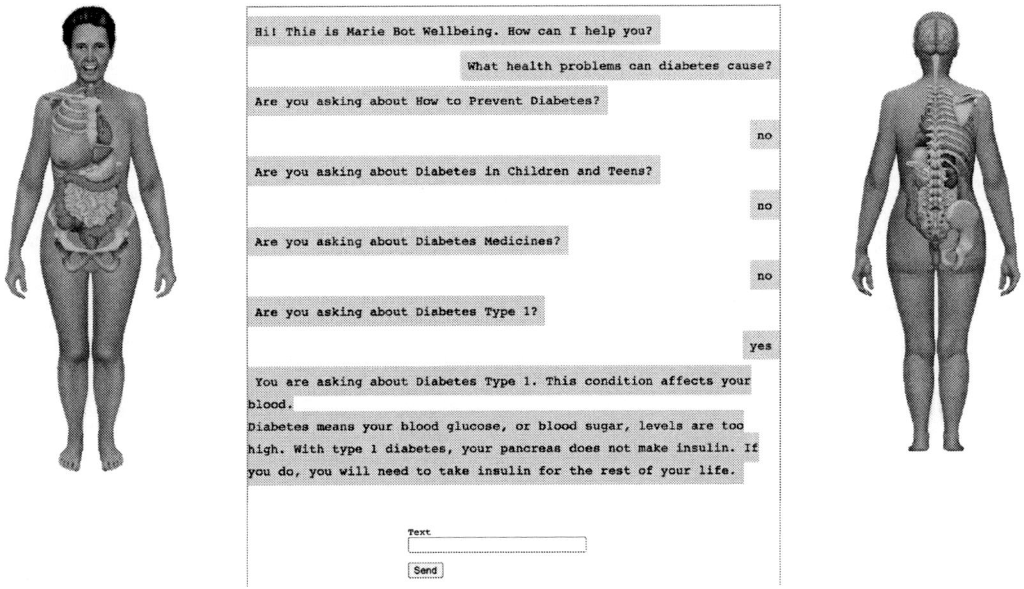

Figure 5: Human Avatar Visual Answer Example From our Prototype: Diabetes/Blood Sugar

and how the avatars help close the doctor-patient communication gap. This study showed that poor communication between doctors and patients often leads patients to not follow their prescribed treatments regimens. Their thesis is that avatar system can help patients better understanding the doctor's diagnosis. They put medical data, FDA data and user-generated content into a single site that let people search this integrated content by clicking on a virtual body.

7 Discussion

7.1 Technical Challenges

Quality and Quantity of Data In order for users to find the agent useful, and for the agent to really have a positive impact, we must provide answers to more questions. We need to extract more questions from a diverse set of reputable sources, while improving coverage.

Comprehensive Visualizations For the visualization, and human avatar grounding to be useful, a more comprehensive avatar is required, with all the parts that make up the human body. Medical ontologies such as the SNOMED CT part of Unified Medical Language System (UMLS)[4] contain a comprehensive list of the human body structures, which we can exploit and provide to a medical illustrator.

7.2 Ethical Considerations

Privacy When we deploy our system, we will respect user privacy, by not asking for identifiers. Additionally, we will store our data anonymously. Any real-world data will only accessible to researchers directly involved with our study.

False Information False or erroneous information in our data sources could lead our agent to present answers with potentially dire consequences. Our approach of only answering medical questions for which we have high quality, human curated answers seeks to address this concern.

System Capabilities Transparency Following prior work on automated health systems, our goal is to be clear and transparent about system capabilities (Kretzschmar et al., 2019).

8 Conclusion

We have presented a high level overview of the design philosophy of Marie Bot Wellbeing, a grounded, multi-interaction mode well-being conversational agent. The agent is designed to mitigate the limited adoption that plagues agents for healthcare despite patient interest. We reported details of our prototype implementation, and preliminary results.

[4] https://www.nlm.nih.gov/research/umls/index.html

There is much more to be done to fully realize Marie, which is part of our ongoing work.

References

Asma Ben Abacha and Dina Demner-Fushman. 2019. A question-entailment approach to question answering. *BMC Bioinform.*, 20(1):511:1–511:23.

Robert N. Charette. 2013. Can Avatars Help Close the Doctor-Patient Communication Gap?

Yu Sun Kilian Q. Weinberger Chuan Guo, Geoff Pleiss. 2017. On Calibration of Modern Neural Networks. arXiv:1706.04599v2.

David R. So Daniel Adiwardana, Minh-Thang Luong. 2020. Towards a Human-like Open-Domain Chatbot. arXiv:2001.09977v3.

Liesje Donkin, Ian B Hickie, Helen Christensen, Sharon L Naismith, Bruce Neal, Nicole L Cockayne, and Nick Glozier. 2013. Rethinking the dose-response relationship between usage and outcome in an online intervention for depression: randomized controlled trial. *Journal of medical Internet research*, 15(10):e231.

Andre Elisseeff. 2007. IBM Research Unveils 3D Avatar to Help Doctors Visualize Patient Records and Improve Care.

Kathleen Kara Fitzpatrick, Alison Darcy, and Molly Vierhile. 2017. Delivering cognitive behavior therapy to young adults with symptoms of depression and anxiety using a fully automated conversational agent (woebot): a randomized controlled trial. *JMIR mental health*, 4(2):e19.

Kira Kretzschmar, Holly Tyroll, Gabriela Pavarini, Arianna Manzini, Ilina Singh, and NeurOx Young People's Advisory Group. 2019. Can your phone be your therapist? young people's ethical perspectives on the use of fully automated conversational agents (chatbots) in mental health support. *Biomedical informatics insights*, 11:1178222619829083.

Evan Mayo-Wilson. 2007. Internet-based cognitive behaviour therapy for symptoms of depression and anxiety: a meta-analysis. *Psychological medicine*, 37(8):1211–author.

Mari Ostendorf. 2018. Building a socialbot: Lessons learned from 10m conversations. *NAACL Keynotes*.

Roy Schwartz, Gabriel Stanovsky, Swabha Swayamdipta, Jesse Dodge, and Noah A. Smith. 2020. The right tool for the job: Matching model and instance complexities. In *Proceedings of the 58th Annual Meeting of the Association for Computational Linguistics, ACL 2020, Online, July 5-10, 2020*, pages 6640–6651. Association for Computational Linguistics.

John Torous, Rohn Friedman, and Matcheri Keshavan. 2014. Smartphone ownership and interest in mobile applications to monitor symptoms of mental health conditions. *JMIR mHealth and uHealth*, 2(1):e2.

Zhongyu Wei, Qianlong Liu, Baolin Peng, Huaixiao Tou, Ting Chen, Xuan-Jing Huang, Kam-Fai Wong, and Xiang Dai. 2018. Task-oriented dialogue system for automatic diagnosis. In *Proceedings of the 56th Annual Meeting of the Association for Computational Linguistics (Volume 2: Short Papers)*, pages 201–207.

Thomas Wolf. 2019. How to build a State-of-the-Art Conversational AI with Transfer Learning.

Lin Xu, Qixian Zhou, Ke Gong, Xiaodan Liang, Jianheng Tang, and Liang Lin. 2019. End-to-end knowledge-routed relational dialogue system for automatic diagnosis. In *Proceedings of the AAAI Conference on Artificial Intelligence*, volume 33, pages 7346–7353.

Guangtao Zeng, Wenmian Yang, Zeqian Ju, Yue Yang, Sicheng Wang, Ruisi Zhang, Meng Zhou, Jiaqi Zeng, Xiangyu Dong, Ruoyu Zhang, et al. 2020. Meddialog: A large-scale medical dialogue dataset. In *Proceedings of the 2020 Conference on Empirical Methods in Natural Language Processing (EMNLP)*, pages 9241–9250.

A Appendix

SubReddit	Question Num
AskPhotography	996
NoStupidQuestions	912
AskHistorians	985
askscience	998
AskWomen	525
AskReddit	925
AskUK	781
AskMen	200
AskCulinary	998
AskEconomics	560
AskAnAmerican	850
AskALiberal	830
askaconservative	775
AskElectronics	842
Ask_Politics	999
AskEngineers	912
askmath	999
AskScienceFiction	652
AskNYC	994
AskTrumpSupporters	357
AskDocs	684
AskAcademia	987
askcarsales	995
askphilosophy	981
AskSocialScience	487
AskEurope	844
AskLosAngeles	400
AskNetsec	995
AskFeminists	978
AskWomenOver30	838

Table 7: Number of questions we extracted from each SubReddit

ankle	arm	breast
cheeks	chin	collar bone
ear lobe	ear	elbow
eyebrows	eyelashes	eyelids
eyes	finger	foot
forehead	groin	hair
hand	heart	hip
intestines	jaw	knee
lips	liver	lungs
mouth	neck	nipple
nose	nostril	pancreas
pelvis	rectum	ribs
shin	shoulder blade	shoulder
spinal cord	spine	stomach
teeth	thigh	throat
thumb	toes	tongue
waist	wrist	

Table 8: Human Avatar Front Body Parts

ankle	anus	arm
back	brain	buttocks
calf	ear lobe	ear
elbow	finger	foot
heart	intestines	kidney
knee	liver	lungs
neck	palm	pancreas
pelvis	rectum	ribs
scalp	shoulder blade	shoulder
spinal cord	spine	stomach
thigh	thumb	wrist

Table 9: Human Avatar Back Body Keywords. Some body parts can be visualized from both the front and back.

Author Index

Association for Computational Linguistics
209 N. Eighth Street
Stroudsburg, Pennsylvania 18360

CURRAN ASSOCIATES INC.
proceedings.com

ISBN 978-1-7138-3382-6

9 781713 833826